RIOTS AND POLITICAL PROTEST

The years 2008 to 2013 saw a new generation of political protestors take to the streets. Riots disrupted many Western cities, and new protest movements emerged, keen to address a bleak context of economic collapse and austerity politics.

In this groundbreaking new study, Winlow, Hall, Briggs and Treadwell push past the unworldly optimism of the liberal Left to offer an illuminating account of the enclosure and vacuity of contemporary politics. Focusing on the English riots of 2011, the ongoing crisis in Greece, the Indignados, 15M and Podemos in Spain, the Occupy movement in New York and London and the English Defence League in northern England, this book uses original empirical data to inform a strident theoretical critique of our post-political present. It asks: What are these protest groups fighting for, and what are the chances of success?

Written by leading criminological theorists and researchers, this book makes a major contribution to contemporary debates on social order, politics and cultural capitalism. It illuminates the epochal problems we face today. *Riots and Political Protest* is essential reading for academics and students engaged in the study of political sociology, criminological theory, political theory, sociological theory and the sociology of deviance.

Simon Winlow is Professor of Criminology at Teesside University and Co-Director of the Teesside Centre for Realist Criminology. He is the author of *Badfellas* (Berg, 2001) and co-author of *Bouncers* (Oxford University Press, 2003), *Violent Night* (Berg, 2006), *Criminal Identities and Consumer Culture* (Willan, 2008), *Rethinking Social Exclusion* (Sage, 2013) and *Revitalizing Criminological Theory* (Routledge, 2015). He is also the co-editor of *New Directions in Crime and Deviancy* (Routledge, 2012) and *New Directions in Criminological Theory* (Routledge, 2012).

Steve Hall is Professor of Criminology at Teesside University and Co-Director of the Teesside Centre for Realist Criminology. He is author of *Theorizing Crime and Deviance* (Sage, 2012), and co-author of *Revitalizing Criminological Theory* (Routledge, 2015), *Rethinking Social Exclusion* (Sage, 2013), *Criminal Identities and Consumer Culture* (Routledge, 2008) and *Violent Night* (Berg, 2006). He is also the co-editor of *New Directions in Criminology* (Routledge, 2012).

James Treadwell is a lecturer in criminology at the University of Birmingham. He is the author of the best-selling textbooks *Criminology* (2006) and *Criminology: The essentials* (2012). He is perhaps best known as an ethnographer, and he has published articles in a number of leading criminology and criminal justice journals.

Daniel Briggs is Professor of Criminology at the Universidad Europea in Madrid. He is the author of *Deviance and Risk on Holiday* (Palgrave MacMillan, 2013) and *Crack Cocaine Users* (Routledge, 2012) and co-author of *Culture and Immigration in Context* (Palgrave MacMillan, 2014) and *Assessing the Impact and Use of Anti-Social Beh* ... *English Riots of 2011* (Waterside Press, 2(

'Are riots a politics of resistance, or just free shopping trips? Has consumerism beaten politics? This engaging, principled and important study is both an exploration of the disturbances in Europe since the financial crash of 2008 and an investigation of the chances and shape of politics in a world where neo-liberalism seems to have won. *Riots and Political Protest* is a powerful call to think – and act – anew.'

Keith Tester, Professor of Sociology, University of Hull, UK

'From New York, to Spain to the North of England, this book gives space to some of the forgotten voices of the last decade. These voices, cast aside by the insistent grasp of neo-liberal economics, are without a politics or a political space in which liberal democracies permit them to be heard. This is a provocative, impassioned, challenging, data-driven, read. If you didn't have a view about the nature of politics and economics before reading this book, you certainly will have after finishing it.'

Professor Sandra Walklate, Eleanor Rathbone Chair of Sociology,
Department of Sociology, University of Liverpool, UK

'In the best traditions of critical scholarship, Winlow, Hall, Briggs and Treadwell take stock of our "post-political present", bringing powerful new insights, and a fresh energy to understanding the nature of contemporary opposition, protest, and antagonism. Written with intellectual precision, wide-ranging theoretical engagement and their characteristic wit, *Riots and Political Protest* will be a landmark text for academics, students, activists, commentators and politicians who have the courage, commitment, and vision to imagine alternative political landscapes.'

Elaine Campbell, Professor of Criminology,
Newcastle University, UK

'In their survey and analysis of recent social movements, riots and protests the authors offer a particular and radical vision of our contemporary world and its potential futures. Anyone with an interest in this field, will undoubtedly want to engage with this book.'

Tim Newburn, Professor of Criminology and Social Policy,
London School of Economics, UK

RIOTS AND POLITICAL PROTEST

Notes from the post-political present

Simon Winlow, Steve Hall, James Treadwell and Daniel Briggs

Routledge
Taylor & Francis Group

LONDON AND NEW YORK

First published 2015
by Routledge
2 Park Square, Milton Park, Abingdon, Oxon, OX14 4RN

Simultaneously published in the USA and Canada
by Routledge
711 Third Avenue, New York, NY 10017

Routledge is an imprint of the Taylor & Francis Group, an informa business

British Library Cataloguing in Publication Data
A catalogue record for this book is available from the British Library

Library of Congress Cataloging-in-Publication Data
Winlow, Simon.
    Riots and political protest: notes from the post-political present/
  Simon Winlow, Steve Hall, Daniel Briggs and James Treadwell.
    pages cm
    1. Protest movements. 2. Political participation. 3. Political violence.
  4. Riots. I. Title.
    HN18.3.W56 2015
    303.48′4 – dc23
    2014048784

ISBN13: 978-0-415-73081-5 (hbk)
ISBN13: 978-0-415-73082-2 (pbk)
ISBN13: 978-1-315-84947-8 (ebk)

Typeset in Bembo and Stone Sans
by Florence Production Ltd, Stoodleigh, Devon, UK

MIX
Paper from
responsible sources
FSC FSC® C013056
www.fsc.org

Printed and bound in Great Britain by
TJ International Ltd, Padstow, Cornwall

CONTENTS

1   Introduction: Name your beliefs; identify your enemy   1

2   Part I: Gulags and gas chambers   29

3   Part II: The liberal attack upon utopianism   61

4   The return of politics: The EDL in northern England   105

5   The consumer riots of 2011   135

6   What was Occupy?   151

7   Spain and the Indignados   169

8   The trouble with the Greeks   185

9   Conclusion   201

     Bibliography   209
     Index   217

1

INTRODUCTION

Name your beliefs; identify your enemy

It is now clear that the global financial meltdown of 2008 was an event of truly historical proportions. Initially at least, when the crisis first hit, it seemed to signal the exhaustion of a particular epoch and open up the possibility that something new might take its place. A strutting, self-satisfied neo-liberalism, beholden to the abstract financial markets that had become central to its economic functioning, appeared to have dropped off the edge of a steep cliff, and only the tax revenues of ordinary workers in the real economy could save it. Before the crash, minimally regulated free-market capitalism had defeated all alternative models of economic organisation to become the pure common sense that all mainstream politicians took for granted. In the months that followed the crash, as the scale of the endemic mismanagement and greed that had carried the global economy to the brink of catastrophe became clear, previously bullish free-market ideologues appeared chastened and contrite. The neo-liberal model itself was subject to stinging rebuke. Once again, it became possible to speak publicly of political and economic alternatives to neo-liberalism without being immediately dismissed as an unworldly utopian or an advocate of totalitarianism.

The crisis allowed us to momentarily extricate ourselves from the dominant economic logic of the neo-liberal era and occupy a new space from which we could look back objectively at the ideological dogma that had led our politicians to believe that the market would find a natural equilibrium, regulate itself and gradually improve the lives of all. We could also begin to see the immutable problems of the debt-fuelled growth model and the staggering injustices that had led to the establishment of new, mega-rich, corporate elites at the top of the class system and the significant growth in 'socially excluded' populations at the bottom. Perhaps most importantly, for our purposes at least, the 2008 economic crash appeared to make it possible to at least begin to imagine a world beyond capitalism.

Predictably enough, the human miseries that followed the crash were concentrated among the poorest and least able to influence the trajectory of mainstream politics. However, this time, the extent of the crash was such that many young people from the middle classes were adversely affected, and this is still the case, now in 2014. Youth unemployment was quickly acknowledged as a problem of genuine historical significance (see Crowley and Cominetti, 2014; Eichhorst and Neder, 2014). Many educated young people were locked out of housing markets and reasonably secure forms of employment, and they would not have the expansive welfare systems of the modern era to support them through the hard times. People across the West were angry, and justifiably so. The certainties of the recent past had evaporated.

However, if the 2008 crash genuinely was a historical turning point, it's not yet clear where history's new course might take us. We remain firmly lodged in an intervallic period, from the standpoint of which it is too early to identify with any clarity the political and economic shape of the future. The crash of 2008 appeared to thaw out the frozen topography of postmodern market societies and open up the possibility of genuine historical change, but, as the months and years rolled by, as new protest movements arose and then returned to the background, it became clear that no new ideology would develop capable of imposing its will on the post-crash landscape. Neo-liberalism, therefore, could continue simply by default.

It is against this rather dour background that we will develop an empirical and theoretical analysis of contemporary riots and forms of political protest. We will address key sites of political and social turmoil and those new forms of activism that suggest to some that a return to history may soon be upon us. In particular, we are keen to develop an account of what many on the left believe to be the long-awaited reawakening of a popular political consciousness that has lain dormant since the 1980s. We want to look at the reality of Western political systems and to think about how political opposition develops. In particular, we hope to see if there is any truth in the claim that political opposition these days has a range of limits imposed upon it. If this is so, what are these limits, who or what imposes them, and how are they imposed?

Of course, in order to understand contemporary forms of political protest, it is necessary to address the context in which they occur. We need to think about the contemporary conjuncture in a reasonably objective manner and develop an analysis of the forces that shape popular perceptions of politics, society and the economy, and those that encourage individuals and groups to see the necessity of political intervention. We must also think deeply about the complexities of motivation. What drives men and women to cast aside the routine considerations of everyday life and take up new political commitments? What are the motivations that propel the individual towards forms of political engagement that suggest a desire to relinquish the possessive individualism of our times?

It is not enough to assume that the political activist is simply a level-headed rationalist who recognises that personal sacrifices are necessary if his living standards are to improve, and we cannot simply reduce the activities of new oppositional movements to an entirely justifiable righteous indignation at high levels of social inequality and injustice. If we are to understand the reality of new forms of political subjectivity, we must develop a theoretical analysis that encourages us to think critically about the forces that drive the individual beyond disengagement and cynical acceptance to dedicated political commitment. We must also reflect further on ideology and subjectivity, and how oppositional political movements might symbolise and act politically upon the anger and dissatisfaction that appear to exist in abundance across the West.

As the book develops, we will build a preliminary response to the fundamental questions faced by the ideological opponents of liberal capitalism today. First, how can political opposition challenge liberal capitalism and seek to move beyond it? What forms should political opposition take? It is certainly true that liberal capitalism has proven to be remarkably adept at assimilating opposition and using its energy to enhance its own functioning (Boltanski and Chiapello, 2007; Hall et al., 2008). What can new oppositional groups do that will not be immediately seized upon and incorporated by liberal capitalism and its ostensibly 'democratic' parliamentary system? The history of the post-1980s neo-liberal period indicates that traditional forms of opposition and protest can achieve only limited success against an incredibly dynamic ideological system that seeks to integrate and domesticate all political antagonisms (Winlow and Hall, 2013), converting enmity and ideological opposition into a bland, insipid democratic negotiation between rational and pragmatic political actors. It should now be perfectly clear that traditional forms of protest can be appropriated by power and used as evidence to support the argument that contemporary liberal capitalism welcomes political diversity and forthright debate (see Žižek, 2008), and that democracy cordially invites all to take part in the creation of our shared future. This is not simply a process of historical revisionism, a process that turns Martin Luther King into a flag-waving patriot and the events of 1968 into a libertarian fight for new economic freedoms. *Capitalism today is ideologically reliant upon actual attempts to subvert its rule*; it needs manifested forms of cultural insubordination and a vocal but domesticated political opposition to convince us that democracy works and that what exists is the will of the majority. Of course, we are not suggesting that liberal capitalism can no longer be successfully opposed. Rather, we hope to encourage the development of new ways of conceiving of opposition that begin with the cold recognition of the titanic power of liberal capitalism's incisive ideological system and the vast amount of labour required to create an ideological account of reality capable of opposing it.

We fundamentally disagree with the post-war intellectual trend that insists that opposition should be limited to constant iconoclasm, with no inkling of what a future without capitalism might look like (see Jacoby, 2013). Given the lessons learned from previous failures, how will the post-capitalist economic and political system be structured? The apparent inability of the political Left to construct a reasonably clear response to this question is quite significant. As we shall see, many contemporary leftist protest movements are capable of constructing a realistic and compelling account of the failures of global capitalism. Protestors know this system to be incredibly unjust. They can see that only a tiny percentage of the population benefits from the operational logic of markets. They know that global capitalism refuses to address the gradual degradation of our natural environment, that the young are, with every passing year, increasingly unable to reproduce the relatively stable and affluent lifestyles of their parents. They know that current austerity policies unfairly affect the poorest, while failing to even inconvenience the rich, and that the current economic model simply cannot produce enough well-paid jobs in the West to allow young people to access the benefits of social inclusion. Leftist protest movements can quite easily identify what it is that they oppose, but they have not yet developed a positive programme for change and a world beyond capitalism. These protest movements are against lots of things, but it is not yet clear what it is that they positively endorse. The removal or reduction of those things they are against does not really count as a positive programme. In academic life too, there is an unusual absence of positive utopian thinking, which contrasts sharply with a surfeit of negative iconoclasm. We like knocking things down, but we seem to have no idea, beyond vague abstractions, what we want to build. Too often, speculative accounts appear to rest upon a disavowed belief that capitalism itself cannot be fully dispensed with, and that the best we can hope for is a *capitalism without capitalism*, a capitalism shorn of its most harmful mid-range causes and effects. In this book, as a political and theoretical backdrop to our analysis of riots and protest, we will try to explain why it has become so difficult to construct an image of a future in which we are not inextricably tied to the profit motive.

We will also look in detail at the dialectical standstill that appears to characterise our times, and our analysis will proceed in full recognition of the huge material problems liberal capitalism faces as it reproduces itself in the twenty-first century. The traditional leftist debate about the end of capitalism should now be more urgent than ever: will capitalism simply collapse under the weight of its own contradictions, or will new ideological projects and forms of political engagement carry us into a new, post-capitalist epoch? Of course, these two positions are not diametrically opposed, and, in order for the debate to move forward in a productive way, it needs to integrate a robust conception of politics and the political 'event' (see Badiou, 2009, 2010a, 2010b, 2011). It also needs to confront the real possibility that capitalism will continue to define the foreseeable future. Throughout its history, capitalism has displayed a breath-taking ability to move with the times, respond to crises and disperse and assimilate threatening forms of popular dissatisfaction. The continuing debate about the end of capitalism needs to revolve around the acknowledgement that capitalism itself has most successfully responded to the periodic crises in the market system. Capitalism changes when it is expedient for it to do so. Historically, it has successfully integrated popular critique and appropriated and reformulated many of the Left's traditional concerns. It is now perfectly acceptable for right-wing politicians to pronounce, without irony, their commitment to equality, social justice, fairness and freedom, once the exclusive clarion calls of the broad liberal Left. We should bear this in mind when our politicians tell us about the actions they have undertaken to end the economic crisis and make our societies stable again. Capitalism, as a genuinely revolutionary socio-economic system, completely transformed what we mean by stability. Capitalism is inherently unstable. It constantly moves and undulates, and, of course, the market system inevitably goes through periods of boom and bust. The political goal of economic stability needs to be placed in this broader context, but it is also incumbent upon all intelligent people to wrestle with the possibility that the economic problems we face now cannot be fully overcome. We are six years into the economic crisis. Austerity and falling living standards are the new normal. This is what stability looks like.

The expansive range of problems associated with the continuation of capitalism, problems that are now known, if not entirely understood, by a significant proportion of the Western population, might well be answered by the development of a new form of capitalism: a capitalism that promises to solve many of the malignant problems that cause such distress today, but capitalism nonetheless. In short, this debate needs to move forward and appraise with honesty the significant ideological successes of global capitalism and its ability to transform itself in order to pacify or sidestep growing antagonism. If it is to draw popular support and mount a significant challenge to the dominance of the market, the political Left must withdraw from the immediacy of ongoing events and, in an entirely dispassionate manner, once again take stock of its opponent. It needs to stop kidding itself that 'the people' are disgusted by inequality and the consumerisation of popular culture and are ready and waiting for an opportune moment to spill out on to the streets to demand a more just and equitable system.

If the Left is to advance from its current position, it might also consider taking a critical glance at its own recent history. With this in mind, we will spend some time in this book taking stock of the basic ideological transformations that have taken place on the left since the 1980s. We hope to interrogate dominant forms of leftist social analysis in order to identify how and why the Left lost so comprehensively, and why it continues to be incapable of developing an analysis of the present that can attract and unify the post-industrial ex-working classes and allow them to understand their frustrations and dissatisfactions in relation to the harms and injustices that are unavoidable outcomes of the normal functioning of today's global capitalist markets. How has the Left changed, and what has happened to its traditional principles of egalitarianism and social justice? Has the Left's traditional utopianism given way to a basic pragmatism that seeks only to mitigate capitalism's worst effects? Why has the Left become uncomfortable with the politics of universality, preferring instead to defend the rights of various cultural interest groups?

Things cannot go on as they are . . .

Our analysis of contemporary political protest develops from an encounter with the manifold evidence that addresses the serious social consequences awaiting us in the near future, as climate change and resource depletion gather pace (Heinberg, 2011; Hiscock, 2012; Pearce, 2013). Against such a background, can liberal capitalism maintain its position as history's most successful socio-economic system? Looming resource wars, ecological disasters and social unrest could puncture even liberal capitalism's mass-mediated ideological bubble and very quickly send this dominant perception spinning into reverse. We have already glimpsed the future in the initial growth of liberal authoritarianism in Western democratic nations: governments are now increasingly willing to discard established civil liberties and legal entitlements in order to ensure that a shallow and ideologically tainted version of freedom is maintained (see Agamben, 2005; Žižek, 2009). Will this trend continue, and, if it does, how will politicians seek to justify such things to the population? How will people respond to this trade-off between authoritarianism and an increasingly one-dimensional form of consumer freedom, and to govern-ments' willingness to discard the basic principles of democracy so that capitalism can continue unimpeded? How will liberal capitalism deal with its fetishistic attachment to economic growth as the global economy reaches its material limits and energy resources become increasingly scarce and expensive? How can liberal democracy and liberal capitalism continue to justify themselves as the 'least worst' of all social and political systems when more and more people find themselves excluded from the social and cultural activities that supposedly constitute the good life? How can Western governments address the chronic unemployment and underemployment that have beset so many post-industrial areas across Europe and North America? Ultimately, can capitalism continue to convince a majority that its market mechanisms, domesticated electoral systems, securitisation apparatus and military operations are the answers to the problems created by its own functioning?

As we write these words, it seems that the ongoing economic crisis has made neo-liberalism a good deal stronger. It appeared to have had its wings clipped in the years that immediately followed the crash, but it continues to exist as pure *doxa* for most mainstream politicians, political parties and cultural commentators across the West. In this intervallic period, we continue to see the reckless exploitation of the natural world; indeed, this appears to be picking up pace, as the desire to drive our economies back to growth supersedes any vague commit-ment to environmental issues our politicians might once have expressed. New commitments to slashing government spending and tackling the structural deficit have further weakened the already half-hearted governmental promise to create sustainable twenty-first-century economies. Relatedly, an obscene land grab is under way across the world, as corporations seek to identify and exploit new energy sources and mineral deposits (see Hiscock, 2012; Pearce, 2013), and there is much evidence to suggest that we simply cannot return to the sustained economic growth of the post-war years, or even the sporadic growth of the early neo-liberal years (see Heinberg, 2011). Here, we are talking about growth in the real economy in which most people earn a living. Abstract financial markets often disguise the worsening reality of the West's economic situation (see Varoufakis, 2011).

Without a radical intervention, it seems entirely likely that we will see the gradual disintegration of the partial achievements of modernity. Liberal capitalism's assumption that incremental historical progress will continue to sustain our flight from barbarism towards the civilisational ideal has now been revealed as mere myth-making. For the time being, it seems inevitable that things will get worse for everyone but the new global bourgeoisie and their hired technocrats and administrators. The great majority of the population will have to get by with less. Given all of these things, and a good deal more besides, isn't it incumbent on leftist intellectuals to once again ask: What hold does neo-liberalism have over us? What is preventing us from fully casting it aside and moving forward towards a more just and inclusive system? The crash of 2008 has allowed more people to recognise their own exploitation amid the fundamental injustices of neo-liberal capitalism, and yet so many people still believe that *any attempt to change things for the better will inevitably change things for the worse.* Despite growing dissatisfaction with neo-liberal capitalism, huge swathes of the population remain unconsciously tied to its continuation. Why is it so difficult to even imagine a positive vision of a world without capitalism?

If we are to develop a realistic account of new forms of political opposition, we need to think carefully about what politics is and what it is not. Too often throughout the academic literature, the word 'politics' is used in troublingly inexact ways. Of course, the adoption of an entirely fluid conception of 'politics' enables the author to identify it in virtually any social context. This, in turn, makes the construction of a clear distinction between 'political action' and 'non-political action' a wholly subjective enterprise. The author can identify a form of politics, or the absence of politics, wherever she chooses and for whatever purpose. For us, the projection of 'politics' on to entirely non-political aspects of everyday social life is a regrettable feature of contemporary leftist social analysis. It suggests a steadfast refusal to countenance the true extent of the Left's failure and the staggering successes of liberal capitalism in reshaping the fields of politics, economics, society, culture and subjectivity. The idea that constantly challenging what are often incautiously deemed to be aspects of cultural hegemony is a political act in itself, insofar as it will clear away ideological obfuscation and allow latent organic politics to flow forth, is now revealing itself to be a fundamental error. In the absence of a coherent and unifying alternative, the endless iconoclastic deconstruction of various bits of liberal capitalism's hegemonic cultural output is not inspiring political thought and action, but furthering the fragmentation, cynicism, pan-scepticism and symbolic inefficiency on which the system thrives (see Winlow and Hall, 2013).

In the chapters that follow, we attempt to develop a coherent and entirely unsentimental analysis of 'the political'. This, we hope, will allow us to think through quite clearly what politics is today, and to what extent it is active or inactive in the creation of the present and the future. For us, it is clear that the social-scientific 'community' must free itself from the ideological injunction to discover politics everywhere and in every social activity. If politics is everywhere, then it is nowhere. We will argue that the liberal Left has expanded the definition of the political act to such a breadth, atomised it into such a harmless spray of globules and dematerialised it to such a degree of abstraction that it has been rendered meaningless, incomprehensible and totally ineffective. For us, the Left must rid itself of this immobilising account of politics if it is to move forward. Politics is the field on which we deal with fundamental antagonisms, where we can determine the basic economic and social coordinates of our shared future. If we discover 'politics' in the most trivial and mundane of activities, then we erode our capacity to identify and address the movement of history and our ability to impose our collective will upon social reality. If graffiti is political, if cross-dressing is political, if pop songs are political, if buying fair-trade coffee is political, then what is the name of the field upon which we determine the structure of global political economy? What is the name of the field upon which we determine the Good? What is the name of the field on which we make collective decisions about our future together? Are we to stretch the concept of politics so that it covers both the small and the mundane and the huge and consequential, or do we simply expect the former to aggregate and become the latter? Could it be that, since the arrival of neo-liberalism, the extent of the Left's defeat has been such that key constituencies within it have strategically withdrawn from an analysis of global political economy, preferring instead to focus on micro-resistance and minor acts of cultural insubordination, after which it can declare its own tiny victories against 'oppression'? Of course, these tiny victories of the post-1980s liberal Left are precisely what the market system needs to reassure the population that democratic politics continues. Capitalism welcomes this kind of cultural insubordination, because the real locus of power lies elsewhere.

But why do we need to define politics in a book such as this? Surely the meaning of 'politics' is perfectly clear, and its role in the world obvious to anyone with a modicum of intelligence? We might believe that politics is clearly an active part of our societies because people continue to vote; because there is widespread disgust at the venal practices of corporate banking elites; because people are angry that the gap between rich and poor appears to be widening with each passing year; and because people often appear quite animated about issues of the day. The ultimate problem in adopting such a simplistic notion of politics is that we end up looking exclusively at the superficial foreground of mediatised cultural politics – the surface once posited as the totality by defunct postmodernist thought – while ignoring the background (see Harvey, 1991; Jameson, 1992). We ignore the fundamental issues – for instance, the socialisation of investment banking credit, land, production and mass media and the shift to sustainable energy and participatory economics – that have the capacity to totally transform political economy and the contours of our social world. To find political opposition in minor acts of insubordination, in momentary disturbances of the normal run of things, is to reduce the potency of political struggle to an argument that takes place *within* the restrictive parameters of the current political and ideological constellation.

In the background, of course, nothing much is happening. Indeed, the background has not changed much since the fall of the Berlin Wall in 1989. Neo-liberalism remains, and, despite its titanic inequalities and injustices, all mainstream political parties continue to be shackled to its economic logic and enthralled by its complex and ubiquitous ideological support systems. If we assume that the cultural foreground of politics is its totality, are we then forced to confront the possibility that 'politics' has lost the ability to fundamentally transform the socio-economic order, or should we accept that there is a general consensus that free-market capitalism, coupled with liberal democracy, is the best of all available systems? Is genuine politics really possible in times of such widespread and enduring consensus? Further, might it be worth briefly pausing to reflect on the possibility that the foreground action of contemporary politics, beamed into our living rooms in news broadcasts every night, acts to reassure the general public that politics and democracy are alive and well, while, behind the scenes, oligarchs work to ensure the con-tinuation of an economy that enriches a tiny percentage of the global population at the expense of everyone else?

Steadfastly refusing to think critically and philosophically about the meaning and constitution of politics means that we remain ensnared in a ruling ideology that shapes the political field and sets firm limits on what can and cannot be understood as legitimate political knowledge and action. Might it not be reasonable to construct an analysis of politics that encourages us to think about the paradoxical *unfreedom* and obvious lack of genuine choice presented to electorates in Western liberal democracies? Might it not be productive to think about who benefits and who loses out when we thoughtlessly apply only the most simplistic, fragmented and superficial definitions of politics and political action to the huge problems we face? Is it conceivable that the urge to identify political motivations in the most banal of everyday activities reduces our capacity to identify that historically – and *despite* the economic crash of 2008 – 'politics' has patently failed to even contain, never mind challenge or replace, current processes of runaway financialisation and the global dominance of free-market ideology?

So, with these issues in mind, we want to investigate the place of politics in contemporary forms of protest and, ultimately, think about the role protest might play in attempts to move beyond capitalism and create a post-capitalist social order free from the gross inequality, avarice, solipsism and competition that characterise contemporary consumer culture. We want to rethink key themes in the analysis of contemporary political activism and, in a clear-headed and entirely unsentimental manner, consider the historical inertia that has accompanied the triumph of neo-liberalism. We also want to consider what a return to politics and history might look like.

Times of cultural inertia

In liberal democratic Europe and North America, we are once again seeing mass unemployment and underemployment. Young people appear to be bearing the brunt of this political and economic failure. There is nothing, absolutely nothing, on the political and economic horizon that might suggest the imminent return of the secure and stable forms of employment that would offer working-class and marginalised populations a reasonable standard of living and a sense of inclusion and satisfaction. At the other end of our radically changed class system, we have seen the establishment of an incredibly wealthy elite that appears to have transcended what remains of the rules, laws and obligations of Western modernity to attain a position of historically unprecedented *special liberty* (see Hall, 2012a). Skilled at negotiating the permeable and imprecise boundary separating the legal from the illegal, they have retreated behind high walls and are now almost entirely cut off from the real world and its pathologies. For them, there are no historical, cultural or geographic loyalties that override their powerful desire to minimise taxation and increase their personal wealth, and so they traverse the globe free from all the restrictive obligations that might obstruct their disavowed commitment to the endless continuation of capitalism's destructive exchange relation.

Across the West, welfare states are under attack, and the hard-won entitlements of public-sector workers are being gradually stripped away. Even in the relatively affluent social democratic states of Europe, a simple but highly effective libertarian discourse is drawing a new audience and seducing disillusioned social liberals with its good old-fashioned economic pragmatism. It argues that the free market is the only game in town and the only chance post-industrial Western states have of boosting employment opportunities and curtailing poverty, welfare dependency and post-industrial urban degeneration. It returns to the apparently timeless appeal of Berlin's (2002) *negative freedom* to argue that the only way to advance liberty is to free the individual from oppressive taxation systems and outdated state paternalism. Even now, during times of extreme crisis, when in Britain more and more people are forced to rely on food banks to survive (see Butler, 2014), this perverse logic of negative solidarity dominates mainstream political debates about taxation, the sovereign debt crisis, welfare spending and the economic viability of public institutions.

In times past, politicians such as Thatcher and Reagan committed wholeheartedly to this ideology. They were willing to argue that the adoption of such policies was right and just. These policies would, in the long run, prove to be of significant benefit to the vast majority of citizens. Now, at a time when our politicians attempt to convince us that they are entirely divorced from ideological commitments and construct their policies in relation to pure economic pragmatism, the logic of negative freedom and unfettered capitalism appears to have cast off its old-fashioned ideological garb. Politicians might like to help the poor, tax wealth to a greater extent or increase the quality and quantity of public services, but they simply cannot do so. Their accountant's pragmatism prevents them from challenging the dominant economic and political logic of our times. As representatives of the people, they must first of all ensure that the economy grows. The hazy categories of 'security' and growth in consumer lifestyles are regarded as the only unimpeachable political goods, the only things that electorates really want and the only criteria of progressive social improvement. In order to make the economy grow, they must reduce individual and corporate tax to a minimum and allow systemic tax avoidance to continue unchecked.

They must loosen or discard employment legislation that prevents summary dismissal and guarantees the basic rights of workers, so that corporate employers might consider the employment of workers to be a risk worth taking. They must recognise that it does no good whatsoever to challenge or seek to modify this system. Any attempt to increase taxes on wealth or corporate profit simply places wealth-creators in the hands of a competitor state. Even supposedly leftist political parties inevitably adopt this logic. They may take office with a zeal for reform and a hazy desire to tame predatory capitalism, but two quarters of negative economic growth are likely to prompt a regrettable about-turn – 'yes we can' quickly and inevitably becomes 'no we can't'.

Idealism is very hard to maintain in contemporary mainstream politics. Pragmatism, punctuated only by a brief flurry of idealist rhetoric during election time, immediately floods back in from the edges and moves progressively closer to the centre, until it reclaims its place as the entirety of politics. Even reformers know that, when the global economy is structured in relation to the needs of the free market, one has to be pragmatic about what is achievable. Reforms must be small enough to be tolerated by 'the market'. What good does it do, when one only has a few years in office to make one's mark, to take on entrenched power and vested interests? This ideology of pragmatism reduces politics to a half-hearted performance in which nothing really changes and tiny victories must be seized upon in the hope that they indicate the willingness of power to change through negotiation.

Of course, the politics of negative freedom are not at all new. They have played a structural role in our shared political life since the Enlightenment and the birth of the modern state. Even during the golden years of post-war social democracy, a period during which the gap between rich and poor narrowed significantly, and the working classes were able to advance their interests against those of capital, this marginal aspect of political and economic theory patiently bided its time and waited for an opportunity to return to the epicentre of politics. That opportunity came during the economic crises of the 1970s, when the Keynesian approach to economic planning appeared to have reached its end point, unable to assuage confident trade unions and incapable of coping with globalisation, resource depletion and the thorny problem of maintaining the high degree of productivity required by modern consumer lifestyles and the panoramic welfare state.

The late 1970s proved to be the perfect time for economic liberalism to have its basic maxim considered anew. Its key motifs were able to stand as answers to the questions posed by the apparent exhaustion of Keynesian social democracy. Since the 1980s, populist anti-tax and anti-welfare state rhetoric has met with huge success in drawing ordinary citizens away from their commitment to the basic principles of the inclusive post-war social democratic consensus. Of course, the dispiriting pragmatism of politics exists throughout the current neo-liberal order. It sees all personal ties and obligations as fetters placed upon individual freedom. It is obsessed with money, deriding all positive ideals of progress or the Good in order to reassert the unassailable value of economic freedom. It ensures that all who talk positively of collective ownership or the common good are seen as callow ideologues who have failed to keep pace with the new political and economic imperatives that appear to be making the world anew. To put forward a positive idea of what a better world might look like, or of a better way of organising the socio-economic order, is denounced by the liberal Right (for example, Friedman, 2000) and the liberal Left (for example, Turner, 2010) alike as a dangerous move towards totalitarianism; only a constant stream of negative, iconoclastic critiques from proliferating single-issue social movements is acceptable.

It is important to keep in mind that this neo-liberal narrative, which asserts the benefits of privatisation and warns of the perils of state involvement in the economy, continues, despite the recent spectacular failure of the privately run financial core of the global free market. The austerity measures now under way across most of the West's liberal democratic states are a further indication of the power of this narrative and its ability to adapt to new social conditions. A new assault is being unleashed upon an already weakened welfare state, but this has followed quickly on the heels of previous assaults. What amounts to a continued war against collective ownership and universal social security provision has been going on so long now that social-liberal ideologues have to put huge effort into their attempts simply to keep it in the public's line of vision.

This latest assault is, of course, justified in relation to the pragmatism we described above. Despite the fact that the dollar and the pound are only nominal fiat currencies and money is generated by private banks' advance of debt to corporations, businesses and consumers, we are instructed to consider the finances of the state to be like those of any household – which is ludicrous simply because a household cannot generate its own supply of currency. On the back of this false analogy, the public can be persuaded that the state needs to restrict its spending and pay down its debt. For too long, the state has spent recklessly and now it is paying the price. We must pass through a period of regrettable austerity – of course, no one *wants* to cut services – so that we can retake control of our financial destiny (see Watt, 2013). In a wonderfully adept ideological sidestep, the perilous economic position of the state is said to be the result of the tendency of left-of-centre governments to spend beyond their means, rather than the outcome of a global financial meltdown that prompted the state to bail out privately owned banks. Be pragmatic, we are told – accept that taxpayers' money must be used to save the banking industry: it is the only way to keep our economy moving and ensure the continuation of paid employment for workers in the real economy. Be pragmatic: austerity is painful, but it is necessary if we are to regain control and balance the books.

The clearest indication that the key facets of neo-liberal governance are now treated as economic pragmatism and basic common sense must surely be when our politicians tell us that taxing wealth is counter-productive. Not only do high taxes dissuade investment, curtail entrepreneurial zeal and reduce the nation's economic competitiveness on the world stage, they inevitably result in *less money* flowing into the coffers of the Exchequer. High-tax regimes immediately increase tax avoidance and drive innovations in the tax-avoidance industry. The nation's demand that the rich pay more in tax inevitably results in the rich paying less. Again, our politicians tell us to be pragmatic. All concerns about social justice and the moral responsibility of the rich to contribute more are dismissed as an unwelcome distraction, indulgences that cannot even be considered if our politicians are to deliver economic growth and lead us to a new era of prosperity.

Neo-liberalism by default

Neo-liberalism is now a veteran power. Across the West, little has been done to challenge its rule for more than a quarter of a century. It was only after the destructive crash of 2008 that new anti-capitalist movements began to draw attention and a little support, but, as we will see, the precise political and ideological content of these new protest movements has yet to fully emerge. They have secured no victory, and they have – in America, Britain and the larger economies in Europe – failed to draw the forms of mass support that might suggest a genuine opportunity to transform our political and economic system, with a view to making it more equitable and just, as well as far less socially and ecologically destructive. These new movements arose quickly after the crash, but most have now faded just as quickly into the background. Abstract finance capitalism and the logic of privatisation continue to structure our economic planning, and the ubiquitous pragmatist who seeks to remain socially included and active in post-industrial labour markets believes that the continuation of this approach is the best available means of securing a degree of financial safety. It is not simply that the logic of free-market economics remains in place. Rather, this logic was allowed to gather more strength as it reasserted itself, in the absence of any coherent, positive opposition, as the only possible answer to the new economic problems it had created. It has established quite firm limits on what is possible politically and economically. Neo-liberalism is both the problem and the answer, a totality that appears entirely capable of assimilating all who are willing to subscribe to its pragmatism.

A new, stripped-back version of neo-liberal governance now dominates, in which all the social concerns of 'third-way' social liberalism have been discarded. The positive vision of social democratic welfarism is a dim and distant memory, an old, flickering, sepia-coloured image of a more naïvely optimistic time. Neo-liberalism is now leaner and bolder, ready to take the tough decisions that will secure the continuation of what currently exists. Its long-running ideological supremacy has afforded it plenty of time to win hearts and minds. It long ago discarded the last remnants of utopianism and idealism from the field of economic planning. It has, for the most part, been successful in its ideological attempt to elevate the field of 'economics' to the status of an objective empirical science. Much of this field is now mere accountancy writ large, the wholesale application of rules laid down by ideologues wedded to reductive mathematical conceptions of the forces that drive men and women to act in the world.

Despite the growing recognition of its inherent flaws, neo-liberalism continues to dominate. It provides the only conceivable game plan, the only tools that can be applied to the task of alleviating some of the huge pressures that now bear down on Western nation-states. But this is not simply a matter of a corrupted polity fetishistically attached to forms of economic planning that, in the fullness of time, simply cannot address the problems faced by distressed communities. A significant portion of Western populations have come to accept the core hegemonic message repeated over and over again throughout our culture and mediascape: we must cut taxes to encourage the forms of investment that create jobs; we must accept that our welfare system is inefficient, and that significant numbers of welfare-dependent people are cheats playing the system; we must accept falling wages, so that businesses can remain competitive; we must accept growing economic insecurity, and fight hard to make ourselves indispensable to our employers, even where this demands that the individual changes core aspects of her personality; we must accept that the people who work alongside us do not form a supportive community, but are in fact competitors in the battle to reproduce our consumer lifestyles. However, acceptance is not belief. They accept this hegemonic message, not because it is 'naturalised' and manufactures consent, nor because it appeals to some timeless competitive work ethic, but because the Left has failed to present a coherent alternative. Whereas specific beliefs can be changed, the destruction of the principle of belief and the adoption of pragmatic acceptance induce a nihilistic political inertia that can last for generations.

Who defines 'resistance'?

This general closure of the discourse on political economy and the depoliticisation of the social consequences of the free market act as the background to our analysis of contemporary forms of political protest. Contemporary neo-liberalism continues to assert its primacy despite the global economic crash of 2008, despite the Left's incessant but increasingly domesticated critique, despite an apparent resurgence in trade unionism, and despite the return of pre-political protests across the West. However, despite widespread dissatisfaction and anger, if we gather together the evidence and appraise it with honesty, we must conclude that there is no significant popular desire for revolution, or even serious social democratic reform of the system's economic core. Dissatisfaction and anger have yet to stimulate the production of a positive vision of an alternative to capitalism, and without that the Left remains stuck in an endless process of identifying capitalism's negative effects and attempting to curb its most harmful outcomes, rather than replacing it with something qualitatively different.

Post-crash capitalism welcomes civilised, lawful and democratic opposition and protest. If the capitalist states of the West were to repress such things, if they were to withdraw democratic elections and arrest and imprison all protestors, this would foment political opposition and greatly increase the chance of a political event that might then be carried forward by a widely felt commitment to a new political truth. The domesticated oppositional marches and protests that appear increasingly common paradoxically reassert the primacy of a liberal democratic system that is patently failing to address the needs of a significant proportion of its population. Media coverage and political commentary after each protest march give the impression that a robust political engagement has taken place, despite the fact that government policy has not budged by a single millimetre. Instead, a government spokesperson can instruct the television audience that they should be thankful that they live in a vibrant liberal society that allows such protest to take place. Contemporary democratic parliamentarianism sees itself as a field of open and forthright debate in which fair electoral practices and the right to protest guarantee that the collective will of an entirely rational and politically engaged population is broadly reflected in the policies of government.

On our nightly news broadcasts, we see a shadow-puppet theatre of intrigue and apparently robust political activity in Europe's debating chambers and corridors of power, all geared to cover up the fact that, underneath liberal democracy's rosy self-image, nothing much is happening over and above an endless sequence of capitulations to neo-liberal economic logic. All mainstream politicians must agree that capitalism is the only conceivable economic system, and all politicians who have a desire to win office or find their way to positions of power must accept that the free-market variant of capitalism is the only means of generating the increased wealth widely considered to be an absolute good and a guaranteed route to re-election.

What we have seen is a movement of robust political debate away from the basic principles of economic practice and towards the field of culture. We are allowed, indeed encouraged, to debate national identity and immigration, to debate whether or not Muslim women should be allowed to wear a niqab in public and if Christians should be free to display religious symbols while at work. There is a clear vitality to such public and political discussion because the ultimate route forwards has yet to be determined. The political class welcomes political input on cultural matters and it is happy to pander to the will of the majority rather than to take a lead on issues of the day. But the enculturation of politics is predicated on an absolute refusal to open discussions on the foundations of our economic system and possible alternatives to it. All popular discussion of the basic principles that structure our economic reality has been systematically removed from politics.

However, it is possible to identify the fundamental economic antagonisms and politics of class submerged beneath many of today's 'cultural' issues. Cultural antagonism often acts as a displaced form of class antagonism. This displacement is an ideological process that attempts to ensure the continuation of capital accumulation, and its key function is to prevent the coalescence of disparate cultural identities into a genuinely collectivist political opposition. The Left's focus should be on driving forward narratives of universality grounded upon the relationship workers of all ethnicities and religions have with dominant forms of capital accumulation. If the Left's principal goals are still social justice and egalitarianism at the point of participation, rather than distribution, then the centralisation of the attempt to identify and condemn any negative view the subject might hold towards its socially constructed Other displaces the fundamental issue at stake. There can be no relaxed conviviality, and no culture of openness, tolerance and acceptance, in a world constituted by brutal interpersonal competition and glaring inequalities and injustices.

Capitalism actively creates, intensifies and reproduces competition. It cannot survive without it. As a basic principle of capitalist enterprise, one must always seek to outdo the Other and receive more than one is willing to give in return. In Western consumer societies, much of our cultural life simply reflects the outcomes of this enduring competition. We seek out cultural distinction by means of the display of luxury goods. We systematically incite the envy of others. It makes no sense to turn away from this reality and hope that, by simply encouraging people and communities to be a little more respectful and tolerant of each other, we can radically improve our world.

We see this displacement of class antagonism most clearly in the United States. The right wing of the Republican Party has done a remarkable job of transforming economic issues into cultural issues. It has convinced an electorally significant proportion of white, working-class voters that the Republication Party acts to defend the American way of life against all who would threaten it. Even though the Republican Party is openly hostile to the *economic interests* of the working class, it can quite easily take on the role of defender of the working class's *cultural interests*. The enemy is, of course, the godless metropolitan liberal who is keen to legalise homosexual marriage, advocates positive discrimination and the advancement of non-heterosexuals in the military and is happy to let immigration continue unchecked. A fundamental economic antagonism between the exploited working class and the interests of capital is pushed on to the field of culture, where it takes a different and fragmentary form. Rather than a conflict about economic justice, we get conflicts about various 'values'. Conservatives are pitched against liberals. Many of the white working class, then, vote against their true class interests because the fundamental economic antagonism has been obfuscated and displaced. Class struggle has been transformed into a forthright debate about the pace of change and respect for tradition. 'Working-class' conservatives are pitched against the 'middle-class' liberals of the Democratic Party, some of whom (admittedly, not very many) still continue to advocate the very policies that might ease some of the genuine hardships experienced by the working class. Instead, they vote for the cultural defenders of the American way, who are also keen to pursue the very policies that will ensure the further immiseration of working-class communities and the eventual destruction of any of the remaining positive remnants of their traditional 'way of life'.

The melodrama of democratic politics

In the economic field, contemporary mainstream political discussion inevitably descends into absurd melodrama, hyperbole and faux-indignation, as our political parties are forced to focus on the minutiae of neo-liberal economic policy. They argue over fractions of a percentage point and throw statistics at each other, while assiduously avoiding any discussion of fundamental changes that might transform our economic future into something other than a continued class war in which only one side appears to be fighting. Of course, our politicians engage in such theatricality, trying desperately to distinguish the nuances of their neo-liberalism from those of their opponents, precisely because, in terms of economic policy, they agree on the fundamentals. Of course, the viewer, watching this soap opera unfold on the TV screen and following the ups and downs of Sainsbury's profit margins on morning radio, almost inevitably arrives at the conclusion that all of politics is entirely bereft of substance. The political class is clearly a world away from the pressing reality of work and bills, cocooned in an incestuous metropolitan bubble of expense-accounted privilege and entitlement. Why shouldn't huge swathes of the electorate come to the conclusion that these public schoolboys and schoolgirls of Left and Right have totally lost touch with the very constituencies they were elected to represent? What experience have these people ever had with hardship and want? Obsessed with statistics, do they ever stop to think about the people whom these facts and figures purport to represent? They crow about driving the economy back to growth and maintaining the nation's credit rating, but what does this mean for the man or woman at home searching for a full-time, fully tenured job that allows them a reasonable stake in society? As no palatable alternative to the present system exists, as the current economic model, with all its periodic and predictable anomalies, is presented to us as analogous to the basic laws of physics, the anger and dissatisfaction generated among the people at the vacuity of contemporary mainstream politics have nowhere to go.

Despite the fact that a shared sense of collective anger has, throughout history, proven to be hugely potent, the popular anger generated by today's domesticated zombie politics remains impotent, unable to identify the ultimate causes of anger or a reasonable plan of action that seeks to set matters straight. Of course, identifying one's political antagonist is a basic feature of any ideological construction of reality that bears at least some resemblance to reality itself, and the failure to reflect the antagonisms that reflect the injustices of the contemporary period is one of the reasons why our politics appears so insipid, stage-managed and ultimately false.

Pent-up anger and obdurate dissatisfaction are usually deeply harmful when experienced subjectively, and the same is true for communities composed of many angry and aggrieved individuals unable to produce for themselves reasonably stable and productive lifestyles. Although there are some notable exceptions, for the most part this objectless anger has yet to be channelled in a productive direction. Without political ideology, there can be no encounter with the objects of truth, no cathexis of the deep anger that intrudes upon and disrupts social experience and subjectivity. Of course, in the absence of fundamental truths about the capitalist system, there is nothing to prevent the dominant ideology instructing individuals to understand their frustrations in relation to their own subjective failures. They should believe that the system itself is broadly fair, and that, if a little more skill and determination had been applied earlier in life, the depressing frustration that clouds their experience would be entirely absent, and in its place would be status, security and boundless hedonistic encounters with the consumer lifestyle that is liberal capitalism's seductive lure. Angry and impotent subjects fall victim to a regressive reimagining of what might have been: forks in the road that offered them the opportunity to take their lives in a radically different direction (see Winlow and Hall, 2009b). It is not a complex ideological operation to turn anger at social injustice into anger at personal failure, and it is not difficult to see why levels of depressive illnesses have skyrocketed in recent years (James, 2007, 2010).

The grinding cynicism of the postmodern age constantly exerts its influence on social experience, subjectivity and ideals. There seems to be nothing pure for us to believe in. We must accept the continuation of the present as inevitable. The only cultural tools at hand to prevent us sinking into a bleak depression are irony, scepticism, cynicism and scorn. As compensation for our ongoing political complacency, we are granted leave to submerge ourselves in the shallow pleasures of consumerised and mediatised culture. Our cynicism encourages us to believe all politicians are corrupt, greedy and self-interested. We assume that all of those at the fringes who are proposing radical alternatives are in some way out for themselves. Even those who are earnest and intelligent – whose plans appear to make sense and suggest a better future – will inevitably fail. We assume that, ultimately, things will continue onwards as they are, and that our anger will become less recognisable to us as it becomes a normalised and irreducible emotional state that colours the way that we see and engage with the social. As we will see, it is the inability of politics to actively negate the logic of neo-liberalism that ensures the continuation of the current mode of destructive capitalism and its theatrically violent culture, and, as we will see, anger must be accompanied by an affirmative political programme if it is to act on the world to effect positive social change.

The conspiracy of opposites

So, we remain for the time being stuck in a perpetual present of gross injustice. The official opposition expresses its righteous indignation, our politicians promise to manage capitalism a little better, but ultimately we remain trapped in a deadening, postmodern *Now* that signifies the termination of history and the persistence of capitalism and its vacuous parliamentary democracy. We will remain stuck here until a genuine historical event occurs that forces a significant number of ordinary people to abandon their cynicism and resignation and demand that the world change.

It is this task of creating a positive image of the new that we seek to address. What influence can protest have, and what are the positive visions and political motivations of those who stridently oppose the current political and economic order? How can the small number of individuals involved with protest movements engage with the masses who remain cut off from politics and sceptical about the possibility of positive social renewal? Will, as some on the left claim, a genuine political event come along of its own accord, provoked perhaps by the publication of yet further details about neo-liberalism's negative outcomes, or does such an event need to be brought into being by organisation, strategy, commitment and personal sacrifice?

In this book, we take seriously the weighty problem of thinking through precisely what a world without capitalism would look like, and what it would mean for those social institutions and practices that remain of considerable value to ordinary men and women. Even now, with new protest groups bursting on to the scene, it is clear that there has yet to emerge a strong desire among the population to move towards a fundamentally different political and economic system. We look around our world and at those things of value to us and we imagine that they are gifts bestowed upon us by a benevolent capitalism. We imagine that the end of this benevolent capitalism would mean the end of technological advancement, the end of social media, the end of reality TV, the end of foreign holidays, the end of consumer lifestyles and so on. The dominant images of the end of capitalism in Western culture are those of absolute economic devastation and crushing hardship, a return to Dark Age repression and poverty. In the popular imagination, capitalism is lively and vivacious, and all alternatives to it are dull, grey and monotonous.

It is clear that anger exists, but are we, the people, really ready to do without those things that we have been taught to believe are the products of capitalist enterprise? Of course, the rise of a genuinely alternative ideological system would be accompanied by the creation of new sources of value. An ideological alternative to capitalism would attempt to wake the people from their slumber and put an end to their dreams of consumerised individualism (see Smith, 2014). It would encourage the people to see consumer items free from their usual symbolic associations and to find value in enriched culture and community rather than competitive individuality, in equality rather than the envy of others, and in a shared sense of social obligation rather than the vague promise of economic freedom.

Turn and acknowledge the truth

If we simply sneer at these ideals and regard the human animal as too innately insecure and selfish for any of this, then the Right will win – forever. This is a profound intellectual error. On the other hand, the idea, common on the left, that 'the people' are naturally orientated towards egalitarianism and, therefore, an inexhaustible source of dissent is the most profound intellectual error of them all. It is a false belief that prevents us from addressing the reality of post-political capitalist realism. Its adherents refuse to consider the possibility that we have already passed through a period of sustained depoliticisation and that the possessive individualism of liberal capitalism and its mass consumer culture has significantly eroded our commitment to the solidarity upon which genuinely progressive politics must rest. This image of egalitarian naturalism is mere wishful thinking that refuses to countenance, and thus wilfully obscures, the true scale of the problem faced by the Left in popularising its narrative of a future age of equality and fairness. It is crucial that we distinguish between, first, the broadly felt anger at falling living standards and failure to achieve success within the structures of capitalism, and, second, a more politically articulate anger directed at the capitalist system itself. If a commitment towards egalitarianism is to grow among 'the people', it must be nurtured and equipped with the forms of political symbolism that might allow the individual to see their social position in a radically new way and redirect libidinal and moral energy towards a new vision of the future.

Let us be honest with ourselves: even given the immense opportunities opened up by the economic crash of 2008, the Left has failed to make significant political headway. After the crash, the Left failed to popularise a narrative that identified capitalism itself as the ultimate cause of the huge problems faced by ordinary men and women across the West. Instead, much of the Left tended to join everybody else in their moral condemnation of the greed, corruption and vulgarity of the banking industry and the failure of the neo-liberal state adequately to regulate the financial system. This problem continues today, as the Left complains about the injustices of austerity but fails to generate any sustained popular discussion about what capitalism is, what it is capable of, and what its continued dominance will mean for our social order and our environment in the near future.

In Britain especially, the Left appears to assume that simply identifying the injustices of government policy will result in a marked swing to the left and the election of a government more in keeping with its political sensibilities. Are we to imagine that TV viewers at home are shocked to hear about the hardships of welfare-dependent families, or about global corporations that are systematically attempting to reduce their tax liabilities? Are they shocked to hear about the growing wealth of corporate elites and the ever-increasing hardship of the poor? Knowledge of neo-liberalism's injustices is already widely dispersed throughout popular culture and has been for some time. The novelty and the impact are wearing off, and no articulate political opposition exists to capture the vestige of our moral outrage.

Indeed, the circulation of such knowledge appears to be an ideological strategy aimed at reinforcing cynical resignation and interpassivity (Fisher, 2009). Our political opposition is now enacted for us by the representatives of the very system we profess to oppose. We are granted leave to remain on the couch, as the media tell us that the government's policies are under sustained attack, and that vocal antagonists are decrying the system's excesses on our behalf. We can openly mock the political elite, denounce the vulgarity of corporate banking elites, dismiss consumerism as a hollow spectacle and argue that the development of sustainable forms of energy is essential for our civilisation. But, if this is all we do, then the system remains firmly in place. Our cynicism and iconoclasm serve only the function of allowing us to delude ourselves that we are not enmeshed in the dominant ideology, and that we see the reality of the system and play no active part in its continuation.

Popular culture actively encourages us to lampoon our political leaders. To dismiss David Cameron, George Osborne and Boris Johnson as braying Bullingdon Club toffs is not in any way subversive. Silvio Berlusconi knew this very well and profited handsomely from his perceived character flaws. Nigel Farage's carefully cultivated image of himself as a bar-room buffoon works to his advantage. We can laugh or sneer at neo-liberalism and those tasked with its management as much as we like, and we are encouraged to do so, as it cathartically releases anger and dissatisfaction. Neo-liberalism doesn't need our approval or wholehearted support. It just needs us to remain disengaged, and our culture of cynicism does this very effectively. We do not need to believe in neo-liberalism. We just need to believe that there is nothing else out there that is better. Our lack of support means nothing to neo-liberalism if we cannot conceive of a more appealing alternative.

The Left must come to terms with this stark fact. Contemporary capitalism does not care if a significant proportion of the population finds its excesses distasteful. It cannot be shamed into adopting pro-social approaches to profit-seeking. Simplistic works that remonstrate against our supposed denial of atrocities and suffering get it hopelessly wrong (see, for instance, Cohen, 2001) – we do not deny, but *pragmatically accept*, these evils because we have no idea how to combat the system that inflicts them on us, which is one very large step worse. Only politics can hold capitalism to account, and only oppositional politics that advocate genuine historical transformation, rather than mere alterations to the regulatory system, truly challenge its continuity. As long as we continue in our appointed role as worker–consumer, focus upon single issues that personally interest us and disengage from unifying politics, then capitalism cares not at all.

Postmodernism has brought with it a historic change in the nature of ideology. For Marx, Althusser and Gramsci, capitalist ideology represented a problem of knowledge. The people were denied access to the truth of their exploitation. During the industrial-modern period, in the vast majority of cases, the people were unable to identify the totality of capitalism and its complex reproductive systems. They continued on in their daily lives, blind to the reality of their position and unaware of the abstract forces that controlled their destiny and structured their experience of social reality. In the liberal postmodernist era, this situation reverses. The various changes that were forced upon the capitalist project during the twentieth century, most notably the attempts capitalism made to integrate the libertarian and anti-establishment discourses of the 1960s (see Boltanski and Chiapello, 2007), allowed the system's excesses to seep out into the public realm. Other factors also helped with this process, but the ultimate outcome was that – as liberalism began to transform politics and economics, and liberal postmodernism began its war against metanarratives and truth claims – the ruling ideology adapted its strategy so that it might continue to grow and maintain its supremacy. With postmodernism, ideology became a problem of action and inaction rather than knowledge (Žižek, 2010; Winlow and Hall, 2012a). The harms of capitalism were, by this time, well known. People knew that capitalism was hideously exploitative. They knew that capitalism actively created and was dependent upon unconscionable inequalities. They knew that capitalism existed only to pursue profit. They knew that capitalism cared nothing about environmental issues or progressive social considerations unless they could be turned into income opportunities.

In a parallel process, the people became disillusioned with political systems and the polity. They now expected politicians to be money-grabbing, power-hungry cynics who danced to the tune set by high finance. They expected anyone who was ostensibly dedicated to representing the people and holding the system to account to have some hidden ulterior motive. We can see an example of this trend when, in 2009, the MPs' expenses scandal broke in the British media. Journalists revealed that MPs had been systematically defrauding the taxpayer for years by claiming the most ridiculous work-related expenses. The dominant reaction of the British public was not shock, disgust and concerted political opposition, but cynical resignation, as if the scandal had merely confirmed what the public assumed to be true all along.

This strategic ideological change tends to ensure that the political potential of conscious realisation quickly fades. Even the governor of the Bank of England and the head of the International Monetary Fund acknowledge the destructive power of abstract financial markets (see Elliot, 2014). Everyone agrees that contemporary capitalism is far from perfect. However, capitalism, in its present form, continues because no creditable alternative exists. It exists only as the least-worst option: it is exploitative, but at least it brings us consumerism. It inevitably produces inequality, but at least we're better off than under communism. Parliamentary democracy is a hollow spectacle, but at least we don't have a dictatorship etc.

The ideology of contemporary capitalism is now perfectly happy to have the system's vulgar excesses exposed to the cold light of day. Our knowledge of these excesses counts for nothing unless such knowledge can be attached to an alternative ideology that offers a disgruntled, disengaged, but essentially passive, population a progressive route forwards. Only the rediscovery of the Good can carry us beyond the debilitating cynicism and making-do of postmodern parliamentary capitalism.

Here, we can see how liberalism's sustained assault upon universality supports the ruling ideology. Our inability to identify the crucial issues that bond us together as a collective ensures the dispersal of radical political sensibilities before they have the chance to cohere into a comprehensible ideological alternative to our present way of life. The deadening climate of possessive individualism ensures that creating and popularising a different political, economic and social model is that much more difficult by a crucial degree. The liberal Left continues with its demand for fairness and its injunction to tolerate diversity, but fails to grasp that genuine change can only come when we move beyond culture to acknowledge our shared political and economic interests. The acknowledgement of these interests, of course, can be a powerful antidote to anxious forms of cultural enmity and conflict. If the poor of all religions and ethnicities are equipped with the political symbolism that enables them to identify capitalism itself as their shared oppressive object, then divisions based on skin colour or which god one chooses to worship become relatively unimportant. Instead, a political community based upon the collective interests of all members will have arisen to put ethnic divisions into their proper perspective.

So, capitalism does not need us to believe in it. We can be as cynical and disengaged as we like, as long as we do not act to oppose capitalism in any meaningful way. Postmodernism ensures the absence of commitment to, and faith in, a broad range of social institutions and practices. It is often said that one of the most dominant aspects of postmodernism is our inability to truly believe. We simply cannot bring ourselves to put aside our cynicism and scepticism and transform ourselves into a true subject of belief. Even the ostensible rise of new postmodern religious fundamentalisms is not antagonistic to this trend. As theologians have long noted, true religious faith is dialectical insofar as it involves wrestling with persistent doubt. Even the most devout are forced to wonder if the object of their belief is an elaborate myth, and if the ecclesiastical guarantees offered by their religion will truly be forthcoming. And how should one seek to address this nagging sense of doubt? Crucially, one must continue to go through the motions of belief. One should continue to pray and profess one's faith, and one should continue to live a devout life in keeping with the Holy Scriptures.

We act as if we believe because in this enactment of faith lies faith's inner truth. It is the ritual that is important. It is submitting oneself to a codified set of rules that seek to apply meaning to our everyday experience. We can also see this in contemporary religious belief and our growing tendency to instrumentalise our faith. We attempt to utilise our faith, to have it work for us. We pray to God, not because we truly believe in a transcendental being, but because it makes us feel better. We eschew religious doctrine and attempt to develop a personal relationship with our god. Despite an obvious lack of genuine faith, we continue to attend service and subscribe to all the rituals of belief. Our religious identity has been transformed into a cultural identity. The true value of the transcendental being to which we profess our belief is that we bestow upon it the power to hand down rules that we feel are legitimate, rules that we feel we must attempt to live by, rules that are shared by a community of fellow believers. To believe in God is to anchor oneself to a set of beliefs and values that can be used to ascribe meaning and by which we can attempt to assess our place in the world. To truly believe is to free oneself from the deep-seated, nagging sense of absence that appears to be a crucial subjective response to the boundless relativism of postmodern society. Our problem is that, these days, there appears to be nothing that can genuinely capture our heart. Every idea is, inevitably, accompanied by a panoply of reasons not to believe it. Every cause is, inevitably, judged to be flawed in some way. Every alternative to parliamentary capitalism is tarnished beyond repair. How do we find our way out of this mess? For Badiou, we must display absolute fidelity to the idea. We must free ourselves from our disabling cynicism and once again submit to belief. And, once we have identified our idea, we must be prepared to fight for it.

Of course, the postmodern subject's inability to truly believe omits one crucial element. We believe in our own lack of belief. We believe that we are fully rational, objective and sceptical individuals who can see the world as it truly is. Despite talk of a supposed post-ideological age, we remain surrounded by ideology. Our absolute, unthinking faith in our own scepticism suggests how the dominant ideology secures its hegemony. As Žižek (2010) has claimed, in the modern era, ideology could be best understood as a process in which *we don't know it but we are doing it*. We can't see the totality of capitalism and we can't understand our subject position within its structure, but, in our everyday behaviour, we are serving capitalism and contributing to its reproduction. With postmodernism, the situation changes so that *we know very well what we are doing, but we are still doing it.* We know of the harms of consumerism, but we continue to engage with it. We know that parliamentary democracy is an empty process that changes nothing, but we continue to vote. We complain about the power of global corporations, but we continue to purchase their services. Our knowledge of the dark side of parliamentary capitalism, by itself, doesn't threaten its continuity by one iota. With no comprehensible alternative anywhere in sight, our knowledge simply tends to reinforce our cynicism and our commitment to turn away from the social and the political and focus on ourselves, our families and our immediate experiences.

The sheer size and ubiquity of the seductive mediated spectacle that affirms greed and competition form a 'shock and awe' tactic far more potent than mere hegemonic 'naturalisation' – so potent that the spectacle can incorporate such knowledge to constantly run a sanitised oppositional narrative alongside, without any fear that it will inspire the return of real politics. When they are viewed in this context, it seems reasonable to suggest that leftist political spokespeople who appear on our news broadcasts, chosen by the corporate media to articulate a general 'leftist' critique of government policy, act as the official extra-democratic opposition, the opposition that neo-liberalism itself appoints in the hope of reassuring the general public that it is continuously being held to account by autonomous antagonists. Inevitably, this process establishes firm limits on political opposition. The Left is effectively being told what it can oppose and how it should oppose it.

Leftist neo-liberalism

Leftist parliamentary parties across Europe have, generally speaking, followed the regressive logic of austerity politics. In Britain, the Labour Party has articulated virtually no substantive opposition to the coalition government's austerity policies. It accepts absolutely that state expenditure must be cut, and that the entitlements already in place must be scaled back. Its opposition goes no further than an entirely fruitless argument about the extent, duration and speed of the cuts. Its message to an electorate suffering significant reductions in consumer lifestyles and the perpetual threat of unemployment and underemployment is simply: 'We aren't quite as bad as the Conservative Party! Although we would cut welfare and state spending, we would cut it at a slightly slower rate than the coalition government!' This is what the death of politics looks like.

Ultimately, after the 2008 crash, the Left failed to make capitalism comprehensible to ordinary people and it failed to allow people to understand their suffering in relation to it. It continues to talk far more about the possibly dangerous social reaction to mounting problems than the problems themselves. The confidence it once had in its ability to solve these problems by means of deep political intervention in their underlying socio-economic structures and processes has now evaporated. This failure of the current Left is simply the most recent contribution to a litany of failure that stretches back through the history of neo-liberalism, indeed through much of the twentieth century (see Sassoon, 1997). Many on the left believe that their critique is holding capitalism to account, and that it is only a matter of time before the people assert their will. However, as we await the final contradiction and the great movement of the spirit, capitalism's ability to destroy lives, corrupt democracy and inflict irreparable damage on our environment remains absolutely staggering to behold. Is the dominant mode of leftist critique really disrupting the onward march of capitalism? Are the new global oligarchs kept awake at night fretting over the Left's cheeky cultural iconoclasm or its incessant call for inclusivity, multicultural tolerance and increased social mobility?

If we are to appraise our current socio-economic reality with a degree of accuracy and honesty, we must dispense with the baseless optimism so common on the left and carefully think through the processes that turn growing anger into an articulate and unified popular opposition to capitalism. Although there are compelling reasons to suggest that a genuine historical and political event may soon be upon us, there is little to suggest that this event will deliver to us a new utopian world of inclusivity, openness, fairness and justice. Those who have identified a return to politics in oppositional movements such as the Indignados, Occupy and UK Uncut must also accept that we can also identify such a return in the rise of far-right groups across Europe. Thus, an important aspect of this book will be a close, empirically grounded analysis of the anatomies of these oppositional groups, left and right. We will also contextualise this analysis in an investigation of the broader composition and trajectory of contemporary leftist politics. We want to see what the new protest movements can teach us about the problems the Left faces in popularising its discourse, and what needs to change on the left if it is to play a genuinely effective role in determining the future of Western civilisations. If Slavoj Žižek is correct in his claim that fragments of the future lie scattered around in the present, we want to gather together some empirical fragments taken from a range of protest movements in order to come to a reasoned conclusion about the potential of these movements and the possibility of the new new Left succeeding where the old new Left failed.

We want to ask what has changed in political opposition. To understand these changes, we will return to Althusser's fundamental question: why do the exploited not rise up in opposition? It is clear that capitalism's economic dynamism continues to produce immense social, cultural and environmental harms, but it has survived crashes and shocks and it has defeated its political opponents time and time again. Throughout its history, capitalism has displayed a remarkable capacity to change with the times and, in so doing, deflect, pacify and assimilate political opposition. However, despite its capacity to change, the fundamental characteristics that constitute its propensity to damage our environment and our collective life remain firmly in place. The core of capitalism is not a 'spirit', an ethico-cultural order, an expression of patriarchy, the sum total of human economic activity or the 'relations of production'. Nor is it a regrettable manifestation of some mythical instinctual human drive to pursue personal interests. Rather, and irrespective of its many cultural variants and its various 'activity-spheres' (see Harvey, 2010), capitalism's core drive is an inhuman, abstracted accounting logic that pursues its own continuation and expansion at the expense of everything else, real or metaphysical. This logic is orientated positively to the expansion of profit and equity, and negatively to the avoidance of its nemesis, the inability to absorb and recirculate its surplus capital as investment. Capitalism will neglect or actively destroy anything that does not help to increase the gap between abstract calculations of assets and liabilities. The presence of ethical subjects within its structures should not be taken as evidence that capitalism as an abstract system of economic organisation can be contained, improved or opposed by basic institutional structures of human morality. As we have seen throughout the system's history, otherwise ethical individuals can become complicit in horror simply by carrying out their institutional roles. A corporate executive can spend his weekends in church or engaged in noble charity work, but, when he returns to his institutional setting and starts signing papers and pursuing profitable investment opportunities, he unknowingly surrenders much of his ethical substance. He finds himself enmeshed in established institutional practices and cultures that stress profit-seeking at all costs, up to and often beyond the boundary of legality.

If we really must insist on attempting to humanise capitalism, if this is a necessary simplification that enables us to grasp what it is and why it does what it does, then we should regard the capitalism of today as a sociopath, perfectly well versed in the outward symbols of human emotion, but entirely incapable of genuine emotional responses to social events. Indeed, individuals who are willing to undertake essentially sociopathic activities can increase their chances of success in both legal and illegal sectors of the system (see Hall, 2012a). We see this today with the tendency of big corporations to give huge sums of money to charity. They do this, not because of some genuine concern for the poor and their problems, nor because they feel a moral responsibility to help those incapable of helping themselves. Rather, corporations engage in highly publicised charitable giving in order to encourage customers, politicians and various interest groups to feel sympathetic towards the corporation and grateful for its largesse. They do this in order to create the impression of considerate corporate citizenship. Despite the huge profits, staggering levels of executive pay and evidence of systematic tax avoidance, they want it to be known that they are committed to the well-being of the social order and its most marginalised subjects. The corporation hopes to encourage the population to think warmly of it, and of course it engages in charitable giving in order to encourage people to develop a closer relationship with its brand and to continue to buy its goods and services.

Post-crash protest

Our goal is not simply a sociology of riots and political protest in which we construct a typology of rioters or objectively analyse the carnivalesque abandon of the crowd. Instead, our goal is to delve a little deeper and address the often entirely apolitical nature of popular dissatisfaction with the current order of things. We will then seek to ask a series of theoretical questions about how political ideology can be connected to popular dissatisfaction, and how alternative political projects might develop as the twenty-first century unfolds – projects that seek to transcend the actuality of capitalism, not simply liberal reformist projects that seek to attenuate some of capitalism's worst excesses. Despite everything we have said so far regarding the reality of our situation, we maintain that change is possible, and opportunities for change can occur with little forewarning. To take these opportunities, the Left should be ready with some sort of inspiring, feasible suggestion for socio-economic reorganisation. Along the way, we hope to investigate a range of issues associated with advanced marginality, changes to the class system and traditional forms of institutionalised opposition. We want to look at what the continuation of liberal individualism and the current retreat into subjectivity (see Winlow and Hall, 2013) mean for oppositional politics that have traditionally drawn their power from collectivism and narratives of universality. In short, we will offer a good old-fashioned, yet updated, critique of ideology that seeks to make some small contribution to the understanding of contemporary politics and political opposition.

2

PART I

Gulags and gas chambers

It is now commonplace to argue that the deep ideological commitments that shaped the twentieth century are almost entirely absent from the sphere of politics. The ideologies that once structured political attempts to put right what was perceived to be wrong – the drive to change entirely the social field so that it might better reflect one's ideological conception of justice, fairness and progressive civility – have been jettisoned from parliamentary politics and systematically removed from social life. Utopianism is now subject to sustained symbolic violence in the liberal democratic states of the West, and all who openly advocate the politics of far-reaching social transformation are dismissed as terrorists or ideological demagogues who would tear down the towering achievements of liberalism's 'open society' and, in so doing, thrust us towards a future of totalitarian brutality.

Why is it that attempts to imagine more ethical ways of living together tend to elicit such a vitriolic response? As we will see, the most famous attempts to imagine Utopia are naïve, but they most certainly are not arguments for brutal dictatorship. Most summon up images of bucolic landscapes free from the excesses of industrial production and individuals liberated from the debilitating effects of material hardships, anxiety and base acquisitiveness. In the most notable utopian texts of the nineteenth and twentieth centuries, the cultural life of the utopian community is structured in relation to openness, fairness, acceptance and the common good: a space defined by expansive freedoms rather than oppression and tyranny. These utopian writers envisioned a world free from social and material pressures, a world in which the unrelenting competition that has such an enervating effect upon our emotional life today is entirely absent. Not one of these texts advocates the enslavement or the slaughter of minorities, or indeed imagines such a thing to be a regrettable but necessary means of moving towards the beatific dream of peaceful coexistence. However, post-war liberalism has transformed our political and intellectual life to the extent that its central tenets – in particular, its piecemeal democratic reformism – are presented as the only means of addressing the perceived social problems that plague our world today. All those who propose to deviate from the well-trodden path of reformism, and all those who advocate political attempts to move beyond our current system, are immediately portrayed as symbols of absolute evil. The dominant ideology demands that we fall into line and accept that only barbarism lies beyond the borders of parliamentary capitalism. Either we will again be subject to a totalitarian barbarism of order, or we will drift towards a barbarism of disorder, in which the rituals, processes and institutions of liberal democracy implode, shattering the basic framework of modern civility (Hall, 2012a, 2012b).

We are constantly warned that comprehensive social and political transformation will inevitably lead to barbarism. Even those who regard themselves as radical liberals chastise utopians for their naïvety. Be careful what you wish for, the utopians are told. Don't let your anger at injustice blind you to the indisputable fact that every economic and social alternative to our present system is immeasurably worse. Instead, put your righteous indignation to a more productive use. Engage with the system and seek to rehabilitate it. Why risk tragedy by abandoning liberalism, when democratically elected governments have before them a range of mechanisms that can significantly improve what already exists? Why bother to revolutionise our world, when we have the opportunity to change our government at the next election? Doesn't our current system give individuals the right to choose, and don't elected governments have the capacity to change the world with carefully calibrated policy interventions? The ultimate message should now be perfectly clear: what we have is the best of all available systems; any attempt at fundamental change will inevitably make things worse.

This narrative has become so ubiquitous that it scarcely registers these days. If leftist or rightist groups are to pursue significant social change, they must first secure a democratic mandate. All political acts that fall outside these borders are terroristic – the folly of dangerous, power-hungry egotists whose blinkered ideological vision encourages them to undervalue the core principles of our current way of life. Their juvenile radicalism is a threat, not just to our political system, but to Western civilisation itself. Their passion and commitment can seduce otherwise cogent members of the public and carry them along the path towards a pathological interpretation of Utopia. It is, therefore, vital that radicals of Right and Left are restrained and brought back into the fold of electoral democracy, history's most advanced form of government.

The standard dismissal of the utopian is to insist that she is a closet Stalinist, willing to sacrifice the freedoms of all so that she might impose her impractical ideology upon reality. Don't these ridiculous ideologues know that capitalism has proven itself time and again to be the best of all available systems and the best available means of boosting the living standards of the poorest? Don't they understand that Soviet-style command economies are hopelessly inefficient and entirely incapable of coping with the complexities of contemporary economic life? Isn't it now clear that economies work best and grow fastest when they are animated by the energies of countless individuals all striving for their own personal advantage? Doesn't it then follow that any attempt to create a less brutal and iniquitous socio-economic system will, in the fullness of time, prove to be an utter disaster? Capitalism dangles the possibility of rapid upward social mobility in front of the individual. It cultivates the belief that even those at the bottom of the heap can completely transform their lives for the better with a bit of hard work and creative energy. Consumerism's sign-value system provides the individual with the means to establish both individuality and social distinction, to stand out from the herd. It claims to be a fundamentally meritocratic system, and it welcomes diversity at the top (see Greenspan, 2013). Capitalism fills our cultural life with desirable objects, and the economic and cultural logic of consumerism is now so well established that these objects become the qualitative measure of our lives. Can we ever show respect to those who would throw all of this away in pursuit of a dream that will inevitably turn into a nightmare?

A similarly aggressive critical response awaits those who hope to explore a politics beyond the horizon of parliamentary democracy. They are reminded of the injustices that existed before the rise of electoral democracy and the sacrifices of those who fought for the right to vote. Don't such people realise how lucky they are to live in an open society in which ordinary men and women are granted the luxury of choosing their own leaders? The diverse advocates of parliamentary democracy – from the social liberals of the Left to the neo-liberal free-marketeers of the Right – instruct utopians to consider countries whose populations do not have such rights, and then to consider countries that have historically suffered under the yoke of dictatorship. Despite its manifold and often quite stark failings, electoral democracy is said to be structured in relation to a base egalitarianism that values the vote of a banker or a bishop no more and no less than the vote of a refuse collector or a call-centre worker. The utopian is portrayed as a dangerous charlatan who stupidly undervalues the great benefits of our current way of life. Adopting the tone of a worldly schoolmaster exasperated by the gullibility of his charges, the pragmatic defender of democracy observes that the utopian may not value democracy now, but, should it ever be removed, they would quickly find themselves transformed into determined advocates of the democratic system. For the established defenders of parliamentary capitalism, there is either democracy or totalitarianism. Either we stick with what we have and continually remind ourselves how lucky we are to have it, or we throw everything away and become mere playthings for some as yet unidentified despot. The message is quite simple: utopians should 'read some fucking Orwell' (Webb, 2013) and accept that our current political reality provides us with the capacity to change the world to suit our collective will. Deeper and more fundamental changes simply aren't necessary, and must be dismissed entirely if we are to avoid the inevitable descent into barbarism that would follow. If you are dissatisfied with the current order of things, engage with it; vote, organise and petition for change. Join a political party and seek to influence its policies. Become an activist and organise peaceful protests to communicate your dissatisfaction to your democratically elected representatives.

Accept that, although the existing order isn't perfect, it's better than all the alternatives. There will always be a few problems here and there, and so there's no point getting too hung up on the difficulties of the current system. Instead, find comfort in the rituals of the electoral process. Accept that what currently exists reflects the preferences of the majority of your peers. There's simply no need for abrupt change. Piecemeal policy interventions will create a better world without any need for disruption and conflict.

Ontology of not-yet-being

Since the close of the Second World War, in a wonderfully adept ideological manoeuvre, celebrated liberal intellectuals have sought to close the gap between naïve utopianism and despotic tyranny. For Karl Popper, Hannah Arendt and Isaiah Berlin, Stalin and Hitler were tyrants made such by their commitment to significant social transformation. Their devotion to an ideologically framed vision of a better world ensured that millions were trampled underfoot, and the lives lost were deemed a price worth paying in pursuit of the utopian dream. Mao and Pol Pot seemed to confirm the thesis. Whenever attempts are made to revolutionise our world, tyranny follows. If we start to take the abstract ideals of utopianism too seriously, it will lead us inevitably to the gulag or the gas chamber.

However, it is very difficult to see *Mein Kampf* sitting neatly within the earlier tradition of utopian writing, seen most clearly in the work of Edward Bellamy, Thomas More, Ernst Bloch and Charles Fourier, a positive tradition of hope and imagination. Stretching the concept of utopianism to include any attempt to intervene in history's trajectory ensures that the original meaning is lost, or, we might suspect, deliberately discarded. What possible sense can it make to position the obviously idealistic and beautifully naïve utopianism of Charles Fourier or the early Thomas More with the industrial slaughter of Nazism? Bloch's (1995) work in particular displays a deep fidelity to the potential of human society to improve itself and actually to realise a future Utopia. His ontology of *not-yet-being* suggests a reality that is not yet ontologically constituted but points towards its future realisation. What has happened to this hope in the *not-yet-being*, this hope that what exists can be improved upon?

For the anti-utopian liberals of the post-war period, the goal was to destroy any possibility that totalitarianism might return. Thus, any 'ideological' attempt to create in reality a conception of the Good must be subject to stinging rebuke. Of course, it is entirely reasonable for these theorists to attack Stalin and Hitler and denounce oppressive forms of governance. Who could possibly argue against that? However, it is also vital that we resist the injunction to withdraw from all forms of utopian thinking and all attempts to imagine a better world. The colossal injustices of contemporary liberal capitalism, when considered alongside a range of crises that lie just ahead of us (see Klare, 2002, 2012; Heinberg, 2011; Pearce, 2013), make the task of imagining a better world more crucial than ever. It is essential that we continue to imagine political and economic systems that are more inclusive and less destructive than industrial capitalism, and social and cultural orders in which insecurity, competition, envy and anxiety are much less apparent. We must never let go of the dream that the future will surpass the present.

For the moment, even though some astute commentators have reassured us that a great event of history may soon be upon us (see Badiou, 2012), firm, narrow limits continue to be imposed on hope and possibility. The received wisdom of our time suggests that we have found the magic formula – liberal capitalism and liberal democracy – and all we need to do is make a slight adjustment here and there to continue to move forward (see Badiou, 2002). Today's dominant positive vision of the future is one in which democracy is more 'democratic' – for example, less manipulated by corporate interests, and more inclusive and representative – and capitalism is more efficient, more concerned with the natural environment and better able to bestow the gift of consumerism upon a much broader population.

Liberal pragmatism furnishes us with the official utopian vision of the future. Casting a dark shadow over it is the orthodox, dystopian view of a future in which the processes and institutions of liberal democracy and liberal capitalism begin to break down, or from which they are entirely absent. Our consumer lifestyles diminish, the diversity of consumer culture is transformed into a dour and unappealing homogeneous whole that allows few opportunities for expressive individuality, and the rights of individuals to actively engage in political life have been suspended. In this view, it is the *relative absence* of parliamentary capitalism's institutions and processes that makes the future unappealing. For the time being, it seems impossible to free ourselves from the horizon imposed by parliamentary capitalism. Both positive and negative visions of the future tend to be structured in relation to what already exists.

It is incredibly difficult to think beyond these borders, but this task has been made much more difficult by liberalism's obdurate drive to censure the utopian imagination. Anyone who attempts to construct new conceptions of the Good, or who attempts to access out-of-date accounts of genuine social value, tends to be greeted by a wave of postmodern cynicism or subject to sustained symbolic violence. Intellectuals who attempt to think, even in the most abstract terms, about a future beyond capitalism are dismissed as silly elitists with no idea or concern about the things that really count for ordinary men and women. The very fact that such intellectuals continue to exist is considered to be a clear indication that the money the state spends supporting the university sector is being thrown away or used to prop up decrepit humanities departments that produce nothing of genuine worth for our economy. Why are these elites being paid to pontificate about a world without capitalism? Shouldn't they instead be applying their intellectual energies to developing new ways of boosting economic growth, or formulating new policies that might improve our experience of civil society? Our world may not be perfect, the defenders of the existing order claim, but we are lucky enough to have a system that allows us to say that it is not perfect and even to change it in a measured, incremental way that guarantees that harms are minimised and the barbarism of collectivist politics is kept at bay. What could be better than increasing the availability of those things we like about contemporary society and minimising those things we do not? In this chapter, we will argue that the first stage of a journey that takes us back to history involves freeing ourselves from the restrictions that have been placed upon our imagination.

Reactionary liberalism

The first task is to contextualise liberalism's anti-utopianism. To suggest that the horrors of the Second World War transformed Europe's political and social order enormously is, of course, an understatement. The war was a truly transformative historical event. Nothing could ever be the same again. There could be no going back to the basic socio-economic and political frameworks that had existed before the war. The shock of war was such that Europe was thrown towards an entirely unanticipated future, totally unimaginable before the war began. In political terms, perhaps the most important aspect of this transformation was the development of a consensus relating to economic planning and the social entitlements that were to be provided to a population that had suffered greatly during six years of total war. The experiences of the Mediterranean states differed, but, for the most part, Western European states developed sizable welfare states and committed to the principle of full employment. Gradually, post-war economies picked themselves up off the floor and, with the assistance of American loans and aid, began to grow. Infrastructural investment improved productivity, and, as time wore on, currency exchange mechanisms and trade arrangements encouraged the development of export markets and diversified national economies. Trade unions became important partners in economic planning and management. As economies developed, and as new energy sources were discovered and exploited, the consumer-based lifestyles of ordinary men and women were significantly improved.

Of course, the long-running post-war economic boom did not appear magically after the declaration of peace in Europe. The initial outburst of relief and happiness that followed the end of the war quickly subsided. It took some time for post-war prosperity to really kick into gear. In Britain, food rationing continued until 1954. But, despite this, when the initial outburst of relief and happiness receded, a mood of cautious optimism appeared to take its place. The working populations of Western Europe were by this time quite used to hardship, rationing and shortages, and the proclamations of mainstream politicians of both Left and Right appeared to give people a sense of hope that the worst was behind them. They appeared to sense that, in their daily labours, they were together creating a better country for themselves and those who would follow. Things were on the up. Democratic socialism had found its way to the centre of European politics, and new policy initiatives suggested that there would be no return to the desperate poverty and grotesque inequalities of the pre-war period.

In economics, Keynesianism was in the ascendancy. In comparison, the neoclassicism of the pre-war period looked simplistic and one-dimensional. Across the West, governments were adapting their approach to fiscal planning and taking a more active role in their national economies. Even politicians of the old order were talking of fairness, justice and progress. Movements for civil rights gathered speed on the runway. For the most part, work was quite plentiful, and a new era of peaceful prosperity seemed to beckon. However, the staggering loss of life associated with the war appeared to temper the mood of optimism. The barbarism of the Holocaust was difficult to fully comprehend. It wasn't until much later in the twentieth century that it was possible for Europe to even begin to come to terms with it. Importantly, the horrors of Auschwitz, Treblinka and Sobibor demanded that we acknowledge our species' capacity for unspeakable evil. This realisation seeped into culture and the political unconscious. The mood was one of hope and optimism, but people now better understood the nature of violence and tyranny. They had witnessed just how bad things could get and the depths to which humanity could sink. Above all, post-war Europe was left with a powerful desire never to let such events happen again.

The perceived threat posed by radical politics demanded that we invest heavily in Europe's institutionalised democratic systems. Throughout the post-war period, electorates seem to have shown great faith in democratic politics and the election ritual. For decades, turn-out figures in general elections remained high, and there existed a much closer connection between the political sensibilities of everyday people and the political parties that sought to represent them in government. Political contestation over our shared future was now to be firmly contained in the democratic process. The upheavals of revolution were no longer necessary. Even the most radical political parties could campaign for office and find their way into government, if they managed to secure a democratic mandate to do so. Parliamentary democracy provided a framework to contain and civilise politics. Formally, politics remained open to all, including those who proposed radical social transformation. Informally, radicalism was forced to the margins, with the tacit ambition of dispensing with it all together. If radicals chose to engage with formal political systems, they were compelled to trade in the bulk of their ideals for pragmatism and small legislative gains, especially in those countries with proportional representation. Rather than fighting for the liberation of humanity from the tyranny of the profit motive, they focused on negotiating the introduction of new legislation that reduced the length of the working day. Rather that fighting for the creation of a new social order built upon a fundamental commitment to equality, they focused on the introduction of new legislation that guaranteed a minimum wage.

Ultimately, however, it was the people who would determine the government of the day. If one could not win a majority, it was assumed that one's ideals or manifesto promises were at odds with the views of the mass of ordinary – and, it was assumed, entirely rational – voters who formed the West's democratic electorates. The people wanted what they wanted, and few were willing to take issue with their choices. The dominant party would form a government and begin to formulate a political strategy in keeping with its sensibilities. If the people didn't like how things were working out, they could change tack at the next election.

Despite the pros and cons of Western Europe's various electoral systems, the government of the day was generally believed to reflect the will of the people. If the government had enough support to do so, it was generally accepted that it could totally transform the socio-economic system by introducing policies that reflected its core concerns.

Despite the dominant assumption that democracy was ultimately fair and that the formation of governments represented the will of the people, post-war Western Europe's democratic systems were strewn with a broad range of problems and injustices. We will not address these problems at this stage, but it is crucial that we note that, after the horrors of the Second World War, parliamentary democracy became imbued with a positive and affective symbolism that extended beyond the perception of equality at the ballot box. In the years that followed the war, parliamentary democracy appeared to become, in the popular consciousness, a basic precept of civilisation itself. It seemed almost natural to conclude that democracy itself had won a titanic battle of ideologies to establish itself at the very heart of a new, progressive and civilised Europe. The war, so it seemed, was not just a conflict between distinct nation-states. It was often perceived to have been a battle between democracy and totalitarianism, between justice and injustice, between freedom and tyranny, and democracy had won because, by every measure, it appeared morally superior to its adversary.

Of course, the Soviet Union had played a crucial role in the defeat of Nazi Germany. The USSR paid an incredibly high price for its involvement in the war, certainly more so than the other allied powers. Its people suffered horribly. Judt (2010: 18) claims some 17 million Soviet civilians and around 8.5 million of its military personnel died in the titanic battle to defeat the Nazis. The Soviet Union was on the winning side, and across its territory there was no 'democracy' to speak of, at least in the most commonly understood meaning of the word. If 'democracy' won, how can we understand the position of the USSR among the victors?

As news of collectivisation, show trials and myriad disappearances found their way into the Western media, this new information merely confirmed our suspicions and reinforced the view that democracy was the very essence of a civilised society. Non-democratic societies were barbaric by comparison. Here was another non-democratic society in which ordinary men and women were dying in huge numbers, as their leaders attempted to impose their ideology upon reality and manifest a warped utopian vision, whatever the cost. Across the West, the post-war social democratic revolution prompted crime to fall to record lows (Reiner, 2007). Poverty and inequality were significantly reduced. Work was plentiful, and consumer lifestyles were expanding (Smart, 2010). On the other side of the Iron Curtain, it seemed as though the opposite were true. In the non-democratic states of Eastern Europe, the horrors of war appeared to be continuing in a different form.

Khrushchev's 'secret speech' in 1956 was a significant watershed moment. In it, he admitted to the barbarism that had occurred under Stalin (see Hobsbawm,

1995; Service, 2010). Until then, many Western intellectuals had continued to argue in favour of state communism. After Khrushchev's speech, communism in virtually all its forms appeared tarnished beyond repair. It was not that Khrushchev was revealing something that had been hidden. Rather, the admission itself removed all plausible deniability from the West's leftist intelligentsia. Even the leader of the Soviet state was willing to admit to its recent tyranny. How could the leftist intellectuals of the West argue otherwise? How could these intellectuals continue to advocate communist egalitarianism, when the Soviet state had engaged in such utter barbarism? One of the outcomes of Khrushchev's monumental denunciation of the former Soviet regime was that a great many leftist intellectuals, even many committed Marxists, felt it necessary to reject state communism and attenuate their critique of parliamentary capitalism.

The great ideological alternative to the capitalist system, and the only genuine challenger to capitalism's global dominance throughout the twentieth century, had engaged in unspeakable tyranny and, unashamed and undeterred, continued to oppress its people. Western democratic populations had quickly come to the conclusion that the freedoms and entitlements that flowed from the post-1945 consensus were essentially 'natural' and theirs by right. Across the Eastern Bloc, the absence of these rights, when placed alongside Khrushchev's admission of wide-spread tyranny under Stalin, appeared to condemn the very idea of communism in the eyes of ordinary men and women in the West. Even in the relatively peaceful East Germany of Ulbricht and Honecker (see Green and De La Motte, 2009) and the 'goulash communism' of Kadar in Hungary (Gough, 2006), many of those things judged essential to the new post-war conception of civilisation appeared to be entirely absent.

Predictably enough, all of this had a profound impact upon the political and intellectual Left and its ambitions. Before leftist scholars would be allowed to present a critique of capitalism and post-war Western democracy, they first had to distance themselves from the state communism of Moscow. This was not simply a form of intellectual censorship or a calculative response on the part of leftist intellectuals. Of course, many Western leftists had been genuinely shocked and appalled by Stalin's tyranny and, later, by the huge and avoidable loss of life associated with Mao's 'Great Leap Forward' and the repression and violence of his Cultural Revolution. Against this background, even the most committed leftist struggled to claim the high moral ground for communism. Communism had become associated in the popular imagination with despotic and destructive leaders who talked of equality and freedom but practised tyranny and repression. The staggering scale of the deaths associated with these regimes boggled the mind. How could something so beautiful, something with so much promise, become so barbaric, so oppressive, hijacked by tyrants completely ignorant of the well-being of the ordinary people for whom they once professed a willingness to die? How had the Left managed to fuck things up on such a colossal scale?

If our intellectual history since these times is anything to go by, the ultimate conclusion drawn from these events was that the very idea of communism contained within it a germ that would spread and grow until, inevitably, the positivity of egalitarianism was transformed into a negativity of brutal dictatorship and authoritarian control. With liberal democracy, however, the people could kick out incompetent leaders at the next election. If a leader was found to be corrupt, or if suspicions grew that he was a warmonger or a corporate stooge, he could be dispensed with, and the country could start again. The horrors perpetrated by the leaders of liberal democratic societies were always contingent, or they were the result of flawed individuals finding their way into high office. The problem could not be reduced to a problem with liberal democracy. With communism, the situation was reversed. Communism itself – the eternal idea of panoramic egalitarianism and common ownership (Badiou, 2010a, 2010b) – was the problem. The horrors that occurred under communist regimes could not be reduced to the shortcomings of any one leader. Rather, these horrors reflected the warped, anti-humanist ideological foundations of communism. Horror was inevitable once communism achieved political supremacy.

In order to remain publicly acceptable to a mass audience – and, in post-war Europe, it was indeed possible for intellectuals to address such an audience – noteworthy leftists were forced to accept the socio-economic and political framework of post-war Western Europe and restrict their critique to its perceived excesses. In fact, the willingness to do this eventually became the fundamental criterion for the leftist intellectual to become noteworthy in the first place. Of course, once communism became so closely associated with tyranny, capitalism seemed that much better by comparison. Even during the decades of post-war prosperity, almost everyone was willing to admit that capitalism was far from perfect, but then almost everyone was also in agreement that capitalism had proven itself to be better than all alternatives to it. The capitalist countries of the industrialised West had their problems, but generally they appeared to be on the right road. At the very least, their leaders were not maniacal despots. Even though, in time, the historical record would prove otherwise (see, for example, Milne, 2004), the people believed that their leaders did not suppress political opposition. The political opponents of the government of the day did not disappear during the night, and a range of democratic and extra-democratic oppositional groups remained in reasonably good health throughout the post-war period. People were living longer and healthier lives. Governments did not feel it necessary to intrude on their privacy, control the media or indoctrinate the young with unrefined ideological dogma. Consumer lifestyles were expanding, and there remained a palpable sense of faith in and commitment to democracy and gradual reformism. In the popular imagination, liberal democracy was the only conceivable political system for a society that strived to be open, progressive and civilised. All alternatives were associated with bleak and enduring immiseration, political and cultural repression and the slaughter of innocent people. The people would take the inequalities of capitalism over the barbarism of state socialism any day.

We should note that the unfolding of post-war history and the dismissal of utopian leftist politics did not occur in an entirely organic way. The CIA and other Western intelligence agencies spent huge amounts of money attempting to ensure that the people of Europe dismissed the radical Left and committed to the pleasures and entitlements of the American liberal democratic model. They hoped to rid the intelligentsia of any residual fascination with communism and Marxism and encourage all to accept the necessity of an American victory in the cold war and the *pax Americana* that would follow. A noteworthy centrepiece of this broad and multifaceted operation was the Congress for Cultural Freedom. At its peak this transatlantic organisation 'had offices in thirty-five countries, employed dozens of personnel, published over twenty prestige magazines, held art exhibitions, owned a news and features service, organised high profile international conferences, and rewarded musicians and artists with prizes and public performances' (Saunders, 2013: 1).

Saunders (ibid.) pays particular attention to the role of intellectuals in the work of the Congress for Cultural Freedom and its numerous offshoots. She provides compelling evidence that the CIA engaged in a 'cultural cold war' against the Left that involved the recruitment or manipulation of such notable figures as Daniel Bell, Hannah Arendt, Isaiah Berlin, George Orwell, Jackson Pollock and many more. These figures worked for, or were subsidised by, the CIA and used primarily to domesticate the Left to the extent that it accepted and committed to liberal democracy and organised itself within the liberal democratic framework. Those willing to endorse the liberal democratic model and wax lyrical about the beauty of Western freedom quickly found themselves centre stage and in receipt of re-muneration and celebrity 'public intellectual' status. Their career prospects magically improved, and their ideas received glowing coverage in both the academic and popular press. The going was that much tougher for talented dissenters who could not bring themselves to renounce their faith in Utopia or curtail their critique of Western liberal democracy.

Saunders (ibid.) ably demonstrates that this organised drive to vanquish the threat of Western Marxism was not a minor and relatively insignificant aspect of America's cold war effort. Huge amounts of US government money were spent building the careers of its representatives in the European intelligentsia and shaping as much as it could the tone and content of post-war culture. Of course, the job of the CIA, and other Western intelligence services, was made that much easier by the genuine horrors perpetrated in the name of communism by the Soviets. That said, we should not underestimate the importance of this kind of behind-the-scenes cultural manipulation in shaping the post-war world of ideas and politics. The ideology that supported the American liberal democratic model hoped to infiltrate the dreams of ordinary men and women across the West. Hatred of the oppressive rich needed to be attenuated, and a new discourse that encouraged all to either admire or at least tolerate the rich for their talent and hard work needed to rise. Dreams of equality needed to be transformed into dreams of freedom and meritocracy. Solidarity and community needed to be adapted to accommodate utilitarian individualism. And, in time, consumerism and the commodity form would need to be elevated to replace the transcendental ideal as the primary source of value throughout Western societies (see Hall *et al.*, 2008).

Of course, the goal was not to entirely vanquish the Left, but to encourage it to start singing a different song. These intelligence agencies recognised that an ostensibly healthy political opposition is vital to the image management of the liberal democratic model. They didn't want to suppress it, and nor did they have any great desire to curtail leftist critique. Rather, they wanted the Left to accept the rules of the game and commit to democracy. Sure, offer a robust critique of inequality and injustice. Go ahead and campaign for reform. Play the game to the best of your ability. Just don't suggest that the game should be abandoned and something else installed in its place. A committed democratic Left was the best available means of suppressing the extra-democratic Left, and the most eloquent and persuasive critics of communism were democratic socialists. When even the system's most strident critics encouraged the people to commit to democracy and rally behind the flag, the ultimate goodness of the liberal democratic model seemed obvious and straightforward. Good guys and bad guys; black hats and white hats; the raw egalitarianism and limited government of liberal democracy versus the barbarism, squalor and want of communist totalitarianism.

Given time, a functional and pragmatic democratic Left could eliminate entirely the need for an extra-democratic Left. A forthright, open and inclusive discourse on policy innovation and gradual social evolution would ensure that thoughts of revolution and lingering dreams of Utopia were cast aside and quickly forgotten. What those who represented the interests of Western liberal democracy wanted was for the Left to split and the pragmatic, democratic and gradualist Left to triumph to the extent that the radical utopian Left could be dismissed as an irrelevance – an excessive, inconsequential and blindly utopian cadre of radicals absorbed in their ideologies, lost in their dream worlds and completely ignorant of the wants and needs of ordinary men and women.

Once the capitalism–democracy dyad was accepted as 'natural' and superior to all alternatives, the system's officially appointed antagonists were unable to go much further than identifying parts of it that needed to be reformed. At this point, the Left fractured, and its component parts began to change. Two dominant and mutually sustaining factions emerged. Many on the left would focus their attentions on reforming the system and petitioning governments to introduce new legislation that would curtail the system's most egregious harms and injustices. Others, of a more libertarian hue, appeared to flip and invert the traditional drive for genuine egalitarianism. They focused instead on a dual-pronged campaign that joined together a fight against biographical predestination with a new, broad-based advocacy for panoramic personal freedoms.

Of course, this transformation of the political and academic Left is precisely what the cold warriors of the American intelligence community envisioned at the close of the war. Throughout the 1950s, 1960s and 1970s, they continued to work assiduously towards this end. They wanted capitalist liberal democracy itself to be seen to have its very own radical cutting edge, in the sense that the views of the majority, no matter where they fell in the political spectrum, and no matter what their sovereign desires might be, would shape the politics of the day. And it should be seen to be fair, in the sense that everyone was entitled to vote, and all votes were considered equal. Only in democracy could everyone play a role in determining the country's leader. Democracy provided its citizens with a codified legal framework that restricted the power of governments and forced them to work within the rules. Democracy allowed every citizen to openly campaign against government policy. All voices were to be listened to. Democracy could be whatever the people wanted it to be. The Left could criticise and mount campaigns whenever it liked, as long as it did so peacefully and remained within the law.

Inevitably, as the winds of change swept across the West, the foundations of traditional leftist politics appeared unable to hold its principles of utopianism and equality firmly in place. Revelations about the Soviet gulag system and Stalin's tyranny appeared to render the basic idea of communism off limits for a new generation of leftists, disgusted by the inequalities of industrial capitalism, yet appalled by the excesses of state socialism. From the 1960s onwards, and partially as a result of behind-the-scenes manipulation and corruption, the radical Left appeared to ditch many of its traditional concerns and principles, or at least to modify them to the extent that they appeared new and more in keeping with the times. The times, after all, were a changin'. Instead of seeking to defend the purity of the communist ideal, and rather than doggedly pursue a future egalitarian Utopia, the newly constituted radical Left combined its fear of capitalist exploitation and communist totalitarianism to establish new fronts from which it could wage a peaceful war of words against the new ideological enemy of capitalist authoritarianism.

This new radical Left rapidly narrowed its focus from the totality of capitalism to 'authority', 'the system' and 'the establishment'. The battle against hierarchy remained, but its discourse, and perhaps even its fundamental ideological commitments, appeared to change. In particular, the Left's roots in political philosophy seemed much less apparent. The language of personal rights and freedoms replaced the language of egalitarianism, solidarity and collective struggle. The academic Left was becoming increasingly libertarian in its social and cultural attitudes, and, as time wore on, large sections of it lost interest in political economy. Capitalist political economy created inequality, sure, but then so did a range of social institutions and practices that were not directly tied to economic activity. The drive to liberate the people remained in place, but it now wanted to liberate them from stultifying tradition and oppressive social norms, rather than the predations of a market economy and the tyranny of the wage form. The new Left's fragmentary cultural Utopia was one in which the individual was free from any demands that might be placed upon her: free to define and redefine herself and her relationship to the world as she chose to, free from all forms of coercion, pressure, moral absolutism and social expectation.

The ideological ties between this new liberal Left and the *pax Americana* were there for all to see, or at least for anyone who had a mind to look. Freedom was, of course, central to America's self-image. Freedom was America's primary selling point, the hypnotic allure that encouraged millions to leave their country of origin and set off in search of something better. The system itself was perfectly able to cope with a situation in which its most vocal antagonists were calling for freedom. Freedom, everyone seemed to agree, was best served by an open democratic system, and the relationship between the state and its subjects was a perennial concern for both major political parties. It seemed as if the representatives of the system could always agree in principle with the system's antagonists. Sure, despite our differences, let's have more personal freedom. The path to freedom begins right here, at the ballot box. And never forget, democracy is absolutely integral to freedom, our most important line of defence in the war against tyranny and oppression.

The primary point of political engagement became how best to facilitate personal freedom. Everything oscillated around this core concern. Should the state tax and spend or shrink and curtail its activities to boost freedom? The other grand ideals of liberalism appeared unimportant by comparison. Of course, the liberal counter-culture and the American establishment it made such a song and dance about despising shared this commitment to freedom. However, reaching a consensus on what freedom was and what should and could be done with it was more problematic, but at least both sides could agree that freedom was great, and that the individual should be given more of it. Even those at the margins who were genuinely disgruntled at the staggering injustices of American capitalism tended to argue that democracy needed to be overhauled and rejuvenated, rather than dispensed with. Beneath the various intellectual and political engagements about the meaning of liberty lay a tacit concern about *whose* liberty, *whose* freedom, *who* should be made free, and how should it be done? Who is being coerced, who is being denied the rights of citizenship? As the 1950s gave way to the 1960s, this unstated concern could be seen in attempts by various cultural interest groups to move to the front of the queue when it came time for the benefits of liberalism to be dished up. Minority sexualities, women, ethnic minorities and so on had clearly suffered disproportionately, and justice demanded that they draw closer to power. Again, the traditional concern with equality – equality for all people, that is – gave way to a multicultural scramble to improve the status and privileges of one's cultural interest group.

This historical battle between the liberal counter-culture and the pin-striped representatives of modern American capitalism was not a battle of opposites. If the primary political conflict of the times is between left-wing cultural libertarianism and right-wing economic libertarianism, then we can rest assured that America's foundations in liberty and the sanctity of the individual will remain in place. Whether or not we should conclude that liberalism's inevitable victory resulted in any significant gains for ordinary men and women is a matter of some conjecture. Certainly, the economic liberalism of the Chicago Boys appeared to benefit from the counter-culture's historic fight to free the individual from the clutches of an overbearing state, and the rapidly growing consumer culture seemed to draw plenty of energy from liberalism's fight against dull social and cultural orthodoxy and its advocacy of the sovereignty of the individual.

Ultimately, especially in the USA, the counter-culture came to dominate the new Left, and eventually it seemed to replace it. Utopianism did not disappear, but it came to address the libidinal dreams of the individual rather than the political dreams of the collective. Utopia was an individual space in which we were free from the encroachments of authority, free to enjoy as much as possible the short time each individual has on Earth. Life ain't a rehearsal. It's a short burst of total self-determination in which we can indulge in pleasurable pursuits and choose only those social obligations that suit us. And the beauty of all this was that one didn't need to overcome capitalism to get there.

The new radical Left of the 1960s and 1970s, especially those elements closely tied to the counter-culture, tended to dismiss the old socialist concepts of 'class struggle' and 'the proletariat' as reductive and one-dimensional. These things, like discredited state socialism, were relics from a bygone age. If the politics of equality and freedom was to be advanced, the Left would need to move with the times and address the concerns of ordinary people who hoped to take a more active role in determining their identities and biographies. The new Left would need to look at other sources of tyranny if it was to continue on the path to social justice. Class inequality was simply one stratagem in a much more complex and multifaceted programme of repressive social control and reproduction that advantaged some at the expense of others. What about gender inequalities and ethnic inequalities? What about sexism, racism and broader systems of social control? What about the stereotyping, oppression and marginalisation of minority sexualities? What about religious and secular tyrannies abroad? All of these things needed to be identified as problems that demand democratic resistance.

Many forms of leftist political thought that persevered with a critique of capitalism became influenced by the liberal humanism of the 1960s' counter-culture. A lot of this new work, especially in Britain and America, centred upon a critique of the capitalist state as the primary agency of dehumanising repression and social control. The capitalist state sought to regulate the population and crush individuality and diversity. It reproduced social divisions and penalised a range of subgroups that were to be denied the full rights of citizenship. It failed to represent the interests of those with little or no social power. As new critical discourses problematised and challenged inequalities and injustices that appeared external to the sphere of production, consumption and exchange, the fundamental immorality of capitalism's basic exchange relation, in which the individual attempts to extract a surplus from the other, became far less important and eventually disappeared as an object of critique. Critique of the profit motive and its capacity to destroy genuine sources of social value and create damaging forms of enmity, envy and competition became far more difficult to find in the discourses of the new Left than they were in the old.

As time wore on, across the political spectrum the trend towards liberalism became increasingly clear. Liberalism was everywhere. Discussions of the old philosophies of socialism and communism became increasingly infrequent, and new discourses of freedom and rights came to the fore. Anti-statism would become as common on the radical left as it was on the libertarian right, and their shared philosophical commitment to personal freedom enabled individuals to move across the political spectrum without appearing to divest themselves of their core political beliefs. Some counter-cultural figures, initially on the libertarian left, moved seamlessly into business while continuing to advocate the politics of individual autonomy and self-determination (see Hall *et al.*, 2008). Their market activities simply represented a new way to be creative, and their products and services could encourage others to find their own freedom. Their radical approach to business, they often argued, was shaking up the stuffy corporate world. The sclerotic and inefficient bureaucratic state was clearly incapable of getting help to people in genuine need. The socially minded entrepreneur, on the other hand, could move mountains with his ingenuity and force of will. They genuinely cared about people; it wasn't all about profit for them. They were keen to encourage marginalised groups to embrace the market and find their own creative route to upward social mobility and personal freedom. If their irrepressible creativity bestowed upon them huge wealth, they were happy to give this money to the needy or to charities that sought to assist impoverished young entrepreneurs to pursue their dreams. In the same way, the savvy businessmen of the libertarian Right could dip into the lexicon of the new Left in order to pressurise governments to reduce taxes and abandon their tyrannical suppression of individual economic freedom. The political representatives of the new Left and the new Right were free to borrow phrases and grand ideals that were once the sole preserve of leftist utopians. Politicians from anywhere on the political spectrum could talk of their commitment to freedom, equality, fairness and social justice. In a new era of panoramic liberalism, who could be against such things?

Of course, not all on the left migrated along this path, but the trend towards liberalism was clear. Parliamentary capitalism had won. Even many of those on the radical left had ceased to talk of alternatives to it. Few held out any hope that there could be a workable alternative that didn't involve totalitarianism and a great leap backwards in consumer lifestyles. Much of the energy that sustained the dialectic of politics drained away, and what remained was scooped up and pushed back on to the field of parliamentary democracy. The overthrow of the system was replaced by a ceaseless drive to reform it. Leftist talk of 'revolution' was increasingly restricted to debates about culture, and the definition of politics was adapted to fit the new cultural frame. Some on the left sought to drop the pretence of a future without capitalism. Instead, the route forwards for the Left was simply to take up a position of permanent critique (see Holloway, 2002).

If the Left were to take power, it would inevitably be corrupted by it. Ultimately it would let down the people and fail in the challenge of creating a future less scarred by competition, injustice and exploitation. While the taking of power would unavoidably lead to disappointment, a position of permanent critique would ensure that the Left was forever unsullied by power and free to offer forthright criticism of the existing order. The politics of the new radical Left, then, should be a struggle *against* power rather than a struggle *for* it. Arguing from a permanently unassailable ethical position would increase the Left's influence and force the incumbent power to listen.

The trend towards liberalism was identifiable even in the more radical and anarchistic literature. Holloway's (2002) proposal, of course, assumes that all power must be opposed, and that there cannot be such a thing as a legitimate power that will not somewhere down the line be corrupted by a willingness to trample over the rights and interests of the excluded or marginalised. In this discourse, both the absence of utopianism and the Left's lack of faith in itself are palpable: here, all of life is to be defined by the struggle against oppressive power. It is not so much that there's no victory in sight: rather, for this branch of the new Left, victory isn't even thought about or dreamed about, let alone planned and achieved.

The field of politics was no longer restricted to debates about political economy, the roles and remits of key institutions and our shared social and historical trajectory. The new Left argued that the restrictive mandate of the old Left omitted a huge range of inequalities and injustices. As the new Left attempted to take up these new emancipatory struggles, everything, it seemed, could be considered 'political'. And, in the developing academic field of cultural studies, it often was. Of course, if political struggle and ideological resistance could be identified in working-class criminality (for example, Cohen, 1955), or in the clothing and musical choices of marginalised subcultures (for example, Hall and Jefferson, 1976; Hebdige, 1979), then we could take a little comfort from the fact that the battle against the capitalist tyrant was being fought in skirmishes over cultural meaning throughout everyday life. With a few creative readjustments and the broadening out of the concept of politics to include the entirety of the cultural field, political defeat could be magically decoded as myriad political victories, and depoliticisation and ideological incorporation decoded as an organic drive towards equality and freedom.

Thompson versus Althusser

As the post-war period unfolded further, a number of key divisions opened up on the political and academic left. Of these key debates and divisions, E. P. Thompson's (1978) aggressive denunciation of Louis Althusser is perhaps the most illustrative of the seismic shift that was taking place in the corpus of leftist intellectual and political life. To reduce this to its basic essence, Thompson was deeply aggrieved at Althusser's depiction of the working class as interpellated into the ideological framework of global capitalism, to the extent that he wrote a book-length refutation of Althusser and structural Marxism. That book is now a foundational text for British cultural Marxists. Although it is certainly true that not all agree entirely with its general thesis, it appears to have set the tone for the development of the British Left throughout the post-war years. *The Poverty of Theory* responded to Althusser's disregard for historicism and empiricism, and, in the book, Thompson offers an impassioned justification of historical method. *The Poverty of Theory* also, of course, displays a marked distrust of 'theory', at least in the way that it was being developed by many leftist philosophers in France, Germany and Italy. One could reasonably argue that that distrust can still be detected on the British left today.

For Thompson and many others working in the British tradition, it was possible to investigate history to discover the truth of class-consciousness and political opposition permeating everyday social life. It wasn't necessary to rely on narcissistic continental philosophers to pontificate on the nature of politics and social reality. One could simply get out there into the real world and gather empirical data that captured reality in a reasonably reliable and objective manner. Althusser had asked an important question: given that capitalism benefits only a tiny proportion of the overall population, and given that the working classes are always cast as exploitable units of production and consumption, why do the poor not rise up in opposition? Thompson's strident response didn't seek to answer the question but to challenge the assumptions contained in the question itself.

For Thompson (2013: *passim*), the history of working-class life, in Britain and elsewhere, was one of ubiquitous and sustained opposition to capitalism and its ruling class. Thompson, a skilled historian keen to excavate historical facts to make his case, believed he could identify among the working class a continuous and very clear refusal to meekly submit to domination. For Thompson, the history of the working class was defined by political struggle and a concerted attempt to defend its own cultures and values, and Althusser's depiction of the working class as ideologically determined automatons was deeply galling. Not only was this factually inaccurate, but it was an outrageous slur that misrepresented the reality of the very group most attuned to the predatory nature of industrial capitalism.

'People', Thompson (1975: 262) declared, 'are not as stupid as some structural philosophers suppose them to be'. His portrayal of the industrial working class draws on those early elements of Marx that are resolutely 'humanist', and these are precisely the elements of Marx's *oeuvre* that Althusser sought to challenge and overcome. Thompson's Marxist humanism stressed the agency of capitalism's most exploited subjects. For him, it was patently obvious that the working class did not simply absorb the values of the ruling class or adopt its world-view. For example, in *Whigs and Hunters* (1975), Thompson draws upon Gramsci's theory of hegemony, but at no stage does he accept that, during the eighteenth century, Britain's lower orders were fully incorporated into the ideological field of the landed gentry. For Thompson, it was clear that the poor did not actively collude in their own oppression. Rather, the poorest retained the capacity to defend their own cultural forms and were never fully dominated and controlled by their oppressors. In *Whigs and Hunters*, Thompson reworked Gramscian hegemony and used the concept to understand the context and form of class struggle within a specific historical conjuncture. This was a technique that would be adopted by the cultural Marxists who followed him, especially those of the Birmingham School. Hegemony, for Thompson, related specifically to struggle and resistance, and that resistance was a matter of historical record. The dominant ideology could never fully bring the working classes to heel; their indomitable spirit could be identified in every epoch.

Ultimately, Thompson's anger at the ongoing developments in continental Marxism – and especially in the work of Althusser and others apparently given to shameless intellectual obscurantism – related to what he believed was its tendency towards dour fatalism and its stupid dismissal of 'empiricism' and 'historicism'. But there were other notable divisions. Thompson defended the law and parliamentary democracy from the aggressive critique of the continental Left. These things, Thompson argued, did not exist in their present form to oppress the poor or to contain them within legitimate structures of power. These things could always be utilised and turned to the advantage of the poorest. They could become the very instruments of social justice. Few doubted Thompson's radical credentials, but he was in fact not ideologically opposed to liberal democracy as such.

His great concern was with the people and their 'experiences'. For him, progressive politics needed to emerge from these 'experiences'. Thompson had no time for talk of intellectual vanguards and he was aggressively opposed to any suggestion that, left to their own devices, the industrial working classes were incapable of transforming their own circumstances. Ideological incorporation, depoliticisation and submission didn't stand up against the evidence. The historical record proved that the working classes had actively opposed the ruling class whenever there was a need to. His overall analysis created the impression of a politicised working class and an immoral ruling class eyeing each other up suspiciously through much of modern history. Whenever the ruling class encroached too far, the working class would rise up in opposition and strike back at those things they found most distasteful, and defend their class interests. History, for Thompson, reflected this enduring antagonism. For Thompson, the working class was cohesive, defined by its solidarity and its own distinct cultural forms. It had a clear sense of itself and its interests. It was creative, improvisational and deeply politicised. It encapsulated, quite clearly, the very best of humanity.

Thompson's *The Making of the English Working Class* is one of the most popular leftist texts to have emerged in Britain during the post-war years. It forced academic history, and other disciplines in the humanities and social sciences, to evolve at considerable speed. It also spurred the development of British cultural studies by displaying the utility of empirical methods and constructing an appreciative analysis of the cultural life of the popular classes. It caught the mood perfectly and provided those on the political left with the impetus to create a new 'history from below'. Thompson offered the British Left the image of an inspirational, never-say-die working class fighting nobly against all odds to defend itself and its values. Despite setback after setback, the working classes were fully capable of overcoming structural constraints to become the makers of their own history. Thompson cast the English working class in a heroic and idealistic light that seemed to satisfy the needs of the British Left during a historical conjuncture that remained overshadowed by the evils of Nazism and Stalinism. The working class was, at once, a sleeping giant capable of rising up to assert its will and the plucky no-hoper who, when pushed too far, was willing to take on a powerful but overconfident enemy.

For Thompson, Althusser seemed to encapsulate all that was wrong with the continental Left. All this navel-gazing was pointless and self-indulgent and completely useless for those sections of the working class who looked to the academic

Left for intellectual sustenance. Both Thompson and Althusser were committed Marxists, and each saw their own discourse as a representation and continuation of the truth of Marx's analysis of capital. Of course, Althusser's analysis of ideology sought to respond to the Left's gradual movement towards humanism. This movement began to pick up pace after Khrushchev's 'secret speech' laid bare the crimes of Stalinism. Althusser's philosophy (for example, 2005, 2008; Althusser and Balibar, 2009) was instead a kind of anti-humanist materialism, and his major contribution to leftist thought, in our view at least, came in his analysis of the ideological state apparatus. Rather than a steadfast commitment to political struggle, Althusser saw in the working class a form of subjectivity structured in relation to the needs and lures of capitalism. The working classes were quite clearly unable to become a class for themselves, fully capable of understanding their shared subjugation and cognisant of their power to affect genuine change in the world.

The spat between Thompson and Althusser is particularly illustrative, as there appears to be no prospect that a middle ground can be constructed between these two leftist positions. This was not a case of the 'narcissism of small differences' that many believe to have held back the development of the Left in Britain. Despite both men being quite clearly committed to the political interests of the working class, the differences in their analysis of working-class politics were huge. The gap between them could not be closed by each conceding a little ground to the other. Althusser identified the capacity of ideology to intrude upon and reshape subjectivity itself. Thompson identified the irrepressible agency of the working classes and their indefatigable political resistance. Althusser saw the working classes trudging off to the factory to be exploited and spending their weekends shopping or partaking in other sanctioned and ruthlessly commodified leisure pursuits. Thompson saw the working classes joining labour unions, campaigning for better conditions and levels of pay, forming democratic and representative bodies to challenge power and rising up violently to oppose the interests of capital whenever those interests threatened to further encroach upon their life-world.

This intellectual jousting proved to be quite important for the development of the intellectual Left, especially in Britain. The shape and orientation of the academic Left in Britain, even now in 2014, continues to reflect the concerns of Thompson and his followers. The idealisation of the working classes and the assumption of class agency and political opposition are very much still with us. The academic Left's commitment to representing accurately the reality of working-class life exposes us to a deeper inaccuracy and a significant, and deeply ideological, misrepresentation of social reality. Even now, after thirty years of political retreat and decades of neo-liberal restructuring and downsizing, in which the working class has been stripped of traditional forms of employment and forced to contend with the problems of unstable and highly competitive labour markets and shrinking consumer lifestyles, we are still exposed to the dogma of perpetual resistance, political solidarity and the open, progressive and creative community life of the working classes. How many anxious, disappointed and angry men and women are ignored by the Thompsonite empiricists as they searched doggedly for the small handful of articulate individuals willing to offer the traditional narrative of political opposition? How many working-class Tories and fascists are ignored? How many criminals, how many men and women suffering with mental illness or addiction? How many dedicated consumers do the empiricists ignore in their desire to research the miniscule number of individuals who see a political resonance in the choices they make while shopping on the high street?

During our early academic careers, we were, like everyone else studying the social sciences in the Britain during the 1970s, 1980s and 1990s, exposed to this dominant left-humanist narrative. We were repeatedly encouraged to adopt the optimistic language and motifs of working-class agency and resistance. Although clearly orientated towards the politics of the working class – the class to which we belong – and leftist politics more generally, this seemed to jar with our real-life biographical experiences of the fatalism and political disinterest that were displayed by members of the working class right through the post-war period, even in those industrial regions judged by history to be the seedbeds of radicalism and oppositional politics.

Very early on, we came to the view that well-meaning and deeply committed middle-class leftists were suffering from a particularly obdurate form of confirmation bias. In their empirical investigations, they were discovering working-class political radicalism because that is what they wished above all else to discover. They found creativity and insubordination only after bypassing the great mass of working-class people who lived relatively humdrum lives free from deep-seated political commitments. Researchers working in the British empiricist tradition often attended community groups and listened with sympathy to the problems faced by working-class communities. They looked on with admiration when members of the community tried to solve those problems, but they ignored the majority of people who didn't attend the community groups, who accepted the lot that had been handed to them, or who were committed to the utilitarian solution of looking out for number one.

Even in the old working men's clubs and union meetings, where industrial machismo seemed to hang in the air, there always existed a clear and uncamouflaged commitment to pragmatism and incrementalism. Workers, reasonably enough, wanted more money and better conditions and, through the middle third of the twentieth century, they fared pretty well. The vast majority of these workers didn't care about communism, nor did they care that much for the vague concepts of equality or social justice. For every working-class firebrand who spoke out at meetings of the need to fight an ethical battle against capitalist authoritarianism, there were a hundred, perhaps many more, who simply wanted a pay rise and extended holidays.

As time passed, they wanted colour TVs and foreign holidays. They wanted a car, and then they wanted a better car. They wanted to buy a house or to send their son or daughter off to university. Of course, these were not bad things in themselves, but we must recognise that, for the huge bulk of the English working class, politics always remained relatively unimportant within the overall structure of their lives. Politics didn't shape the way ordinary workers saw the world, at least not to any significant degree. The English working class, simply by accident of birth and circumstance, was not predisposed to politics and opposed to the continuity of capitalism. It did not attempt to resist corporate culture when making consumer choices at the supermarket or in the shopping mall. Capitalism as an economic system was, for the vast majority, not fully understood. Work was a timeless fact of life. This, it seemed, was as it had always been. Work and struggle. The comforts of family and community. The great majority of the people were confirmed pragmatists who hoped that things would improve and that their children would fare a little better. They wanted to ensure the continuation of their employment, and they wanted to improve their lifestyles.

The everyday experience of exploitative industrial work was capable of fomenting forms of solidarity and togetherness in the workforce, and this in turn could facilitate what Lenin (1993) called a 'trade union consciousness'. However, we should bear in mind that, in most cases, trade unions wanted employers to remain profitable and their businesses to grow. If the employer succeeded – which often meant putting other companies out of business and some of their comrades out of work – they would be more receptive to pay demands and more inclined to bestow other benefits upon the workforce. Although there were obvious exceptions, most trade union representatives were unconcerned with broader issues of economic management. They focused instead on the material interests of their members. Rather than a utopian dream of equality, they wanted a bigger share of the spoils.

It is too simplistic to suggest that anti-capitalist politics emerges from the 'experiences' of ordinary working people. It makes far more sense to claim that the 'experiences' of the worker were politicised only when he was equipped with the means of grasping his political and socio-economic position, only when he became aware of capitalism as a global economic system, and only when he began to see his own disappointments, fears and frustrations in relation to the abstraction of market forces. The next developmental stage is for the worker to become cognisant of alternative ways of organising the economy, or at least be aware that such alternatives exist. If anti-capitalist politics is to be extended outwards from the cosseted metropolitan cocoon of the liberal middle classes to connect with ordinary men and women, workers need to believe that a better world is possible. As we have already argued at length, knowledge of capitalism's inequalities and injustices is, by itself, not enough to drive political interventions that seek to move beyond capitalism.

In Britain, members of the old industrial working class voted Labour when the Labour Party seemed to represent their interests. A strong link between the unions and the party still existed, and those at the top of the party seemed to be, generally speaking, 'like them'. You could imagine having a pint and a natter with Aneurin Bevan or Harold Wilson. With Blair, Brown and Miliband, indeed the entire front bench of the party since the mid 1980s, not so much.

To be sure, up to the Thatcherite era, the English working classes often begrudged the ruling class its privileges. And, of course, they displayed forms of community solidarity, certainly far more so than working-class communities do today. Generally, they recognised that, if they stuck together, they had a shot at improving their standards of living. They knew that family and friendship networks were important if one was to defend oneself against the periodic hardships of working-class life and find one's way to the pleasures and beauty of intimacy, altruism and enduring support and commitment. But these spaces were not packed with organic intellectuals debating the role of the state in a post-capitalist society. Some members of these communities certainly were politicised and quite strident in their opposition to capitalism, but the English working classes were not dyed-in-the-wool humanists, nor were they particularly liberal or 'progressive' in their social and cultural attitudes. Rather than commit to the creative recoding of consumer products, young working-class people wanted to have a good time, develop and move forward with their lives. And, despite what many on the Thompsonite left said, there is nothing inherently revolutionary about that.

The rise of the Thompsonite Left

Thompson played a crucial role in establishing what became known as cultural Marxism. Marxism in Britain had atrophied since the end of the war, but, throughout the 1960s, it underwent a mild renaissance. This renaissance was, of course, connected to the forms of cultural opposition that were synonymous with that period. Some young people, dissatisfied with the rigid class and gender hierarchies of modern capitalism, were demanding change in quite strident terms (see Borabaugh, 1992; Ross, 2004). They demanded an end to the American imperialism that appeared to be driving new global conflicts, and they seemed generally unwilling to settle for the restrictive expectations handed to them by the older generations who had lived through the Second World War. The time for the return of Marx seemed to be at hand.

Cultural Marxism has its intellectual roots in history and English literature. 'Marxism' exerted its influence from its background location, structuring critical accounts of injustice as they related to the field of 'culture'. The 'Marxism' advocated by the cultural Marxists was, of course, a humanist Marxism concerned with the agency of the great mass of people exploited and dehumanised by capitalism. In the foreground, cultural Marxism sought to develop new empirical accounts of everyday life and the experiences of ordinary men and women. It was, for the most part, uninterested in dour political and economic accounts of class formation, and instead it hoped to place the diversity and complexity of post-war cultural life centre stage. Cultural Marxism was, then, an attempt to move beyond the limitations of formal Marxist political economy and leftist political theory more generally. It hoped to communicate new truths about the reality of working-class life and, right from the outset, it tended to follow Thompson in accentuating the agency of the poor and the capacity of the post-war proletariat to resist the ideologies of the market as the major economies of Europe grew and became more complex.

As a school of leftist thought, cultural Marxism stood in marked contrast to the Frankfurt School, which offered a much darker depiction of the human condition and a much bleaker analysis of the incisive nature of market ideology. Both of these schools distanced themselves from Marxist economism and both identified the crucial importance of the field of culture in post-war Western societies. Having agreed on these things, these two schools of thought parted ways to develop accounts of culture that had virtually nothing in common.

The Frankfurt School saw a disconsolate and individualised consumer trudging forlornly through the momentarily alluring, mass-produced tat of the culture industries, manipulated, incorporated and placed in competition with those who would once have formed his political community. The cultural Marxists saw a rational and discriminating consumer making active choices and determining his own cultural engagement in a manner suited to his tastes and dispositions. They believed they could identify the capacity of the proletariat to appropriate the symbolism of corporately manufactured commodities and refashion them in ways that suggested a desire to subvert the hierarchical structures of cultural domination. For the Frankfurt School, in the act of consumption the consumer was immediately incorporated into the cultural symbolism of the market and the process of commodification.

For the cultural Marxists, and especially those at the Birmingham Centre for Contemporary Cultural Studies, the act of consumption could be loaded with counter-cultural significance. Buying corporately manufactured consumer items didn't necessarily signify absorption into capitalism's meaning system. Rather, the consumer retained the capacity to creatively rework consumer symbolism and transform its significance for political use by his cultural in-group. The symbolism produced by global corporations could be creatively transformed and used to subvert the system itself. For the Frankfurt School, there could be no resistance at the point of consumption. For the cultural Marxists, resistance was everywhere.

Of course, the caricatures we have just drawn ignore the complexity that existed in and between both of these schools of post-war leftist thought, but they are nonetheless based on a crucial kernel of truth that is quite useful in offering a quick comparison between the two positions. The fundamental issue that separated the cultural Marxists from the theorists of the Frankfurt School related to the difficult theoretical terrain of 'subjectivity'. Without digressing too far, we can say that the cultural Marxists imagined as their starting point a fully rational subject, capable of understanding its place in the world and constructing its own social identity, tastes and dispositions as it entered the social field. They were, above all, dedicated humanists, keen to develop a positive and essentially optimistic analysis of the rational human subject and its 'agency'. Here, we can begin to see the connections between cultural Marxism and other aspects of liberal philosophy. Their opponents on the political and intellectual right tended not to be so optimistic about the 'ethical' substance of raw subjectivity, but they could certainly agree that the subject possessed the ability to make calculative decisions about its identity and social activity. Of course, the subject imagined by the cultural Marxists was capable of seeing the injustice of the capitalist economic model and mobilising in opposition to it. Thompson, in particular, did not see this as a process led by intellectuals capable of equipping the working class with the conceptual tools necessary to understand and structurally locate their exploitation. Nor did the working classes need leaders capable of stirring their blood. Instead, the development of political opposition was a reasonably organic process that flowed from basic perceptions of their shared 'experiences'. The subject imagined by the English liberals of the Enlightenment, and the neoclassical and neo-liberal economists who have played such a crucial role in determining the shape and content of our global economy, was capable of rationally calculating its own best interests and then using these interests as a basis for social action. At the fundamental level of the ontology of subjectivity, there is no great disagreement between British cultural Marxists, social liberals and right-wing liberals. The Frankfurt School's account of subjectivity varies somewhat from author to author, but generally it dismissed the simplistic phenomenology and rationalism of liberal philosophy and, drawing upon Hegelian philosophy and Freudian psychoanalysis, created a more complex account of the subject that incorporated conceptions of ideology, drives, desires and the unconscious.

In a detailed analysis of the development of cultural Marxism and the considerable changes that the British Left underwent during the 1960s and 1970s, Dennis Dworkin (1997) draws our attention to the roots of cultural Marxism in leftist political organisations during the 1930s, 1940s and 1950s. This connection to real politics and the struggles of ordinary working people, Dworkin believes, shaped the character of British cultural Marxism and encouraged a degree of romanticism and idealism, which are largely absent from other leftist schools of thought. The Frankfurt School, for example, comprised unapologetic intellectuals who saw their work as a form of psychosocial analysis and political practice. They were, for the most part, unconcerned about closing the gap between the intellectual elites of the Left and the industrial working classes. Their work and their contribution to the understanding of capitalism and politics represented, they believed, an important and entirely necessary contribution to political, social and economic transformation. It's also worth noting that most of those who worked in this tradition were educated in philosophy. They knew their Hegel and Plato, as well as their Marx, and they tended to be more comfortable with abstract thought.

The cultural Marxists on the other hand were often quite dedicated to the task of using their understanding of capitalism and history to advance the causes of ordinary working people. They hoped to engage the proletariat in a mutually beneficial relationship that advanced the politics of the working class and allowed the intelligentsia to see the reality of this particular social group. They avoided unnecessary abstraction and attempted to make leftist theory comprehensible to the masses. They wanted it to have a utility for the very people most likely to benefit from it. Cultural Marxists often came from the academic disciplines of history or English literature, or else they were a part of the rapidly developing field of cultural studies. Their background in these fields tended to ensure they were less comfortable with the abstractions of philosophy and a good deal more comfortable with the empiricism and historicism that Althusser dismissed as impediments to truth.

Dworkin also suggests that the British tradition of workers' and adult education reinforced cultural Marxism's tendency to idealise ordinary people and overestimate their capacity to understand and politically oppose modern capitalism. Many of those who were at the very forefront of this new school of thought had spent a good deal of time interacting with and learning from ordinary workers, especially those disposed towards the benefits of education and political opposition. These workers were, no doubt, complex and thoughtful men and women, fully capable of comprehending their position as exploited units of production. They could grasp the basic essence of Marxism and were capable of talking in an informed manner about their own experiences and cultural practices. In talking in this way about the reality of their lives and their attitudes to popular culture, consumption and work, they could educate a deeply committed, middle-class, left-wing intelligentsia keen to learn more about the working classes, as capitalism embarked upon a new phase in its development. How could one underestimate the complexity, creativity, humour and intelligence of the modern working class when faced with this evidence? How could one adopt an account of ideological interpellation and position the worker as a passive, uncritical recipient of capitalist propaganda?

Of course, the problem here is what is omitted. Were those politically engaged members of the working class, who attended evening classes to learn from enlightened middle-class Marxists, truly representative of the great mass of proletarians who chose not to attend? Isn't there an apparently 'natural' drive to defend the self against any suggestion of external political or ideological manipulation? Don't we all like to soothe ourselves with the belief that we see the world as it really is and that we are fully capable of rationally engaging in it? Even those individuals who engage in the most shamelessly commodified aspects of our culture like to retain the belief that they are doing so on their own terms.

E. P. Thompson probably made the most important contribution to the establishment and development of British cultural Marxism, but there were many other notable influences. Raymond Williams (for example, 2005) and Richard Hoggart (1969) both wrote important books that set the tone for the movement. Later, Stuart Hall, Paul Gilroy, Paul Willis, Angela McRobbie and Dick Hebdige helped to carry the banner forward. As time wore on, and the structures of modernity began to exhibit the first signs of loosening up and breaking apart, cultural Marxism responded quickly to changes in British society and became more concerned with the experiences of women and ethnic minorities. The critical analysis of racism and sexism and our empirical understanding of the experiences of women and ethnic minorities developed at least partly as a result of the work of these individuals and their colleagues across the social sciences. The work of the Birmingham School, the European Group and the early National Deviancy Conferences sits firmly within this tradition of British Marxist scholarship. Their collective influence has been enormous.

Post-crash cultural Marxists on contemporary riots and protest

Importantly, for our purposes at least, we can continue to detect the influence of modern cultural Marxism in contemporary accounts of riots and political protest. The English riots of 2011 were given their character by the unprecedented looting of symbolically loaded consumer goods. Empirical research seems to indicate that many rioters saw the breakdown of law and order as an opportunity to do some free shopping (see Topping and Bawdon, 2011; Treadwell *et al.*, 2013), and there was no obvious articulation of political opposition to the dull uniformity of contemporary consumer culture or the grotesque hierarchies and exclusions of post-crash capitalism. However, many on the contemporary political and academic Left have followed Thompson's lead and proclaimed these riots to have been a legitimate political response to social injustice. The crowd acted when it felt that the ruling elite had abandoned the established protocols of economic, political and moral conduct and pushed the poor into a corner from where they had no option but to strike out to defend themselves and their class interests. Harvie and Milburn (2013) suggest that the rioters were not opportunistic looters or depoliticised consumers but rational, calculative and politicised subjects defending traditional entitlements, keen to punish those whom they perceived to have acted in a predatory manner upon their community. They argue that the looting that tends to characterise the riots in the popular imagination should be understood 'as a defence of certain customary entitlements' (ibid.: 564). The rioters, Harvie and Milburn claim, stole consumer items that they believed to be theirs by right, but to which – as austerity began to bite and reasonably well-paid employment opportunities fell away – they were denied legitimate access.

This argument appears to rest in part upon the standard rhetoric about the social benefits of democratised luxury consumption. Everyone, apparently, has been granted the right to own big-screen TVs, games consoles and branded clothes. We can measure the accomplishments of a society, not by abstract concepts, such as equality, justice and fairness, but by levels of ownership of commodified material goods. The broader context of consumerism is completely absent. The ecological problems caused by vapid, short-term consumerism – in which we buy and throw away and buy again – are simply ignored. The envy and social competition upon which consumerism depends, and the corrosive effects of these forces upon political, social and community life, are free from any critical consideration.

The criminologist Roger Matthews (2014) makes a similar point, claiming that consumerism is one of the great benefits of Western capitalism, the saving grace of an otherwise oppressive social system. According to Matthews, when the system is one day transformed by the weight of accumulated pragmatic reforms, this aspect of Western culture should be retained and embedded in a post-capitalist social order. This is precisely the kind of intellectual blindness the Left needs to overcome if it is to stand any chance of renewing itself and popularising its narrative in the years ahead. Matthews clearly sees no problem in the way consumerism tends to mediate social relationships or drive new exclusions or forms of discrimination (see Hayward and Yar, 2006). He has no problem with the vacuity of commodified forms of culture that exist solely to sell, and he sees no problem in consumer symbolism's role in the depoliticisation of the working class and displacement of the collective identity-building that was once sourced in class, community, locality, family and history. He appears unable to distinguish between consumption and consumerism, and his analysis ignores crucially important changes within capitalism itself, most notably Western de-industrialisation and the growth of Eastern economies built upon production for export to the consumerised and debt-laden West. His idealistic pragmatism, in which a future democratic socialism continues to be animated by the lures of consumerism's sign-value system, must come as cold comfort for those workers forced to toil in appalling conditions in sweatshops across the East. And why should we care about the degradation of our ecosystem, the depletion of our natural resources, impending resource wars and the problems that await future generations? Fuck it: the liberal Left's slow-motion revolution proclaims iPads and PlayStations for all. It is the right of every exploited Western worker to own a pair of Nike trainers made by hyper-exploited Eastern workers.

If these authors are to be believed, the contemporary British Left should forget about the desperate state of our labour markets and the growing inability of a significant proportion of the British workforce to find reasonably rewarding employment. Instead, the liberal progressives of the Left should be arguing for reduced prices at the corporate behemoths that dominant our high streets. Branded consumer items, after all, are a basic entitlement, the great reward of modernist progress and a right offered by neo-liberalism to all citizens. Rather than addressing the structural causes of immiseration and social disintegration, and rather than thinking about the complexities of subjectivity or the ability of ideology to shape our drives and desires, these authors appear to be arguing that the Left should instead be defending the rights of consumers to bag a better bargain on the high street.

Harvie and Milburn (2013) suggest that rioters targeted stores considered to be the most predatory on the community. Sports stores selling high-end trainers attracted the attention of the rioters, not because they stocked commodities valued by the rioters, but because the rioters considered the prices that predatory corporations and shopkeepers charge for these items to be too high. The rioters weren't particularly interested in the designer trainers they stole; their primary motivation was to punish excessively profit-motivated businesses. The end-point is, of course, that the riots should be understood as a fight for (consumer) justice rather than an outbreak of destructive apolitical violence and disorder occurring against a background of depoliticisation, consumer incorporation, capitalist realism and neo-liberal consensus. Despite clear suggestions to the contrary, Harvie and Milburn (2013) can't see the triumph of consumerism in the riots. They can't see resource-poor, angry and forgotten populations engaging in blind, apolitical forms of acting out, desperately seeking recognition, mobilised by shallow consumer gratification rather than the dream of an egalitarian society. Instead, the Thompsonite fantasy is invoked without any critical reflection, and the 2011 riots, just like every other riot in British history, take their place in the great historical saga of the poor rising up to express their righteous indignation at social inequality and oppression. For Harvie and Milburn (2013), and many others, there is no consideration of ideology or the ability of consumer culture to shape our dreams and desires, and no consideration of the apparent inability of the rioters or their representatives to clearly articulate a plan for a more just society.

Sutterlüty (2014: 38) goes even further. For him, the rioters were rebels fighting against an oppressive state that 'failed to live up to its promise of equality'. We are not entirely sure when the neo-liberal state promised equality to marginalised, unemployed and underemployed urban populations struggling to make ends meet. Neo-liberalism does not and never has 'promised equality'. In the neo-liberal framework, inequality is believed to be entirely functional, and it is assiduously constructed and reproduced as such. It propels people back out into the market to innovate and work harder. Failure is the individual's own fault. The sight of the obscene wealth of the elite and the simpering, lustful press coverage their consumer lifestyles receive act as motivational tools to encourage the talented from each social class to take on the task of mimicking the elite's success and earning the entitlement to display its associated symbolism. If the working classes can't see this and adjust their political discourses, strategies and practices accordingly, they are not as intellectually switched on as the cultural Marxists would have us believe. And neither are the cultural Marxists.

Neo-liberalism has no interest in creating or promoting equality. Equality, properly understood, is the death knell of neo-liberalism. The furthest neo-liberalism goes along this road is to construct a myth of 'equality of opportunity', which, we must now understand, is directly antagonistic to really existing equality. Equality of opportunity is the enforcement of a democratic framework that gives everyone the chance to win in a game that will inevitably produce many more losers. It seeks to enrich the game and pacify the players, rather than seeking to abolish it. Giving everyone the opportunity to change their circumstances and move from the ranks of the exploited to those of the exploiters has nothing whatsoever to do with the traditional goals of the political Left. 'Equality of opportunity' enforces and naturalises competitive individualism and positions the individual firmly within the structures of consumer capitalism. The opportunity to do what exactly? Flee one's immediate social circumstances? Fulfil one's dreams? And what is the substance of those dreams? What does the individual who climbs from the lowest social stratum to the very top really want? Recognition? Social distinction? To attract the envy of others? Are we to accept that the desire for more material possessions is an objective and unproblematic aspect of social organisation? Is it too outlandish to imagine the drive for social distinction connected to positive social ends, such as artistic or technological achievement or simply doing one's duty to care for others, rather than advancing one's own consumer lifestyle?

'Equality of opportunity' doesn't care about those who are left behind. This supposedly progressive discourse, born of the decidedly non-leftist American Dream, argues for all to be equipped with the capacity to rise up through the class system. But of course, for this to mean anything, some must remain at or descend to the bottom. The individual's success is predicated on someone else's socially mediated failure. We cannot all be at the top, and the fact that some rise from the bottom to the top immediately provides the system itself with a degree of legitimacy, while at the same time erasing all sympathy for those who fail to make this journey. If 'equality of opportunity' were to become a reality, what comfort could those at the bottom draw from their experience? Even in a terribly unequal class system, those at the bottom have the advantage of explaining their disadvantaged position in terms of injustice, bias and good old-fashioned bad luck. Social acceptance of the 'equality of opportunity' doctrine applies debilitating pressure upon the poorest, as it encourages them to accept that they are worthy of nothing else.

This point notwithstanding, it is salutary to note that, in an era in which the failure of abstract markets has condemned millions to poverty and many millions more to significantly reduced lifestyles, so many on the left continue to follow the classical liberal line and focus their critical attention on the oppressive state. Although a critique of the ideological character of austerity politics is entirely justified, these critics usually ignore entirely the transformation of the market and the stark fact that capitalism now has absolutely no need for a mass industrial workforce in the West. Very little is said about the reality of contemporary capitalism or the failure of abstract markets, or the growing disparity between those sections of the economy that thrive on financial speculation and those that provide employment for ordinary men and women. The market and the profit motive are generally spared any critical consideration. Instead, the state is identified as the principal enemy, and of course the state can always be reformed. The politicians who instigated austerity policies can be dispensed with, and the good honest folk of the parliamentary Left can take their place. It is when we listen carefully to the liberal Left's unrelenting critique of the oppressive state that we can begin to comprehend the close intellectual and ideological relationship between this group and their opponents on the liberal right. The general tone at some leftist academic conferences, even now, is one of marked antipathy to all forms of authority, and the domineering state and its institutions in particular. For many, capitalism itself is still off the menu, too complex and old-fashioned to warrant further consideration.

Of course, we do not deny the importance of rising poverty, falling living standards and the advance of exclusion and marginality in helping to explain the context in which the riots occurred, but we reject the assumption that the fundamental motivations of those engaged in the looting of stores across numerous English cities in 2011 emanated from an enduring orientation to equality and social justice. The assumption that the rioters saw the reality of contemporary capitalism and reacted with proto-political fervour against it seems to us hopelessly naïve, a knee-jerk ideological reaction rooted firmly in the domain assumptions of an exhausted cultural Marxist paradigm. This prevents us from coming to terms with a far more troubling reality. We investigate the English riots of 2011 in detail in

Chapter 5. All we will say before closing this chapter is that, just as we must avoid making the mistake of confusing the frustration caused by the individual's perception of failure within capitalism with a collective desire to overthrow capitalism, it is also a mistake to underestimate capitalism itself and its ability to influence and shape our goals and values. To see the proletariat as a moral and nimble-footed David, willing to rise up against a ponderous and dull-witted capitalist Goliath, is to make a fundamental error that mis-characterises both parties. The Left today must accept the reality that capitalism is as nimble, fleet-footed and quick-witted as it would like the proletariat to be. Further, capitalism has proven time and time again that it can change its form in order to survive. Its profit motive and basic exchange relation remain in place, but its drive to survive and to grow ensures that it is able to change its appearance and mode of social engagement quite significantly. We are living through just such a period today. Abstract finance capitalism appears no longer to need labour, and the gap between the real economy and the abstract financial economy seems set to grow further. In the current situation, characterised by declining resources and ecological destruction, it is quite simply impossible for the economy to grow at the rate required to soak up the world's adult population as well-remunerated entrepreneurs and wages labourers (Heinberg, 2011). As the super-rich see their wealth race ahead at a staggering pace, the old middle and working classes of developed European nations are seeing their standards of living diminish and their material ability to reproduce themselves fall to a critical level, where the vast majority of Western workers are now precariously employed and threatened with a precipitous fall into the ranks of the excluded. It is precisely now that the Left needs to abandon its domain assumptions, forged in qualitatively different times, and look again at the reality of post-crash capitalism.

3

PART II

The liberal attack upon utopianism

Post-war democracy

Despite the horrors of totalitarianism and war, and in spite of the desire for political tranquillity and incremental economic progress, the early post-war political scene continued to be animated by forms of measured ideological commitment. These commitments were, of course, expressed in a less strident and combative tone than during the pre-war years, but they continued to exist. Democratic communist parties remained quite popular in Italy and France for many years, and the numerous social democratic political parties that populated the European mainstream often contained within their ranks countless 'socialists' of one type or another. The far Right was of course disbarred from mainstream politics, and comprehensive 'denazification' programmes were instituted in both East and West Germany. These programmes did not meet with immediate and unambiguous success. Of course, many ordinary men and women who were not obvious beneficiaries of the Nazi regime, and who had not taken part in the slaughter of minorities, saw themselves and their communities as victims rather than as perpetrators. First, they had been victimised by an oppressive elite who had thrown their country into a destructive war and committed horrific crimes in the name of the German people. Second, they had been the victim of an allied war machine that had reduced many German towns and cities to rubble and whose armies had committed their own atrocities as they progressed on to German soil in the final years of the war (see Cook, 2010). After the war, their country was carved up between the two remaining power blocs, and the German people were forced to endure significant poverty and want as they adapted to a new post-war reality.

In the popular German imagination, at least for a decade or two following the war, the people had little to apologise for and much to be quite aggrieved about. It was not until much later in the twentieth century that one could say with confidence that Germany had finally come to terms with its own recent past and the slaughter of its Jews (see Judt, 2010). Nevertheless, as the post-war period began to take shape, fascism remained formally excluded from mainstream politics, and the central tenets of its ill-defined populist ideology were reviled throughout post-war Europe, especially after the true extent and nature of the Holocaust became clear. However, as we will see in the chapters that follow, variants of xenophobic nationalism were certainly not entirely expunged (Hobsbawm, 2012). They never became, as we once hoped, a deeply regrettable historical curio, unimaginable in our present time. The break-up of the Soviet Union was at least partly precipitated by the return of nationalism, and the unravelling of the former Yugoslavia after the death of Tito resulted in prolonged and utterly barbarous ethnic conflict, which the European community did little to address (see Glenny, 1996). As the cold war came to an end, nationalism gradually returned to mainstream politics, and the hypnotic siren call of the imagined community was once again reverberating across the continent.

In some instances, the new nationalism draws upon the old symbolism and iconography of Nazism, and in others it has sought to move gradually closer to the centre, hiding ethnic and religious antagonisms beneath the rhetoric of economic pragmatism. Predictably enough, as new nationalist political parties have drawn support, the political terrain has changed. The mainstream social liberal and neo-liberal parties have warmed to the idea of restricting immigration and now recognise that a vocal commitment to multiculturalism and open borders risks alienating disillusioned and angry voters keen to find someone to blame for their falling standards of living and the miasma of insecurity that hangs over the postmodern urban experience. If we gather together evidence from across the continent, it seems that ethnocentrism is very much back in vogue. What was once, only a decade or so ago, considered vulgar, insensitive and politically incorrect is now scarcely remarked upon. Of course, key figures in most mainstream parties talk of the value of openness and the benefits of multiculturalism, but this does not appear to dampen their enthusiasm for placing new barriers in front of aspirant immigrants keen to avail themselves of Western Europe's relative prosperity or those fleeing tyranny in their homelands.

We should keep in mind that the post-war European project never constructed a policy of open admittance. The religious and ethnic diversity of the major European states today results from, first, internal migration from poorer Eastern European states to the more affluent West, especially after the Treaty of Lisbon in 2009. Second, it results from Western European states' desperate need for cheap industrial labour as post-war rebuilding programmes began to get under way. Third, it results from the imperial and colonial history of militarily powerful European nations. We could go beyond this, further back into history, to identify the movement of religious and ethnic groups and the factors that drove them to move from the place of their birth to pastures new, but instead it seems reasonable simply to conclude that Europe's self-image as an open and tolerant collection of mutually supporting neighbouring states tends to omit important truths about its history and its present reality. Of course, nationalism is not a uniquely European malady, but it is one that has played a significant role in its long and often turbulent history.

So, if Nazism and fascism were formally excluded from mainstream politics after 1945, how can we understand the politics of the Right during the post-war period? In the powerful economies of Western Europe, the political Right tended to be populated by both traditional conservatives and free-market liberals, an alliance that was not always plain sailing. Both of these groups tended to oppose the increasing power of organised labour and the tax regimes that enabled the construction of Europe's new 'cradle to the grave' welfare states. Despite this opposition, when the democratic Right found its way into office, it tended to be pragmatic enough to accept that the political topography of Europe had been transformed. In Britain, for example, the Conservative Party did little to challenge the general acceptance that it was the state's responsibility to ensure that the welfare system was maintained, standards of living continued to rise and reasonably remunerative and integrative employment was available for all who wanted it. Even the graduated taxation systems that compelled the rich to contribute proportionally more than those lower down the class system stood unchallenged. The fact that the representatives of organised labour were invited to Downing Street by the representatives of Britain's ailing aristocracy to discuss the organisation of key industries and the country's economic well-being was a powerful indication of how far the country had travelled since the Depression years of the 1920s and 1930s.

The British Conservative Party was, throughout the post-war period, significantly influenced by the tradition of one-nation Toryism, which draws from the ancient principle of *noblesse oblige* but is most commonly associated with the nineteenth century and the political sensibilities of Benjamin Disraeli. One-nation Toryism held that it was the responsibility of the naturally superior elite to ensure the welfare of all. It expressed a measured degree of sympathy for the suffering of marginalised populations, treating them rather like errant children in need of a firm hand to direct them back on to a godly path of hard work, discipline and asceticism. Adopting what appeared to be an updated, twentieth-century form of this aristocratic paternalism, they hoped to perform their duty as Christians and ensure that a reasonable standard of living was available to those under their care. For the one-nation Tories of the mid-twentieth century, in particular the Conservative Prime Ministers Stanley Baldwin and Neville Chamberlain, it was both right and just that the rich were rich and the poor were poor. It was, however, a matter of honour for the rich to take the responsibilities of social management seriously, and so they benevolently bestowed their favour upon the unfortunate commoners of the lower orders, who, without the leadership of the natural elite, would lapse into godless depravity and squalor.

Of course, the one-nation Tories were dedicated to preserving what was left of the old order, and they were certainly not so progressive as to advocate policies that might challenge the continuity of Britain's entrenched class system. It was this aspect of British conservatism that contributed to post-war 'Butskellism', a phrase coined to communicate the consensus that existed between the post-war Labour and Conservative Parties, specifically in the form of the Conservative Chancellor of the Exchequer, Rab Butler, and his Labour equivalent, Hugh Gaitskell. With the one-nation Tories dominating senior party positions, the British Conservative Party was a full partner in a comprehensive programme of social transformation that significantly narrowed the gap between rich and poor and improved the life chances of ordinary men and women throughout the country (see Hennessey, 2007).

During these years, the free-marketeers represented only a small but not entirely insignificant minority within the British Conservative Party. Their roots were in the nineteenth-century 'free-trade' movement, and they had been at the forefront of the party during the 1920s and 1930s, but suggestions of growing class consciousness in the industrial heartlands and the towering problems of post-war reconstruction appeared to require the party to adopt a more progressive political bearing. This was to change quite significantly during the 1970s, as the social democratic Keynesian model of economic management appeared incapable of coping with the complexities of increasingly competitive and interconnected global markets. The neo-liberal Right had patiently waited in the wings, rehearsing its doctrine and refining its theories of economic management.

The election of Margaret Thatcher to the party leadership in 1975 flipped the usual arrangements in the Conservative Party on their head (see Denham and Garnett, 2001; Jenkins, 2007). The economic liberals were now in the ascendancy. In comparison with the iconoclastic Thatcher and her followers, the old one-nation Tories seemed like dusty old men, unable to keep pace with the rapidity of social change. With Thatcher at the helm, the role of one-nation Toryism in the consensus politics of the 1950s and 1960s appeared to condemn the grand old men of the party in the eyes of the new breed of thrusting go-getters who were appearing everywhere, keen to liberate the nation's entrepreneurs from their enslavement to the social democratic state. Hopelessly out of place in their own political party, the old one-nation Tories did the decent thing and shuffled off, leaving the young Turks free to pursue their revolution.

Thatcher's Conservative Party appeared entirely unconcerned with the traditional themes of British conservatism (Jenkins, 2007; Bale, 2011). She revolutionised both her political party and British society. Despite being a singularly divisive figure, she met with remarkable electoral success. Her Conservative Party was a party of government. She won three successive general elections before being eventually deposed in 1990 by members of her own party. The leadership was then taken by John Major, who promptly secured a fourth successive election victory for the Conservatives. Thatcher had become prime minister in 1979, and the Conservatives remained in office until 1997, a full eighteen years in which to embed their ideology into all the branches of government and into the deepest fissures and ravines of British culture and society. From here on, the Conservatives were to be a party defined by their commitment to the free market. In essence, it was now a classical liberal party rather than a conservative party, dedicated to liberating the oppressed individual from the existing order, rather than conserving the old order's traditions, hierarchies and cultural values.

Thatcher's conservatism related only to her cultural politics, and her theatrical invocation of 'back to basics' decorum and family values stood in the shadow of a range of socially destructive monetarist economic policies for which she displayed remarkable zeal (Vinen, 2010). She was committed to dispensing with the restrictions of the post-war consensus and utterly dedicated to the task of establishing a new political path towards freedom. Thatcher might have offered occasional conservative platitudes, but she was a hard-line liberal individualist down to her very marrow. She saw it as her duty to identify the waste, inefficiencies and mollycoddling dependencies of the old consensus. Instead, she would fight to free the overtaxed and over-regulated entrepreneur from the yoke of an aggressively interventionist state. For her, the nanny state had no right to take such a comprehensive role in social and economic management. Doing so introduced lethargy, sloth and inefficiency, which in turn prevented the country's wealth creators from taking their rightful place at the commanding heights of the global economy. Everyone would be better off if the state were to shrink and concern itself solely with the limited spheres of life that demanded intervention.

Of course, as is now clear, Thatcher was successful in dispensing with an existing consensus and establishing a new one in its place. Thatcher revolutionised both the Right and the Left of British politics. She cited the transformation of the Labour Party as her most important political accomplishment. During her time in office, the Labour Party moved away from its traditional social democratic commitments to full employment and common ownership of the means of production, distribution and exchange. In order to gain ground politically, it appeared necessary for it to accept that Thatcher had won the economic argument and follow her in adopting policies of privatisation, state minimalism and low taxes. It would need to ditch any lingering suggestion of socialism and distance itself as much as it could from the trade union movement.

Of course, by this time, the 'industrial heartlands' no longer contained a mass industrial workforce. The nature of class identification had changed (see Winlow and Hall, 2006, 2013). The Labour Party needed to modernise and talk to an increasingly consumer-orientated and media-savvy electorate. It needed to stop restricting itself to the old politics of class and equality and instead focus upon the new politics of multiculturalism and tolerance in order to prevent an increasingly competitive and atomised population boiling over into internecine hostility. Throughout the 1980s and 1990s, the Labour Party purged itself of its remaining Trotskyites and aggressively promoted a new breed of university-educated specialist attuned to the maximisation of media impact, keen to draw upon the findings of opinion polls and focus groups in the construction of policy (see Gould, 2011) and entirely without deep ideological convictions, save the ambition to win office and stay there.

The British Labour Party returned to office in 1997 under the stewardship of Tony Blair. Perhaps as much as Thatcher herself, Blair symbolises the politics of British postmodernism. His appearance, demeanour and political orientation were radically at odds with Britain's traditional working class and its labour movement.

He rebranded the party 'New Labour' in order to make it absolutely clear that Labour's tax-and-spend, welfarist history was at an end. The New Labour Party would no longer be a party of dour, stern-faced old union officials sitting in smoke-filled clubs and plotting how best to hold capitalism to account. It would be a diverse and multicultural party in which everyone was encouraged to become actively involved. The engrained industrial machismo of the 1950s and 1960s was escorted firmly to the door. The party now hoped to assist as much as it could those who strove to better themselves and climb through the class system. The party clad itself in the trendy new garb of 'diversity', 'social mobility' and 'equality of opportunity', the plain old ill-fitting rhetoric about equality and social justice bagged up and dropped off at the charity shop of history, an unpalatable reminder of a bygone age.

Blair accepted early on that industrialism was a dead duck (Seldon, 2005). One might even be forgiven for thinking that he was glad to see it go (all those scruffy men working in factories – it really wasn't the image that Britain should be projecting on to the world stage). Instead, following Thatcher's lead, Blair's Britain would throw itself into the ferocious competition of the global economy. Aware that Britain simply couldn't compete with developing countries for productive jobs, he hoped to up-skill the nation's workforce with a view to making it attractive to the new hi-tech and 'creative' industries that were transforming global media and culture. The university system was expanded, daubed with the symbolism of personal opportunity and positioned in the sky like a giant advertising blimp. In the financial sector, he scaled back regulation still further and tried to steal a march on the Tories by portraying New Labour as the party of business. The City of London grew considerably, and Blair was perfectly happy to let it continue on its merry way. Salaries and bonuses for city high-fliers grew exponentially as British culture adjusted to its economic dependence upon high finance. The country's business leaders were deified, and its young were instructed to develop their entrepreneurial skills as means of freeing themselves from their communities and journeying un-encumbered towards a good life laden with consumer goods. CEOs, asset strippers, union busters, rentiers, venture capitalists and a variegated assortment of asocial profiteers became fixtures on prime-time television, asked to comment on the issues of the day and advise government on how it might further assist the corporate sector in its interminable quest for greater profits.

Unions, once the institutionalised representatives of working men and women across the country, were increasingly cast as archaic, undemocratic and instrumental institutions willing to hold the entire country to ransom in order to advance the interests of their members. As work became increasingly insecure, union membership fell away quite significantly, particularly in the private sector. Now, many private-sector workers despise trade unions, a clear indication of the success of neo-liberalism's crude but effective divide-and-rule strategy. Trade unions disrupt the lives of ordinary workers going about their day. Trade unions ensure businesses are less profitable, and so the national economy lags behind its global competitors, and fewer new jobs emerge. Trade unions ensure that workers in the shrinking public sector have higher rates of pay and better pensions, whereas workers in the private sector struggle with endemic low pay and minimal pension cover. A race to the bottom ensued. Workers in the private sector increasingly saw workers in the public sector as their enemies. The continued strength of the trade union movement in the public sector meant that workers in the private sector were paying higher taxes. The logic of neo-liberalism was everywhere. Why not ban trade unions and let the market set a rate of pay for teachers, police officers, firefighters, lecturers and council workers? Working-class solidarity and the politics of universalism never really took hold in Britain in the way many on the political left like to imagine, but even the slightest semblance of it seemed to have disappeared from view by the time New Labour left office.

The gradual decline of industrial production in Britain had a huge effect upon the nation's culture and economy. In a global free market, it was incredibly difficult to compete with low-wage economies in the East, and, in Westminster, there remained no political desire to protect British workers from competition. De-industrialisation, unemployment, insecurity and poverty were the tough medicine Britain had to swallow to emerge fitter, stronger and ready to reclaim its place at the very forefront of the global economy. The British economy would henceforth be reliant upon consumerism, its low-wage service economy and the ability of the City of London to generate profitable investment opportunities. Of course, as we know to our great cost, underneath both of these economic sectors was an ever-growing ocean of debt.

Blair's drive to develop a comprehensive, hi-tech, knowledge-based economy in Britain failed to bear fruit. Although opening up the university sector to a broad range of 'non-traditional' students may well have produced quite considerable, but very hard to measure, cultural benefits, there simply were not enough graduate-level jobs awaiting the millions of new graduates. The outcome was that, in a new 'accredited society', jobs that would previously have been given to non-graduates were now reserved for graduates. Employers – even those operating in the lower reaches of the service sector – became increasingly demanding. An even yet more competitive age dawned for British labour markets. The rather depressing reality that lay underneath Blair's drive to create a knowledge economy was that Britain's economy was becoming increasingly polarised.

In the City of London, staggering amounts of money were being made. Never before had CEOs and city financiers received such extravagant remuneration packages. The collective economic power of this new and increasingly globalised elite transformed both the national and the global economy. Of course, their collective buying power and their ability to move money around the world in order to avoid taxes were only two aspects of their collective economic influence (see Shaxson, 2012). Perhaps more important were their deep ideological commitment to the logic of the unfettered market and their hatred of financial regulations and restrictive tax regimes. These regulations were always judged to inhibit market performance and, therefore, to restrict economic growth. For them, the market was king. Left to its own devices, it would find a natural equilibrium that benefitted all. Surely everyone benefitted when the national economy grew? Didn't the economic dynamism of the feted elite boost the living standards of those less gifted? Didn't the tax revenues they paid allow the government of the day to continue to provide services to the unemployed, the sick and the elderly?

As the 1990s gave way to the early years of the twenty-first century, this new elite came to possess staggering economic power and huge political influence. Few British politicians dared to ignore the financial services industry and its political lobby, and most of those who found their way into government felt compelled to put in place policies that would keep them relatively happy. Their collective power had risen to such heights that even the democratic Left did not dare challenge their supremacy. Of course, the social outcomes of their instrumental calculations were enormous. Even now, in 2014, after five years of recession, caused at least partially by a failure to regulate the institutionalised greed and avarice of the city, there is no political will to address this trend.

Elsewhere, low-level service work came to predominate (see Toynbee, 2003; Ehrenreich, 2010). In a new and increasingly fluid global economy, corporations needed to cut costs to an absolute minimum and remain responsive to fluctuations in the market. Fixed costs were slashed. Wages stagnated, and work became increasingly precarious. Industrial labour markets were often exploitative and dangerous, but they had the benefit of being relatively stable, and this stability gave the employee some capacity to plan for the future. Many workers in the post-industrial economy would not be so lucky. Short-term contracts became common across the private sector, and the great bulk of these jobs were low paid and non-unionised (Southwood, 2011; Lloyd, 2012, 2013).

In both crude and subtle ways, Blair sought to move beyond the politics of social class. He revised into non-existence his party's historic commitment to the ownership of the means of production and purged the party of its radical leftist groups (see Frost and North, 2013). New Labour was to be a party of optimism, energy and drive; a party dedicated to social mobility and rewarding talent. The radical Left in the party were an excremental stain from a bygone era that needed to be wiped clean if the party was to convince a consumer-orientated electorate that Old Labour was dead and buried and the good times were just ahead. Towards the end of his time in office, Blair announced that 'we're all middle class now', and it seemed as if he wanted this pronouncement to stand above all others as a lasting testament to his premiership. Uncouth industrialism was at an end, and the old working class had been reintegrated into a new and progressive civil society centred upon a new discourse of individualism, rights and the joys of consumption.

Of course, Blair's third-way politics were built upon a commitment to economic growth, and the principal means of securing that growth was the removal of virtually all of the restrictions that the social democratic state had placed upon corporate business activity. It continued Thatcher's policies of privatisation and accepted that the drive to accumulate profit made the private sector more efficient and dynamic, whereas the ailing public sector was wasteful and unwieldy. Of course, Blair attempted to balance his advocacy of private business by displaying a willingness to help the poor. He established a Social Exclusion Unit (see Levitas, 1998) to address a new form of obdurate poverty that was the inevitable product of a new epoch of neo-liberal marketisation and competitive individualism. New Labour's attempts to reintegrate the poorest produced no discernible benefits whatsoever.

As we write these words, poverty and social exclusion in Britain remain unconscionably high. Defenders of New Labour in the academy argue that, without these policies, things would have been significantly worse. If the Tories had remained in office during the early years of the twenty-first century, income inequality, poverty and relative deprivation would have been much higher than they were under New Labour. This argument is a powerful indication of the negative character of New Labour's political discourse, a discourse that continues in the Labour Party today. The Labour Party has no positive message. The only thing it can offer the poor is that, with it in charge, things won't be quite as bad as they would be with the Tories in office.

Even if we strip away the rhetoric and the populist veneer, Blair's third-way politics remain admirably uncomplicated. He would give the market free reign. A booming economy – even if the boom only benefitted a relatively small percentage of the overall population – would mean a significant growth in tax receipts, and this money could then be used to fund social programmes aimed at alleviating some of the inevitable problems experienced by the poorest. During the 1990s and the early years of the twenty-first century, this is what mainstream progressive politics looked like in Britain. Social democracy was nowhere to be seen, and any thought of socialism was dismissed out of hand.

In truth, Blair's 'we're all middle class now' slogan suggested a wilful and dogged refusal to engage with the reality of British society in the post-Thatcher era. The abstract statistics used by civil service mandarins and the think-tanks of Whitehall may have suggested that the British economy was growing, but they were totally averse to communicating the fundamental truth that lay underneath the supposed economic miracle of Blair's third-way, neo-liberal variant. The Labour Party – the party of labour, the historic party of Britain's working class – had presided over a staggering movement of wealth and political influence from the poorest to the richest. A more fitting assessment of the Blair era was offered by key Blair aide and former business secretary, Peter Mandelson, who admitted to being 'intensely relaxed about people getting filthy rich'. Mandelson also made the rather stark admission that, 'we're all Thatcherites now' (see Tempest, 2002). This was the core of New Labour. Its approach to economic management was simply to continue where Thatcher had left off and, in an effort to convince the voting public that it wasn't quite so nasty as the Tory Party, it would continue to pump money into welfare and state services.

During this period, New Labour became wedded to economic growth measured through gross domestic product (GDP), and, for all politicians and the middle-class metropolitan media elites who hung on their every word, growth was a clear indicator that the country was on the right track. Of course, GDP is a poor measure of post-industrial economic reality, and it is even worse as an indicator of a country's collective well-being (see Fioramonti, 2013). Crucially, the growing importance of GDP during the 1990s drew critical attention away from the fact that the country's overall wealth was increasingly concentrated in the hands of the new elites created by the global free market. Perhaps more to the point, the downward pressure placed on income and the continued growth of productivity and profit had created a huge amount of capital ready for reinvestment. However, the onward march of economic globalisation was reaching its material limits. New investment opportunities, energy resources and mineral deposits were not as readily available as they used to be. New markets needed to be created. This drive to push capital back out into the market in search of yet more profit resulted in the huge growth of the financial services industry and the creation of new abstract mechanisms that allowed investors to seek profit in ways that had almost nothing to do with the creation of jobs in the real economy. As the trend towards financialisation gathered pace, investors could grow rich, while workers sat idle or worked in insecure services jobs for minimum wages, and the country's GDP figures could show growth, while, for many, real living standards declined.

New Labour appeared resolutely committed to a less beastly version of Thatcherism, and it believed that this new approach would carry the country away from the class antagonisms of its past. If the lifestyles of the poor improved only marginally, while those of the new elites leapt forward at a staggering rate, this mattered little. In an enthusiastic invocation of the dogma that 'a rising tide lifts all boats', improvement was the key, even if the rise in consumer lifestyles during the Blair years appeared tied to the liberalisation of markets, a concomitant rise in household debt and the deepening of insecurity, both real and perceived. The huge growth in debt also disguised the stagnation, and in some cases the fall, of incomes in real terms (Harvey, 2007, 2010; Varoufakis, 2011; see also Keen, 2011).

Despite initially surviving the horrors of Yugoslavia and Iraq, Blair left office under a cloud. Like Thatcher, he was deposed by members of his own party keen to divest themselves of a leader whose image appeared hopelessly tarnished in the eyes of the electorate. It is perhaps more fitting to say that it was Blair's *brand* that was tarnished. Blair seemed indicative of the historical trend towards game-show host politicians, a trend that transforms the politician from the committed conduit of political ideology to a mere celebrity whose real interest to the voting public lies in the titillating mysteries of his private life rather than his proclamations about progress and social renewal. He tried hard to cultivate the image of a statesman who commanded respect on the world stage, but, as growth began to dip and the horrific aftermath of the invasions he supported became increasingly clear, his formulaic gravitas and his stage-managed earnestness could no longer be counted upon to win the day.

It is worth considering Blair in depth because he was a consummate populariser of ideological dogma. He presented neo-liberalism and the staggering growth of the wealth of the richest as mere common sense; after all, these were economic processes that ultimately benefitted all. Under his stewardship, the economic liberalism of Thatcher was stripped of the last vestiges of class privilege and presented to the people as unadorned meritocracy and fiscal pragmatism. For Blair, there was no need for conflict or for factionalism. We could all get richer together. A growing economy, driven forward by the removal of regulatory impediments and the introduction of new programmes to boost entrepreneurship, would allow the government to spend more on those state services that remained after years of neo-liberal asset-stripping. For example, New Labour was deeply committed to the country's ailing National Health Service – at least in part because opinion polls consistently suggested that the country's voters were deeply committed to it – and it pumped huge amounts of money into the NHS in the hope of improving its performance. However, New Labour's utter faith in the efficiencies of private enterprise ensured that profit-making corporations were now involved in the provision of services to citizens in need of health care. Although the NHS's performance remained fairly static, significant profits accrued for those who had secured competitive contracts to provide services within the NHS itself, and, predictably enough, the drive for efficiency was accompanied by a torrent of expensive bureaucratic innovations that appeared to impede efficiency (see also Whitehead and Crawshaw, 2013, 2014). Throughout the Blair years, health secretaries were forced to talk of how much money they were spending on the NHS, rather than of the benefits patients were receiving as a result of that spending.

Despite the hype that grew up around Gordon Brown's chancellorship and the supposed economic miracle of the Blair years, unemployment remained relatively high, and underemployment grew significantly. New Labour continued the old Conservative government's drive towards flexibilisation. Labour laws were watered down, and work became increasingly insecure for a growing proportion of the nation's workforce. It is not hard to imagine workers in the dominant service sector of the economy listening to TV broadcasters tell them of the successes of New Labour's economic strategies while wondering when the economic miracle they were hearing so much about would get round to elevating their own lifestyles. If the good times were here again, why were their workplace benefits being run down, and why were their jobs increasingly insecure? Why were they not experiencing the wage rises that historically had tended to follow growth in production and consumption and the expansion of GDP? Still, household and consumer debt was easily obtainable, and interest rates seemed quite competitive. The democratisation of lifestyle consumption had already become a seemingly timeless fact of life.

What should we take home from the rise of Thatcher and Blair? How should we understand their place in history? For us, the most important issue at stake is the transformation of both the Left and the Right of British politics. The Conservative Party under Thatcher shed its skin and became a party utterly dedicated to the ruthlessly competitive economic logic of neo-liberalism and the liberation of the business class. Today, under the leadership of David Cameron, the Conservative Party again seeks to conserve, but the object of conservation is neo-liberalism itself, rather than any of the old ideals of traditional conservatism. The Labour Party under Blair made a similar transition, abandoning socialism and the principles of social democracy. It ditched its commitment to welfarism and a managed economy and committed wholeheartedly to the logic of the free market. The fact that today it is still considered a party of the Left should give us pause for thought. We must now acknowledge that the field of politics has, over the previous two decades, changed beneath our feet.

What does it mean today to say that one is on the left of British politics? If the Labour Party remains a tacit follower of Friedman and Hayek and totally accepts the logic of the free market, and yet still proclaims itself to be a party of the 'Left', what has happened to the founding principles of traditional leftist politics in Britain? When all of those involved in the democratic system agree on key political principles, especially those that relate to political economy, the entire field of politics narrows. Politicians must find alternative issues on which to focus their attention. Set against the stage-managed action of the contemporary political scene, in which political correspondents gossip like schoolchildren about cabinet reshuffles and back-stage conflicts, the aspiring British statesman attempts to distinguish himself from his competitors. The current trend suggests a growing desire to present the self as a 'conviction politician', in the hope that they can draw the attention of the 24-hour news channels, which in turn might lead to a groundswell of popular support. The aspiring statesman draws upon focus groups and opinion polls to discover what the British people really care about and then issues proclamations designed to curry their favour. This creates only surface action, because the basic foundations have already been agreed upon and are no longer presented to the people. There is no discussion whatsoever about alternative forms of economic organisation and their likely social and cultural outcomes. As far as the British mass media are concerned, there are no alternatives. Only an idiot would dispute the utility of the market system. When positioned against this deadening reality, what sense does it make to continue with the pretence that the traditional spectrum of British politics is still operative, and that there exists a genuine conflict between 'Right' and 'Left' about the future of our country? Can we now admit that the Labour Party is on the 'left' simply because it is not quite as far to the 'right' as the Conservative Party?

When the mainstream political 'Left' has set up camp on terrain traditionally associated with the political Right, when the Conservative Party is in fact a neoclassical liberal party, and when the economic policies of the Labour Party are directly antagonistic to the interests of labour, why shouldn't significant numbers of young people display a marked disinterest in organised politics in Britain? Why shouldn't growing numbers of voters report a general lack of faith in the political class, believing it to be populated by corporate stooges, profiteers, shysters and power-hungry egotists? The underlying ideological structures of contemporary British politics are fixed firmly in place and there appears to be no prospect of progressive dialectical movement, nor any concerted attempt to come to terms with the reality of our situation. Within the restrictive framework of contemporary democratic politics, it is difficult to identify any possibility that hope can return to reanimate the dead corpse of parliamentary politics in Britain. It is precisely now that we need to rediscover utopianism.

Dead politics and developing opposition

In general terms, it is possible to identify a similar trend towards neo-liberal consensus in all of the major economies of Europe. We do not seek to deny the particularities of European nations or the unique processes that transformed politics and economy throughout the post-war period. However, it is the end-point that concerns us most. That end-point is one in which neo-liberalism has triumphed, and all alternatives to it are dismissed out of hand. It is one in which conscious ideological commitment has been discarded, and the logic of the free market has become so ubiquitous that it has taken on the status of basic common sense. The political scene has become drab and uninteresting, and only fleeting scandals can jolt jaded electorates out of their lethargic disregard for politics and politicians.

If there is any action in mainstream politics, it tends to be at the margins. New political movements can now rise quickly, if they are understood to be in opposition to the stultifying sameness of the political mainstream. It doesn't seem to matter too much if these new parties or movements haven't yet developed a compelling strategy or a broad range of policy initiatives to put before the electorate. What matters most is simply that these new political movements are new. Their novelty ensures they are not tainted by the scandals and failures of the established mainstream parties. Momentarily, the interest of the electorate stirs. These new parties and movements seem to suggest that action can indeed be returned to politics, but this action threatens to take the form of *anti-politics*, a politics structured in relation to a dissatisfaction with politics as such.

We may judge this to be no bad thing. It's clear that dissatisfaction with contemporary politics is fully justified. However, we should not confuse the rise of new, anti-political movements with genuine political attempts to reclaim the field of politics in the hope of rejuvenating society and setting it on a progressive new course. Those who vote for these new movements appear to be motivated by the opportunity to register their dissatisfaction with the general shape and content of politics, rather than the opportunity to express their commitment to a positive programme of policy change. By voting for these new, anti-political movements, electorates hope to deliver a clear message to politicians of Right and Left. They want to admonish the polity and make it plain that their misdeeds will no longer be countenanced. Ultimately, voting for a new, anti-political movement is an instruction for politics to correct itself.

The rise of the Five Star Movement in Italy is indicative of this trend. Rather than construct a positive image of progress, those involved seek election in order to be granted the opportunity to clean up politics and fight endemic corruption. The positive image they present to the people is simply a version of the present in which the venality that plagues Italian politics has been expunged and the Italian people are treated with greater respect. If their great hope is to fight corruption, criminality and nepotism in government and the mainstream political parties, we might reasonably judge this to be a compelling programme that signifies a meaningful return to politics. 'At last', we appear to be saying, 'someone dares to say what needs to be said; someone is talking honestly about the anti-democratic tendencies of contemporary parliamentary capitalism.' The general programme of the Five Star Movement grows from the identification of a problem within the present, and indeed it is not too difficult to identify a huge range of problems with political systems throughout Europe. These problems are serious and should be addressed, but we should keep in mind that the basic goal of the Five Star Movement is to create a *future that is the present minus some of its excessive characteristics*. There is no fundamentally ideological commitment to something beyond what already exists. Unconsciously, they accept the limits that have been set on politics. Progress is reduced to the removal of a perceived negative that exists within the system. There is no attempt to construct a positive programme that attempts to address the system itself, and no attempt is made to build something new as an alternative to it. If we listen closely to Beppe Grillo's critique of the Italian polity, it becomes clear that he has a general commitment to the structures of Italy's market democracy; he just wishes to remove those things that he perceives to be inhibiting its maturation and representativeness.

Electorates now actively solicit political movements that propose to hold the establishment to account. An electorally significant number of voters appear willing to vote for anybody who is not associated with the major parties of the centre. Deep dissatisfaction with the uniformity of the neo-liberal centrist parties is already quite widespread. Anger is everywhere these days, but the problem is that anger can be manipulated and dragged off course. By itself, it is never a force for good. In order for it to fuel a genuinely political response to the towering inequalities and injustices of the current neo-liberal epoch, anger must be accompanied by a coherent political narrative that positively endorses an alternative. That alternative needs to be clarified and debated until its broad principles are understood. The alternative must be named.

The anger of so many ordinary citizens these days remains impotent unless it is equipped with the political symbolism that can enable individuals to begin to understand their own anger, where it comes from, and what they might do about it. Politics needs coherent ideologies that allow individuals to objectify the ultimate source of their anger and discuss models of social improvement and creative accounts of what human societies can become. Without these things, politics becomes merely a system of social management that seeks only to administer what already exists.

As things stand, we are forced to look at our political and economic reality and accept that it will continue indefinitely, even though, in practical and material terms, *things simply cannot go on as they are.* We are already seeing the signs of global warming, ecological harm and resource depletion, and even mainstream, non-radical economists are beginning to wake up to the fact that our economic model inevitably concentrates wealth at the very top, and that abstract financial markets produce no real economic growth that might benefit society as a whole. Even these mainstream economists are arguing that a radical change is needed to prevent the collapse of capitalism in the West (see Picketty, 2014). Despite the mass of persuasive evidence that we must now think seriously about significant social reconfiguration, we remain lodged in a societal form of fetishistic disavowal (Žižek, 1992, 2008): we know that things cannot go on as they are, but we do not want to know, and so we block this knowledge from consciousness and carry on as if the problems we face are manageable and can be fixed with a little piecemeal reform here and there. It is not yet possible to find fault with the entire edifice of liberal capitalism and liberal democracy, or to construct a comprehensive alternative to it. Only a genuine political Event can transform our situation.

The long-running processes that constructed and normalised Western atomised individualism reach their apogee in the post-political present. The individual's anger cannot yet be adequately connected to the anger of others who are, in fact, angry for the same objective reasons. We remain cynical about alternatives to what currently exists, and we baulk at the suggestion that we should submit to a new collectivist politics in which the interests of the individual are submerged within the broader interests of the collective. Postmodernism encourages us to shrug off all forms of collective identity and embrace an image of ourselves as unique and distinct from those others who would have once formed our political community. It is now commonplace to suggest that, when we vote, we vote in accordance with a basic assessment of our own best interests. Increasingly, we are believed to have no firm political convictions beyond improving our own lifestyles and advancing the causes of our own distinct micro-community. There seems to be little place in contemporary politics for deeply felt ideals. Politicians are attuned to this and construct policy accordingly.

Only a broadly felt desire to create in reality something better and more just than what currently exists can break through the politics of possessive individualism, the blind faith in the logic of markets and the cynical dismissal of utopianism. However, desire is not enough, even when that desire for political change grows from a deep fidelity to an ideological truth. A collective desire for change must, in turn, be accompanied by hard work and the willingness to make sacrifices. Part of that work involves the recruitment of others as part of a process that creates the ground upon which a transformative political Event can take place, but an event is not an Event until it is interpreted, carried forward and enacted in social reality. An Event may arise 'out of nowhere', but, unless we display fidelity to its message, it can quickly return there.

There are many other issues worthy of consideration in relation to the rise of new political parties and movements. We will touch on some of these throughout the remainder of the book. We should, however, return to the central concerns of this chapter. Can we identify any utopianism in new political movements such as Five Star? If we remove the attractions of novelty and the vague hope that the power elite might someday be knocked off their lofty perch, can we really identify a genuinely alternative politics? If we are to name Five Star a genuinely oppositional political movement, why is it that opposition to neo-liberalism – the economic bedrock upon which the contemporary social order rests – is entirely absent from its critique? This absence, we propose, tells us much about the nature of political opposition these days, but it also indicates the extent to which the ruling ideology has penetrated the porous rock of postmodern civil society. Thatcher's famous TINA dictum – 'there is no alternative' – appears to have been almost universally accepted across the social and political fields. Neo-liberalism now appears to exist as a permanent background to the present, prompting, even in those who are aware of its inevitable inequalities and injustices, a tired resignation punctured only by an occasional burst of anger. Once political opposition to the dominant order accepts neo-liberalism and the rule of markets as a regrettable but unavoidable reality, the anger and enmity that have, throughout much of our history, driven society and history forwards are neutralised. Rather than oppose neo-liberalism and hold out for the prospect of something better taking its place, political opposition focuses on some aspect of its cultural life that needs to be addressed. Anger and anxiety that, in reality, result from the continued rule of markets can quite easily morph into anger at something else.

A troubling example of the democratic backlash against the stultifying sameness of mainstream politics can be seen in Britain. The right-wing UK Independence Party (UKIP) has drawn a great deal of support precisely because it is new and not yet tainted by decades of political failure. UKIP has sought to separate itself from the dour political correctness of the mainstream. The party plays upon traditional concerns about nationhood, culture and the threats posed by immigrants to Britain's labour markets and social fabric. Its main support comes from the post-industrial working classes who, since the 1980s, have seen traditional forms of employment disappear, their communities fragment and their political representatives desert them. These people are angry, and they want their anger to be acknowledged and acted upon. They are completely alienated from the two main political parties and blame those parties for the problems they face. They hope to identify a political party that will address their concerns and construct policies that reflect their interests. For the time being, UKIP fits the bill.

Nigel Farage, the party's leader, has been particularly successful in creating an image of himself as a man of the people. Many people appear to like him because he seems quite different from the identikit politicians that roll off the Westminster production line. He is impulsive and talks with an openness that other political leaders do not. He drinks beer and smokes. He shows nothing but disdain for the mainstream's political correctness. When he is chastised by mainstream politicians, he shrugs it off and insists he is simply representing the views of ordinary men and women from across the country. When the broadsheet press expresses dismay at his policy proposals and labels him a racist, he responds that there is nothing at all 'racist' about proposing tougher immigration controls. He argues passionately about the need to defend the interests of British workers and tells his audience that his adversaries would rather defend the interests of immigrants who care nothing for Britain's culture and heritage. He rallies against the banality of the Labour and Conservative Parties and talks of how these parties are now totally disconnected from the needs and views of the majority of the British people. He suggests that mainstream politicians are now nothing more than a self-interested metropolitan elite who know nothing of the reality of contemporary urban life or the pressures that are bearing down upon voters. It is not difficult to see why his popularity has risen so high so quickly.

Again, the rise of UKIP seems to suggest that action can return to Britain's worn-out electoral system. There appears to be a genuine chance that, at the next election, UKIP can make significant inroads into the country's long-established two-party system. However, we must ask, what will justifiably aggrieved UKIP voters really be voting for? We should not be so stupid as to dismiss UKIP supporters as idiotic racists, driven solely by a hatred of minorities. UKIP's anti-immigration policies appear very attractive to many of the country's ex-working-class population, who are justifiably anxious about the safety of their jobs. They want their political representatives to address this issue in a direct manner. The more politically attuned and engaged ex-working-class voters know that another Labour or Conservative government will simply mean more of the same: a further reduction in their lifestyles, a contraction of the life chances of their children, and yet more labour market insecurity and competition. Crucially, many among this group want change, and one gets the sense that they will vote for any party that appears likely to deliver it. The direction of that change seems to matter much less than we might imagine.

It is vital that we recognise that, beneath UKIP's anti-EU and anti-immigration policies, there lies a deep commitment to the free market. The news media understandably focus on the party's desire to close the nation's borders to immigrants. Unfortunately, this means that there is almost no discussion of its drive to create in Britain a pure free market in which government regulation of business is kept to an absolute minimum. UKIP also hopes to massively reduce taxation and shrink still further the current neo-liberal state. This is not simply a matter of the ex-working classes voting against their interests. What is really important is that an energetic political opposition to the neo-liberal mainstream ultimately accepts the logic of neo-liberalism, seeking to cut taxes and government spending and generally operate in the interests of 'British business', which, of course, in an era of global free-market liberalism, appears antagonistic to the economic logic of our times. Again, we see that opposition to the dull uniformity of neo-liberalism takes the form of a marginally different form of neo-liberalism. The underlying political and economic structures remain firmly in place and are not even discussed. What ex-working-class voters would get with a UKIP government is hard-core Thatcherism with tougher immigration policies and a vote on Britain's continued membership of the European Union (EU). Again, UKIP's supporters seem destined for more of the same, with an added element of regressive nationalism.

Of course, UKIP's understanding of markets is confused, but its confusion reflects the distorted logic of postmodern politics. New political movements and parties often offer contradictory messages and divergent accounts of the categorical 'values' that structure their discourse. UKIP wants a free market, but it also wants to free Britain from the authoritarian bureaucracies of the EU. UKIP no longer wants Britain to be a part of a pan-continental union that was first conceived as an instrument of economic growth across all member states. UKIP wants Britain to be a fully independent democracy that operates outside Europe and the bureaucratic structures of the EU, but, if it were to achieve this goal, UKIP would also be separating Britain from its main export market. By implication, Britain would be forced to return to a form of modern protectionism, even though UKIP imagines itself to be a party of the global free market. UKIP wants to free capital to move across the globe in search of profit, but it wants to protect British business. It wants small government liberalism, but it wants to inhibit the flow of bodies across borders. As is the case with a whole host of variants of neo-liberalism, UKIP wants to have the cake and eat it. It wants the benefits of the free market without any of its cultural outcomes, in the same way that neo-liberal ideologues argue against the interventionist state when it comes to welfare and social provision, but for an interventionist state in order to extend the reach of markets or provide subsidies for non-profitable industries.

Again, with UKIP, the real political action is restricted to the sphere of culture. A vociferous debate rages about the threats posed by immigrants to some nebulous 'national culture', and almost nothing is said about UKIP's absolute fidelity to neo-liberal orthodoxy. UKIP may offer the opportunity for some social groups to vocalise a deeply felt anger, but these groups cannot yet appreciate that the real source of their anger is allowed to carry on unchecked. Their entirely justified anger and fear have been captured by the reactionary Right, when these things could quite easily have mobilised a leftist response to the insecurities and hardships of ordinary people trying to find a secure foothold in the formal economy. Again, neo-liberalism exists as mundane orthodoxy. It is almost never discussed or challenged in our media or in public culture. The result is that the people cannot problematise its continuation. They cannot see or understand a connection between political economy and the accumulation of humiliation, insecurity and anger in ex-working-class areas, nor can they discern the link between the logic of markets and their own inability to build a secure and reasonably rewarding life for themselves and their families. For the moment at least, the commonly felt desire for something genuinely different has no representation on the field of politics.

We can identify no utopianism in UKIP's policy pledges. It offers no positive account of genuine historic change. Like Italy's Five Star Movement, it simply hopes to reproduce a version of the present shorn of its perceived negative characteristics. Even oppositional movements that have correctly identified the towering problems associated with the continuation of liberal capitalism further into the twenty-first century seem unable to imagine a future without democracy and the market system. If an articulate alternative to our present way of life exists at all, it tends to take the form of a new regulated market system in which the state is far more active in the economy and, by manipulating the taxation system and redoubling its commitment to welfare, seeks to truncate inequalities and actively create a shared sense of mutual cooperation. If we are willing to accept inevitable economic disruption and a significant reduction in our consumer lifestyles, then this is a compelling and reasonably realistic alternative to what currently exists. This approach has the benefit of being immediately comprehensible to ordinary people, even if the great allure of a market society – that one day the individual might, against all odds, overcome every impediment to take her place among the gods – appears to have been withdrawn. Let us be honest with ourselves: the middle third of the twentieth century was indeed a golden age for the working classes of Britain, France, Germany, the Scandinavian states and the Benelux countries. Not perfect by any means, but certainly better than the long-running depression that preceded it and the neo-liberal age that followed. A return to the politics of that time would be beneficial to a great many people across Europe. Of course, the huge economic growth of that epoch was dependent upon an abundance of energy, an absence of concern about the environment and a profusion of under-developed markets ripe for exploitation. Were we ever to return to social democracy, these great advantages would be absent. It is unlikely that the sustained economic growth of the golden age can ever return (Heinberg, 2011; Klare, 2012), at least not in the real productive economy inhabited by ordinary working men and women.

If social democracy or any of its variants is to be used to drive an alternative politics then we must first acknowledge that, in effect, the image we have created of a better future is also an image of our past. It represents a return of the politics of the post-war period, rather than the positive construction of a genuine alternative to contemporary parliamentary capitalism. Perhaps we may judge this to be entirely unproblematic if the manifold harms of contemporary capitalism are curtailed and a new era of inclusive social democracy emerges. Perhaps it is time to once and for all ditch our attachment to the conceit that we can, through hard work and innovation, incrementally improve what already exists. Perhaps we should all become realists and learn to live with those things we cannot change. Perhaps a no-growth social democratic system would provide the most realistic political and economic framework to protect us from the daunting challenges that lie just ahead. The present authors certainly wouldn't argue against the rise of a new social democracy capable of sweeping aside neo-liberalism. However, if social democracy is the best that we can hope for, then it is clear we must start to think about the limits that have been imposed upon our imagination.

The politics of anxiety

Would it be too churlish to suggest that mainstream politics today is increasingly populated by a tangle of competing interest groups, fighting to have their grievances acknowledged and their fears addressed? Why is it that so many of these groups claim for themselves the status of 'victim' and seek to further their interests by demanding that power accept this status and place them next in line to benefit from small adjustments to policy as recompense for their victimhood?

Of course, it is now commonplace to suggest that, as we have drifted into an era of 'post-ideological' politics, bespoke micro-causes have come to play a more active part in our shared political life. However, as we have disengaged from the party political system and come to accept the impossibility of moving beyond parliamentary capitalism, the remaining residual political energy has been displaced and reallocated to a range of micro-issues that may be of considerable significance to the individual and the individual's community but of little interest to others. Here, our advanced cynicism and ideological resignation encourage us to accept the continuation of the present. We accept that the war cannot be won, yet hope we still have the chance to be victorious in small skirmishes here and there. The political framework of the present cannot change, but there appears to be the possibility that minor adjustments can be made to government policy. If one campaigns effectively, new laws can be passed that can advantage one's own cultural interest group. Tax breaks, subsidies and direct government investment can be offered in assistance, even if such practices tend to advantage one group at the expense of another.

The rise of political micro-causes suggests the exhaustion of politics rather than a new trend that can breathe new life into our sclerotic liberal democratic system. It reflects the fragmentation of publics into isolated and competitive defensive enclaves that see their particular causes and their particular interests as entirely separated from everyone and everything else. Victories are, of course, small and immediately absorbed into the general tumult of mediatised democratic politics, and in many cases the immediate benefit that accrues from a change in policy is clawed back in some way by the neo-liberal state, as it attempts to assure markets that national debt and expenditure are manageable and do not threaten the state's ability to meet liabilities. Of particular interest to us is the role of fear in the composition of these instrumental micro-communities.

Fear, these days, is a key component of all politics. The postmodern attack upon fixed forms of truth greatly assisted our journey from the politics of hope to the contemporary politics of fear. The certainties of modernity are clearly at an end. Of course, there are also parallel changes in ideology and political economy that have served to foment fear. The most important of these changes relates to the arrival of post-politics, which we have already discussed at length. One of the outcomes of our arrival in the current post-political epoch is the development of a postmodern bio-politics, a new politics concerned with the safety of the body. As Žižek (2008: 34) notes:

> Once we renounce big ideological causes, what remains is only the efficient administration of life . . . almost only that. That is to say, with the depoliticised, socially objective, expert administration and coordination of interests as the zero level of politics, the only way to introduce passion into this field, to actively mobilise people, is through fear, a basic constituent of today's subjectivity. For this reason, bio-politics is ultimately a politics of fear, it focuses on defence from potential victimisation or harassment.

Žižek's basic point is entirely correct, and his identification of the importance of our fear of victimisation and harassment to the composition of contemporary society and politics can certainly help us to understand policy innovation since the 1980s. The disintegration of the social and the retreat into subjectivity encourage the development of a discourse that focuses on the sanctity of subjective experience and the individual's 'right' to live a life free from the over-proximity of the other (see Winlow and Hall, 2013). However, Hall (2012a) claims that, if we are truly to grasp the reality of our situation, we must distinguish between fear and anxiety. Fear, Hall claims, is caused by objects, whereas anxiety is caused by our inability to discern objects. It is the nagging sense that something unknown is out there that possesses the ability to radically change our lives for the worse that is our primary problem. Of course, if we can objectify the cause of our fear, we can start to do something about it. We can seek to understand the object that causes our fear and then begin to mobilise against it. However, if we are stricken by a general, imprecise but immovable sense of *anxiety*, there is very little we can do to address our discomfort, save continue to search fruitlessly for an objective cause. We cannot conclusively identify the object that causes our anxiety. We may momentarily believe we have found the cause and enthusiastically set about extinguishing its effect, but inevitably we discover that anxiety remains, and our search continues. It is the persistent, nagging sense of anxiety that most disrupts our being-in-the-world.

These days, fear appears to be everywhere in politics. We are afraid of impending ecological catastrophe, afraid of meteors wiping out life on Earth, afraid of unemployment, afraid of the poor, afraid of immigrants, afraid of another economic calamity, afraid of walking the streets after dark, afraid that the fabrication that structures our social identity will be discovered. But, underneath these fears, a general anxiety continues to grind away, making us doubt that the positive substance of our lives and identities can continue to be protected, nurtured and enjoyed. Of course, anxiety and fear are closely related, and there appears to be a cross-pollination taking place that means our objective fears encourage the development of new anxieties. The same appears to be true in the opposite direction. Our drive to identify the objective cause of our anxiety can encourage us to misidentify its source. As history regrettably shows, we can project an image of pathological threat on to essentially neutral populations, who can then be repressed or destroyed, in the form of a displaced antagonism that enables the true source of conflict to maintain its pretence of social neutrality.

We can see this process played out in the politics of UKIP. The former working-class population who appear to be flocking to UKIP's cause are angry about what has become of their communities, livelihoods and identities and anxious that things are about to get a good deal worse. Of course, they have falsely identified the immigrant other as the ultimate cause of their anxiety. The regressive politics of xenophobic nationalism always exists as an ideological remainder that can be picked up and used to frame a growing sense of anger, uncertainty and obstinate anxiety. The almost total absence of a serviceable leftist alternative to what currently exists means that the justifiably pissed-off and anxious ex-working classes of Britain are unable to discharge their aggression upon the true cause of disturbance, the true reason they cannot find reasonably fulfilling work, and the true reason they face the disintegration of their communities, their identities and their status. The same is true in many other European states threatened by rising nationalism. Throughout history, the rise of the far Right evidences the failure of the Left to objectivise capitalism itself as the ultimate cause of the troubles faced by ordinary people. This failure means that it is quite easy for right-wing political movements such as UKIP to position immigrants and ethnic minorities as the ultimate source of working-class anxieties. Rather than the totality of global capital, it is the immigrant who prompts the disintegration of community, the immigrant who threatens one's livelihood and so on. As we will see later, the contemporary liberal Left appears entirely incapable of reconnecting with the ex-working classes and totally uninterested in engaging honestly with their fears and anxieties.

The liberal dismissal of Utopia

Why is it that we so often refuse to see consensus politics for what it is? Why is it that so many on the contemporary liberal Left continue to argue for piecemeal social reform, when there is more than enough compelling evidence to suggest that radical change is now absolutely necessary? Why is it that so many on the Left continue to seek to reform liberal capitalism, and why is there so little talk of actually attempting to build a viable alternative to it?

Many of our colleagues in the social sciences continue to investigate the social world in search of new policy initiatives that they believe can improve the lives of those in need. They petition government in the hope of having their ideas acknowledged and picked up by the harried, pragmatic administrators who run government departments. Yet these same social scientists know better than anyone that good ideas and policy suggestions, even on those rare occasions where they are picked up by government, are invariably diluted until anything that was once good and important is removed, and any chance of genuine social improvement disappears. Despite setback after setback, they continue, hoping that one day their research and expertise will be acknowledged and used to make important changes to policy and governance.

Other colleagues are campaigners and activists and adopt a more forthright approach to engaging government. They identify flaws in government policy and demand that action is taken to prevent the accumulation of harms in under-represented and marginalised populations. Some of this work bears fruit, but, again, these campaigners know better than anyone that other problems will quickly arise to demand their attention. There is no end to it. The problems of contemporary neo-liberal governance are such that piecemeal reformers, even radical leftist piecemeal reformers, set themselves the task of Sisyphus. All of this activity is not re-moralising the system, nor forcing it to work harder to represent the needs of ordinary men and women. In fact, the opposite is true. All of this work enables the neo-liberal state to identify occasions when it has listened to the people and reformed itself, or drawn upon scholarly evidence when creating new policy initiatives. It provides the neo-liberal state with further opportunities to argue that it welcomes informed critique and creates its policies with a view to driving new efficiencies and improving the popular experience of social life.

Can we now look back at the history of neo-liberalism and acknowledge that all of this admirable work has not prevented things getting considerably worse for a significant proportion of the overall population? Can we see that capitalism doesn't need an industrial workforce in the West, and that the relatively stable work cultures that accompanied modern industrialism cannot easily be brought back? Can we acknowledge that capitalism in the West now thrives upon insecurity, precariousness and mountains upon mountains of debt? Aren't we caught in a fetishistic desire to reproduce our own discourse and our own position as vocal antagonists of the system? Is it not time to abandon all hope that our institutionalised activism will eventually reform the system? Should we not instead seek to build something new in its place, something that is sustainable and ethically and morally superior to contemporary liberal capitalism? How is it possible for so many on the Left to look at our social and economic reality and then argue that a little reform here and there will cure the system of its most egregious harms and injustices?

In order to help us think through some of these questions, we now want to look again at the popular rejection of political radicalism as the post-war consensus began to take hold. In addition to the well-funded activities of various Western intelligence agencies in attempting to domesticate political radicalism during the 1940s, 1950s and 1960s (see Saunders, 2000), we must also acknowledge the role played by notable liberal intellectuals in discrediting all forms of utopianism and assisting with the imposition of a liberal democratic horizon that sets firm limits on politics and the ambitions of the political Left.

As we shall see, in important ways these liberal intellectuals also set the stage for the development of the neo-liberal epoch. Many of the ideas they developed were incorporated into the very foundations of this new, post-1980s liberalism, and the influence of these academic superstars remains huge to this day. It can be detected, not simply on the neo-liberal Right, but also on the social liberal Left, which, for the most part, continues to argue for the democratic reform of capitalism and a gradualist approach to social improvement. In this section, we will use the work of Hannah Arendt, Karl Popper and Isaiah Berlin as exemplars of this body of liberal theory, but they are by no means the only individuals who played an active role in the aggressive denunciation of the radical Left and its dismissal from the political stage.

Hannah Arendt, who is often considered to be a political radical and standard-bearer for contemporary critical theory and leftist scholarship more broadly, produced a particularly vitriolic dismissal of the radical Left and its tendency toward oppressive and inhumane totalitarianism. Arendt (1973, 2009), who was particularly well connected with establishment figures in Washington, despite her early flirtation with revolutionary Marxism (see Saunders, 2000), believed Stalinism to be just as barbarous as German Nazism. She also believed she could identify a shared foundation that bonded these two ideologies together. Her analysis of these twinned totalitarianisms is rooted in a cluster of intellectual commitments that tend to characterise the fundamental belief system of the post-war liberal class: a deep fear and loathing of utopianism; a deep distrust, at the very least, of 'ideology';

a deep commitment to 'freedom', hazily defined; faith in 'common sense' and rationalism; and an unyielding conviction that liberal democracy represents humanity's best shot at advancing this hazily defined 'freedom'.

Like many other scholars who warmed to the task of denouncing political radicalism in the wake of Nazism and Stalinism, Arendt talked of the capacity of ideology to disturb the basic foundations of our social and moral life. Ideology was dangerous, and she imagined herself and those she admired to be entirely untainted by it. The intellectual commitments and political bearing of the post-war liberal class were, for Arendt and many others, based on rational and objective analysis of the facts. Unlike the ideologues of the radical Left, the minds of the liberal class were open, and their scepticism protected them from being dragged into ideology's dark trap.

For the liberal class, the word 'ideology' suggested a pathological attachment to ideas, rather than a reasonably cohesive suite of ideas used to structure social and political life. For it, ideological commitment was like an illness that overcame the individual, forcing her to value ideas more than anything else that might command attention. The ideologue's unwavering commitment to ideology denies him access to a reality that is perfectly straightforward to the liberal critic. Of course, the liberal class judged its intellectual position to be entirely free from ideology simply because its position was anti-ideological. Trapped in this tautology, it could not turn and critically appraise its own discourse. For the liberal class, ideology was always a problem of the Other, and never of the self. Its members argued that they valued human life and the well-being of ordinary men and women more than they valued ideas, and so, in their definition at least, they were completely free from the deathly pallor of ideology. However, if we understand ideology in the more conventional sense, then it's clear that they too were dedicated ideologues, engaged in a no-holds-barred conflict with their ideological opponents on the radical Left. They simply refused to accept that their position could be considered ideological. They understood their own position to be rational, logical, ethical and objective, whereas the radical Left's ideological commitments separated it from rationality and rendered it capable of absolutely horrific actions in pursuit of its goals.

Arendt, Popper and Berlin assumed utopianism and ideology to be tightly connected. In some cases, the words are used interchangeably. Popper talks of utopianism and Arendt of ideology, but the central arguments of these two authors are very much the same. Popper's writing is clear and unadorned. Arendt's analysis wanders, but, of the three, she is clearly most comfortable in the realm of theoretical abstraction. Berlin's writing is rather baroque in style: learned, interesting, but often lacking in substance. For all three, ideology and utopianism present a significant threat to civilised post-war social life.

For them, believing that a better world was possible, and then formulating a plan to make it so, encouraged the masses, and the ideologues who manipulated and indoctrinated them, to change the world entirely in order to justify their faith in ideas. Ideology, Arendt wrote, strives to 'make the world consistent, to prove that its respective supersense has been right . . . [and] it is chiefly for the sake of this supersense, for the sake of complete consistency, that it is necessary for totalitarianism to destroy every trace of what we commonly call human dignity' (Arendt, 1973).

Karl Popper's monumental work *The Open Society and Its Enemies* (2011) was written during the Second World War and published in English at the war's end. Popper had fled his native Austria, moving first to New Zealand and then on to a fully tenured academic post at the London School of Economics. Born in Vienna in 1902 to reasonably affluent middle-class parents, Popper was initially attracted to the promise of socialism and 'for about two or three months' regarded himself as a communist (Popper, 2002a: 32). It seems as though Popper's early radicalism was driven by a desire to help people, especially those he deemed less fortunate than himself. Popper's brief flirtation with radical politics came to an end when a number of unarmed socialists and communists organised a demonstration against the detention of some of their comrades in a police station in Vienna. Shots were fired by the Viennese police, and a number of protesters were killed (ibid.: 32–3).

Writing towards the end of the twentieth century, looking back upon his youthful politics at the end of a long life, Popper makes it clear that living through these events changed his political and intellectual trajectory enormously. Before the deaths of these young people, Popper was a communist committed to changing the world. Perhaps his traumatic experience had brought him to the decision that incumbent power is simply too brutal to confront, but we know for certain that, when he had fully reflected upon what had transpired, he was firmly of the conviction that political radicalism was hopelessly naïve and potentially dangerous. Justifying and popularising this view would take up a significant portion of his life's work.

'The whole experience', Popper writes, 'produced in me a life-long revulsion of feeling' (ibid.: 33). Understandably enough, Popper appears to have been haunted by the deaths of his comrades and his own role in the protest. He admits to feeling partly responsible for what happened. But his reaction to these deaths was not the only consideration that prompted him to abandon radical politics. Popper was ill at ease with the 'scientific' Marxism that appeared to play a structural role in leftist accounts of social change. He had read Plato, Hegel and Marx and was already beginning to formulate an aggressive critique of their 'teleological historicism' (Popper, 2011). Here, we can begin to see a connection between Popper's political philosophy and his philosophy of science. In particular, Popper's construction of what he calls 'critical rationalism', which he believed would sweep aside all inductivist accounts of scientific knowledge, places falsifiability central to the construction of scientific knowledge. Only those theories that survive testing by both their proponents and opponents can progress to shape the development of science (see Popper, 2005). He sets science the enormous – some would say impossible (see Hall and Winlow, 2015) – task of testing both all conceivable and all proposed hypotheses, and he dismisses all proposed forms of knowledge that can be neither proven nor falsified.

Popper adopts a similar approach in his attack on the philosophies of Plato, Hegel and Marx. For Popper, the three greatest figures in the history of philosophy were, ultimately, responsible for creating an unscientific account of historical change that encouraged totalitarianism and political repression. All three, Popper claimed, offered accounts of history that rest upon the existence of universal laws that lead inevitably to a particular destination. For Popper, this kind of historicism was faux-science in its worst form. There was simply no scientific basis for the claim that history developed in relation to universal laws that carried societies from one historical epoch to the next. Popper believed that there was no way of accurately predicting what age would follow this one. Historical change developed in relation to contingent events that could not be forecast. Worse still, and for Popper this was the nub of his argument, this kind of historicism fuelled totalitarianism and authoritarianism. It encouraged people to believe that the death of individuals was a price worth paying in furtherance of historical necessity.

Popper (2012) gives an instructive example that relates to the death of his leftist comrades outside the police station in Vienna in the spring of 1919. Popper recalls discussing this incident and the tragic loss of life with his surviving leftist colleagues. He was shocked by their response. Apparently, they expressed the belief that the death of their friends was a necessary sacrifice that would hasten the socialist revolution. Popper uses this brief story as a means of capturing the stupidity of leftist utopianism, and especially those forms of utopianism that appear to rest on a series of faulty assumptions about the forces that determine the movement of history.

Popper's two major works of political philosophy, *The Open Society and Its Enemies* and *The Poverty of Historicism* (2002b), were both hugely influential. They cover similar ground, insofar as they offer what became the standard liberal critique of continental philosophy and its treatment of historical processes. Popper is most concerned with demolishing the basic precepts of Marxist thought and disabusing leftist radicals of their passionate enthusiasm. He is noticeably less concerned with fascism, and we might judge this a little odd given the nature of fascist crimes during the twentieth century, Popper's Jewish roots and his flight from Austria–Hungary before the war. Despite widespread awareness of the Holocaust during the years in which these books were in production, fascists certainly have a much easier time of it than 'Marxists', broadly considered. First published in 1957, *The Poverty of Historicism* contains barely a mention of the Nazis, concentration camps or 'the final solution', and, on the rare occasion these things do crop up, they are directly conflated with the crimes of 'Marxists', and the ultimate cause of their collective crimes is then immediately identified as the flawed belief in 'Inexorable Laws in Human Destiny' (Popper, 2002b: vi; emphasis in the original).

For Popper, all 'utopians' were ultimately the same. There was no need to tease out ideological distinctions or to explain precisely what in Nazism might be considered 'utopian'. Popper was not much interested in the social model the utopian hoped to create or in how she planned to create it. Popper ascribes faith in universal laws of history to all utopians, and his argument develops on that basis.

He then identifies a commitment to radical social transformation as the second defining characteristic of all utopians. With these two dominant characteristics of the utopian established, Popper then feels ready to make a huge ideological leap in claiming that all utopians possess a willingness to countenance human suffering on a monumental scale in order to clear away obstacles and accelerate the arrival of their utopian society.

Popper's most substantial treatise, *The Open Society and Its Enemies*, captured the mood perfectly. At the end of the Second World War, there existed a notable distrust of political radicalism. People wanted peace, and there existed considerable faith that liberal capitalism's market economy and democratic political system would deliver incremental social improvements. Europeans were appalled by the crimes of the Nazis, and there was a growing realisation that the communist revolutions in the east were proving to be an utter disaster for millions of ordinary working men and women. In what appeared to be a partial confirmation of Popper's thesis, radical social transformation appeared to bring with it a disregard for human dignity and the right to self-determination. With a reinvigorated post-war democratic platform firmly in place, there seemed little need to pursue radical change.

Popper's enthusiastic support for liberal democracy and his forceful dismissal of all alternatives to it immediately found an appreciative audience among the liberal intelligentsia of the West. A number of notable figures arranged Popper's departure from New Zealand and his employment at the London School of Economics, ostensibly in recognition of his earlier work on the contours of scientific knowledge. It was the kind of elevation that happens in the academy when one constructs a new argument that powerful institutional figures immediately recognise as 'truth'. Because this new argument is 'true', these powerful figures ennoble the individual as much as they can. They also seek to popularise his discourse, so that it might, at some point in the future, take on the appearance of basic common sense. Gradually, the basic building blocks of disciplinary knowledge are adapted to reflect the particularities of the new landscape.

However, Popper's influence extended way beyond the restrictive enclaves of the liberal metropolitan intelligentsia, and way beyond the common room and the campus. His thesis spoke directly to those democratically elected politicians who were attempting to rebuild shattered nations after a long and destructive war. It spoke to those fearful of the politics of the east and keen to construct a broad alliance against the Soviet threat. It spoke to Fabian social liberals on the left and radical economic libertarians on the right. Popper's thesis received support from liberals and democrats of all kinds, working in economics, the arts, the humanities and the social sciences, in fact right across the academy. It was a broad-spectrum antibiotic targeted at the dangerous bacterium of utopianism. It subtly infiltrated popular culture and, in its own way, contributed to the new post-war consensus.

Popper's opponents on the utopian Left might reasonably have claimed that his thesis was immediately captured by, and used to re-energise, a ruling ideology reshaping its discourse in response to significant external threats, or that Popper's philosophical work delivered on behalf of the dominant ideology a range of new proclamations on what one should believe and how one should believe it. In any case, if, after the war, democracy emerged as the clear winner, it was accompanied to the winner's rostrum by a newly powerful liberal capitalism that set firm limits on the political field and the nature of contestation within it. Arguments continued to rage, of course, and some of them became more than a little heated. However, these arguments were in most cases arguments between liberals of the Left and liberals of the Right, and they tended to focus on who got what when it was time to cut the cake and distribute the economic spoils of unprecedented productivity and economic growth. A new golden era of liberal progressivism beckoned, and Popper's powerful advocacy of liberal democracy appeared to set the tone.

Popper's rapid rise to prominence placed him alongside such notable figures as George Stigler, Friedrich Hayek, Milton Friedman and Ludwig von Mises, and together they established the Mont Pelerin Society in 1947. The society – which has gone from strength to strength and continues to exist to this day – is dedicated to the advancement of personal and economic freedoms. On eight occasions, a member of the Mont Pelerin Society has received what is commonly – and mistakenly – known as the 'Nobel Prize in Economics'. In fact, the prize in question is actually called the Sveriges Riksbank Prize in Economic Sciences in Memory of Alfred Nobel. Sveriges Riksbank made a donation to establish the prize; there is no Nobel Prize in Economics.

The Mont Pelerin Society has, since its formation, functioned as a partisan 'thought collective' keen to advance the neo-liberal project (see Mirowski and Plehwe, 2009). In this undertaking, the group has been spectacularly successful. Its influence can be seen in virtually every aspect of contemporary free-market thought, and it draws much of its philosophy from Popper's aggressive denunciation of political radicalism and his deep commitment to the measured pragmatism of liberal democracy. Of course, Popper's faith in liberal democracy sits perfectly alongside the neoclassical and free-market economics of his colleagues in the Mont Pelerin Society. The simplistic ontological framework, developed first by Descartes and expanded and institutionalised by the Enlightenment liberals, is taken as a given in classical, neoclassical and neo-liberal economics and in the liberal thought of Popper and the countless others who followed in his footsteps. Above all, the individual is rational and preoccupied with his or her 'best interests'. The individual determines his or her own social identity by weighing things up and selecting a route forwards. For liberals of both Right and Left, the social exerts little influence upon the individual's decisions, desires, tastes and dispositions, and all are blessed with similar gifts and the capacity to engage rationally with economic and social life.

It is worth spending a little time outlining Popper's position, mostly because it is almost diametrically opposed to our own, but also because it provides the foundation for so much liberal political and social thought today. In particular, one can discern how his theory, and the theories of his brethren in the Mont Pelerin Society, helped to establish the boundaries that were placed upon the post-war political field and set the scene for the contemporary neo-liberal epoch.

In *The Poverty of Historicism*, Popper compares what he calls 'historicist' and 'nonhistoricist' approaches to reform and social change. He is, in fact, counterpoising utopianism with anti-utopianism and the politics of radical change with the politics of small-scale reform. The nonhistoricist employs 'piecemeal engineering' (Popper, 2002b) and focuses upon small adjustments based loosely on models of scientific testing and falsification. Rather than changing the system in its entirety and inviting tragedy, the dispassionate nonhistoricist works within the system as it exists and focuses on those aspects of the system that can be fixed or improved. Gradually, through carefully controlled interventions here and there, the nonhistoricist improves social well-being and boosts progressive civic sentiments. Deploying the caution and scepticism of scientific method, the piecemeal reformer slowly creates the ground upon which freedom can set down roots and begin to blossom.

The nonhistoricist reformer is governed by pragmatism and does not succumb to passionate desire and 'strong thought' to create perfection. Instead, he sets himself the task of removing impediments to freedom. He focuses on ridding the system of blockages and identifying new and more efficient ways of delivering services or managing economic practice. Rather than focusing on distant goals, he focuses upon concrete problems that can be remedied. Above all, he realises that, in his desire to create perfection, the utopian is on a fool's errand. There is no feasible blueprint for a perfect world, and attempting to change the social field to better suit one's preferred image of Utopia risks absolute catastrophe.

For Popper, there can be no rational justification for radical social transformation. There is simply no scientific basis to justify utopian social blueprints of any sort, and so, because it is impossible to fully justify utopian goals in the eyes of rational men and women, violent authoritarianism tends to be the political outcome of the utopian imagination. The utopian has only his conviction to support his blueprint for Utopia. He can volunteer no evidence to support his model over others that might be constructed, and so, in Popper's view at least, the committed utopian inevitably draws upon violence to build a new society in accordance with his blueprint.

Throughout Popper's work, it is possible to detect a commitment to genuine social improvement. He is not at all opposed to improving the life-chances of the poor or furnishing them with significant social provisions. He simply wants changes to be small and based on rational judgement. For example, despite the probability that many of his friends in the Mont Pelerin Society would have loathed the idea, it appears Popper would not have been ideologically opposed to a national health care system provided by the state, *if* there was sufficient reason to argue that this system would be an improvement on the existing model. That is, if it could be proven to significantly improve public health, and if this improvement could be considered to be a reasonable return on the initial investment when weighed against other possible social interventions. For Popper, it would be reasonable to attempt to change the provision of public health services because society as a whole could afford to make a mistake in this regard. Tragedy would not result from an attempt to overhaul the public health system. However, if one were to change the whole of society on a similar basis, the potential harms would be of an entirely different order. Tyranny might well be the outcome of such an attempt, and society could not easily withdraw from a colossal social experiment of this kind without significant human costs.

Many rallied to support Popper's intervention. It reverberated across the intellectual landscape and throughout much of politics. It was precisely what democratically elected politicians wanted to hear, and the same was true of all who possessed a stake in preserving the post-war status quo. There was simply no need for radical transformation. Throughout history, or at least throughout Popper's partial reading of it, radical social transformations had resulted in tyranny and slaughter. Liberal democracy allowed for careful deliberation and informed decision-making over all proposed reforms. It provided a fair and representative system with inbuilt checks and balances and it required political leaders to pursue change through a series of small-scale adjustments. These adjustments, especially when taken cumulatively, were capable of improving economic efficiency and social well-being, and they were not accompanied by the risks large-scale intervention inevitably carries.

Popper was sure that there was no such thing as Utopia. It was idiotic to even countenance the possibility. Utopianism was dangerous, the preserve of dreamers so intoxicated by the allure of their imaginary Utopia they were willing to throw away the essence of civil society in pursuit of it. The careful rationalists of liberal democracy could instead improve the world, one policy initiative at a time. They would form their plans in relation to evidence and never get distracted by dreams of perfection. Small-scale adjustments could be made that would dispense with those concrete social problems that reduce the sum total of happiness in society. Improvements would be incremental, but real and, above all, safe.

This argument became the orthodox defence of liberal democracy and the standard critique of all alternative models of social and political organisation. Its influence grew as supporters were recruited and carried the thesis, or at least its general orientation and key concerns, back to their own academic disciplines. It contributed to the armoury of self-satisfied liberal ideologues keen to draw attention to the economic growth and social improvement of post-war social democracy and the violent authoritarianism and hardship that existed in non-democratic systems. As the economic recovery gathered pace, and the cold war began to take shape, it was clear who the good guys were. Democracy was about freedom, prosperity and gradual and incremental social improvement. Communism was a boot stamping on a human face for all eternity (see Orwell, 2013).

Popper's thesis, especially in *The Open Society and Its Enemies*, develops from a general desire to explain the root cause of twentieth-century totalitarianism. Despite his professed deep commitment to scientific objectivity, Popper's thesis is pure ideology. It ignores whole chunks of history, and, in the absence of compelling data or a reasonably coherent theoretical account, Popper is forced to take a leap of faith in connecting the utopian imagination to the rise of destructive totalitarianism. His definition of utopianism is hazy to say the least, and the characteristics he ascribes to utopians are overly generalised. One could be forgiven for thinking that his unwillingness to engage in a detailed analysis of German fascism reflects the fact that, were he to do so, he would find very little 'utopianism' in it, and certainly no obvious connection to the universal laws of human history that he so despised. He appears totally unconcerned about, and blind to, the tragedies that have occurred under the auspices of liberal democracy (see Losurdo, 2011; Seymour, 2012). For him, it is almost as if the history of human suffering is exclusively confined within political attempts to transform the social, which in turn reflects the pathologies of utopianism, which in turn reflect flawed philosophical accounts of historical change. It is worth reminding ourselves that Hitler and his Nazi Party won democratic elections in 1933, formally disbanded the Weimar Republic and established the Third Reich with an Act of Parliament. And hadn't the liberal democratic USA dropped atomic bombs on Hiroshima and Nagasaki, killing hundreds of thousands of innocent civilians, just a year or so before the publication of *The Open Society and Its Enemies*?

Whereas Popper offered a firm advocacy of liberal democratic reform, Isaiah Berlin was more concerned with the threats posed to 'value pluralism' by utopianism and political collectivism. Like Popper, Berlin was born into an affluent, middle-class family, and, like Popper, some of his most powerful memories related to the rise of 'totalitarian politics'. Berlin was born in 1909 in Riga, in what is now Latvia. Later in life, he recalled vivid memories of the Russian Revolution and made it clear that witnessing these events shaped his work and his distaste for authoritarian populism, and communism in particular (see Ignatieff, 2000). Berlin moved to England with his family in 1921 and spent most of his adult life at Oxford University, where he quickly became a fixture in the intellectual establishment. He was awarded a CBE in 1946, the Chichele Professorship in Social and Political Theory in 1957 and a knighthood in that same year, despite being, for the most part, an essayist and occasional lecturer rather than a *bona fide* philosopher and discursive architect of new ways of conceptualising the world and our place within it. During the war, he worked for the British Diplomatic Service, and it is rumoured that he maintained his connection to the British intelligence community after the war (see Saunders, 2000). Over his long career, he became the most revered of Britain's small band of public intellectuals.

Berlin is remembered as a genteel man of remarkable erudition. He saw himself as a historian of ideas rather than a philosopher in the traditional sense. His lectures were said to be spellbinding, and his written work eschews all unnecessary abstraction. In truth, it has something of a literary quality to it, suggestive of a kind of informal but high-minded intellectual conversation, rather than a complicated treatise constructed to advance a particular point. At no time during his career did he attempt to write or publish an original work of philosophy. This seems odd given the esteem in which his work is held across the arts and humanities. Instead, Berlin produced a great many essays on a variety of topics, although it is, of course, possible to identify an enduring concern with liberalism and the nature of freedom.

Despite the fact that he produced no notable books of his own, Berlin's work has been anthologised and republished quite regularly since his death in 1997. The influence of his work is as great now as it has ever been. However, for such a celebrated public intellectual, his position on liberty is rather obtuse and difficult to pin down. He both endorses and castigates negative and positive freedom and hints at an unresolvable competition between the two. Ultimately, like earlier English liberals, he is forced to confront the old Hobbesian problem and declares that a decision must be reached about the extent to which we are willing to sacrifice freedom in order to advance other social goods. He politely shepherds his readers to the conclusion that we should be deeply suspicious of all who seek to change society for the better. Instead, we should accept, indeed celebrate, society's imperfections. We should recognise that we cannot have everything just as we like it. It is wrong to assume that diverse values can be brought together harmoniously.

If we take in the broad sweep of his published work, it's clear that ultimately Berlin saw freedom negatively, in terms of the absence of obligations and controls. The freedom that most attracted Berlin was the freedom to do whatever one liked, prefaced, of course, with the assumption that the free subject would immediately know how to use this freedom and to what end. We will try to draw together key parts of Berlin's work in the pages that follow, but we do not have the space necessary to fully explore his contribution to liberal philosophy. Our focus is on his dismissal of utopianism and his enthusiastic championing of liberal pluralism.

Throughout his work, he draws upon such a remarkable assortment of intellectual figures and with such ease and alacrity that some have doubted that he had full command of all of the work to which he alludes (see, for example, Arblaster, 1971; Anderson, 1992; Jacoby, 2013). Berlin often quoted Kant, who once briefly opined that, 'out of the crooked timber of humanity no straight thing was ever made'. This phrase appeared to capture the essence of Berlin's advocacy of pluralism, and he quoted it so often that it was later used as the title of a posthumous collection of Berlin's essays (Berlin, 2013). For Berlin, the phrase suggests the necessity of accepting pluralism and dismissing grand schemes and plans that hoped to change humanity or set it to a particular task. Ultimately, human timber could not be made straight. It was best to accept diversity and the messy and unmanageable business of human societies and leave individuals free to forge their own path. What good does it do to seek to mould men and their collective life, when their very nature suggests such a task is impossible? Surely the desire to transform men in this way, to manage and control human societies and instruct individuals on what is good, proper and right is a dangerous and destructive undertaking, antagonistic to the principles of human freedom?

Anderson (1992; see also Jacoby, 2013) notes that Kant did not coin the 'crooked timber' phrase in support of liberal pluralism. Berlin appears to have ripped the quote from its original context. Perversely enough, the essay from which the quote is taken in fact endorses an account of universalism and the possibility of Utopia (see Jacoby, 2013). This does not render Berlin a fraud, of course, but, when taken together with other evidence offered by Jacoby and others (Manuel and Manuel, 1979; Hitchens, 1998; Bird, 2000), it does give us a sense of his character and the context of his intellectual elevation to the status of peerless scholar, visionary and determined advocate of human liberty (see, for example, Gray, 2013).

Ignatieff's (2000) biography paints a picture of a modest man who avoided conflict. He carefully side-stepped the task of directly engaging with his established leftist contemporaries and was more comfortable in the company of long-dead philosophers unlikely to answer back. Berlin was consummately polite. Even when engaging with ancient philosophers, he did what he could to identify their achievements. He misinterpreted and simplified Marx's overall philosophy, but he then seeks to make amends by talking in glowing terms of Marx's analysis of politics. He did this often; it appears he could always find something in any philosopher's *oeuvre* that was interesting and worthy of congratulation.

Hitchens (1998) sees Berlin as a confirmed establishment figure, dedicated to the continuation of the status quo. In Hitchens's view, Berlin risked nothing. He equivocated, fudged and backtracked. Hitchens paints a picture of Berlin as a supreme raconteur, raising the tone of conversation at court, capable of impressing a lay audience with the breadth of his philosophical knowledge, but steadfast in his refusal to actually commit to a position and then defend it. Rather than breaking any new intellectual ground, he was a 'skilled ventriloquist for other thinkers' (ibid.).

Bird's (2000) biography of the Bundy brothers, key figures at the heart of the American establishment throughout the cold war and architects of America's policies in Indo-China, reveals that Berlin was a great supporter of, and friend to, the Bundys and a sponsor of the so-called 'special relationship' between Britain and the United States. Berlin, it seems, saw the necessity of America's war in Vietnam and believed in the Bundy's 'domino effect' policy. His support was gratefully received and not forgotten. The Ford Foundation, a benevolent organisation of great wealth dedicated to maintaining the key principles of the American way of life, gave a huge sum of money to establish Wolfson College at the University of Oxford. Berlin was its first president. Can this be the same man who eschewed violence and warned us all of the consequences of committing to abstract ideas? The same determined defender of messy pluralism and the sanctity of self-determination and human life?

Berlin's most important and oft-cited contribution to knowledge is his analysis of positive and negative freedom, which appeared in his 1958 essay 'Two Concepts of Liberty' (Berlin, 2002). In this essay, we get Berlin in full flow: expansive, learned, illustrative and persuasive, his prose a languid and aesthetically pleasing stroll down the leafy lanes of liberal thought. The essay contains a remarkable breadth of reference. It is easy to see why he considered himself a historian of ideas rather than a creator of new ones. As in much of his work, Berlin is long on educated discussion and short on conclusive and coherent argumentation. As many other notable philosophers and theorists had already done, Berlin draws a distinction between two forms of liberty. It is also possible to detect a kind of liberal intellectual pragmatism that runs counter to any conception of utopianism. The essay is concerned with the choices made by societies and individuals in relation to values.

It presents freedom as the highest form of value, a barometer that allows us to calibrate the achievements of any society.

For Berlin, if we sacrifice our freedom in order to address justice or inequality we suffer a net loss in human freedom. If we give up our freedom to ensure that others have enough food to eat, those others who benefit from our largesse do not necessarily experience a growth in their own freedom. Rather, freedom has been sacrificed in order to bolster some other aspect of our shared social life. We have, for example, chosen justice and equality over freedom, and this is the crux of Berlin's dour and pragmatic account of liberty. We must make a choice and engage in a trade-off between social values. A compromise must be found. We cannot construct a perfect social system. We must accept that the world is imperfect or accept the repercussions of seeking to change it.

Here, we can see Berlin's debt to Hobbes, Locke, Smith and Bentham. It is assumed that a quotient of freedom must be sacrificed and ceded to the state, so that rules of social conduct might be established that protect men from the pure freedom of other men. However, the sacrifice should be as small as is practically possible. The state should not seek to intrude upon the private life of the individual and regulate her behaviour any more than is absolutely necessary to guarantee a reasonably civilised social order.

Berlin is particularly enthusiastic about the work of the French liberal philosopher Benjamin Constant. Indeed, Berlin returns to Constant again and again in a great many of his essays and lectures. For Constant, and many other notable liberals, we must preserve personal freedoms or else 'degrade or deny our nature' (quoted in Berlin, 2002). For Constant, religion, opinion, expression and property occupy a stratum of things that absolutely must be free from the intrusions of the state. It is self-defeating to surrender these things, for in the act of surrender we deny the very essence of our humanity. Here, Berlin uses Mill to suggest that an overweening state deprives society of the spontaneity, originality, dynamism and genius that it needs to advance and improve itself. The surrender of personal freedom to the state ensures a form of collective mediocrity that stunts human development. For both Mill and Bentham, man is a being with a life of his own, to live as he chooses. To intrude upon his personal space, even when this intrusion is spurred by the best intentions, is to 'sin against the truth of . . . man' (Berlin, 2002). As Berlin admits, this is the *negative* conception of liberty in its classic form. Characteristically, Berlin offers some criticism and holds this account at a distance, but his tacit endorsement of it can be detected both in this essay and throughout his writing. He acknowledges its inadequacies and challenges the assumption that democracy is the system of governance best able to preserve the freedoms of the individual. He does not openly commit to pure negative freedom because he is most concerned with the defence of messy pluralism and keen to draw our attention to the difficult and value-laden choices society faces in determining its character and primary values. For Berlin, there can be no perfect balance: there is always a downside, always a sacrifice to be made, and this is true of both negative and positive freedom.

In comparison with his conception of negative freedom, Berlin's account of positive freedom appears rather vague and flimsy. It certainly fails to engage with the work of those who have stridently advocated forms of state intervention or investigated fully the place of justice and equality in conceptions of the good society. Berlin is resolutely committed to an analysis of freedom and refuses to be dragged off course to reflect upon those other values capable of driving forward civilisation. For Berlin, we may choose to sacrifice our freedom in pursuit of other forms of value, but we must not lose sight of the fact that freedom has been sacrificed. It has gone. We have traded it for something else.

At its most basic, of course, positive freedom is simply the 'freedom to'. Positive freedom requires an authority to push past Mill's concerns with the sanctity of self-determination and intervene in the lives of individuals to equip them with the tools necessary to create their own freedom. This requires a self-assured authority with a clear conception of what is good for the individual, and, for Berlin, therein lies the problem. The authority that intervenes to equip the individual with the capacity to be free imposes its conception of value on free-willed individuals. It transforms the individual from an autonomous being capable of creating and responding to her own values into mere human material to be moulded by the values of others. The motives of the authority that intervenes might be entirely benevolent, but 'to treat men in this way is to treat them as if they were not self-determined' (2002: 183). Quoting Kant, Berlin argues that this kind of 'paternalism is the greatest despotism imaginable'. It is to treat men as if they were 'subhuman . . . as if their ends are less ultimate and sacred than my own' (ibid.). Again, Berlin backtracks a little. In a long and winding discussion of philosophical rationalism, he stresses the importance of knowledge and understanding in positive accounts of freedom. If the rational individual consciously submits to particular rules, he is not oppressed in the same way as the subject who has these rules imposed upon him, either against his will or without his fully understanding their context. Berlin stresses self-direction and self-control as integral elements of positive freedom. If the individual rationally determines that it is in his best interests to live in accordance with rules created either by himself or by some external agency, then we should not assume that he has sacrificed or been robbed of his liberty.

Berlin's essay closes with a mild critique of those aspects of philosophy and political theory that hold out faith in the discovery of 'a final solution', that is, a future society in which positive values can be realised and brought together in harmony, a society of expansive freedoms and social justice, a society of truth, happiness, innovation and fairness. Of course, Berlin is doubtful that all good things are compatible. Advancing one is likely to mean reducing another. 'The belief that some single formula can in principle be found whereby all the diverse ends of men can be harmoniously realised', Berlin argues, 'is demonstrably false.' The realisation of some social good inevitably means that another must be sacrificed. The end-point is that we must accept pluralism and remain resolutely distrustful of those who hold out the prospect of a future Utopia. Pluralism was, for Berlin, 'a truer and more humane ideal than the goals of those who seek in the great disciplined, authoritarian structures the ideal of 'positive' self-mastery by classes, or peoples, or the whole of mankind' (ibid: 216). Berlin closes the essay by encouraging his readers to recognise that human goals are many, that humans are free-willed agents, and that values are not commensurable and are in fact 'in perpetual rivalry with one another'. Pluralism 'does not . . . deprive men, in the name of some remote, or incoherent, ideal, of much that they have found to be indispensable to their life as unpredictably self-transforming human beings' (ibid.). Above all, and as always, we must keep in mind that, 'Out of the crooked timber of humanity no straight thing was ever made'.

Conclusion

It is now commonplace to argue that liberalism has, since the end of the Second World War, cut many of the ties that bound it to its founding principles. Liberalism is often talked about as if its meaning is self-evident, but liberalism today is so plural and amorphous, and contains so many striking contradictions, that its precise meaning has been lost. Its broad expanse stretches from interventionist social liberalism on one side to hard-core economic libertarianism on the other.

For us, liberal democracy came to define Western political economy and culture after the defeat of the twentieth century's specific historical forms of totalitarianism – by no means the only ones imaginable – but the philosophical liberalism on which this system was based gradually appeared to lose a clear sense of itself. In contrast to the clear universal symbols of liberty, equality, fraternity and progress that inspired its birth, its core meanings became woolly and inexact. As it transformed itself into the metacategory of Western political discourse (Bell, 2014), it became little more than a gatekeeper for all sorts of traditional and novel cultural forms whose members applied for entrance into capitalism's socio-economic race and pleaded for tolerance as they were compelled to compete against each other with increasing vigour. It lost much of the positive political identity at its core and gradually mutated into the negative category of *non-totalitarianism*. All that remained was a degenerative and non-dialectical post-political debate between the state and the individual, centred upon the point at which the state must intervene and the extent of the intervention necessary to secure a balance between the individual's 'freedom' and 'security'.

Our primary goal with this section has been to highlight the role liberal intellectuals have played in closing off discussion about significant social change and forcing all to accept the framework of liberal democracy. Repeatedly, we have been told that anything that exists beyond the borders of liberal democracy involves totalitarianism, repression, murder, genocide and a prolonged assault upon human rights and dignity. All who believe that they can identify the limits of liberal democracy and all who are dissatisfied with liberal democracy's apparent inability to enact genuine change in the world are, for these great intellectuals, potential tyrants so besotted with their ideologies that they would ride roughshod over the whole of humanity to make the world fit with their mad utopian dreams and blueprints. Repeatedly, we have been told that there is simply no need to make any significant changes. We can accomplish humanitarian goals by using the instruments of government and by engaging with the democratic process. We can still make capitalism work for us by drawing upon its legendary productive and organisational efficiencies. Capitalism's tendency towards boom and bust cycles can be overcome. Its drive to privatise the commons and its propensity to squeeze the last drop of surplus value from labour can be contained and strictly policed. Why invite tragedy with wholesale social and economic change, when a series of small-scale interventions can improve what we already have? Why risk a return to totalitarianism? We can return capitalism to the cage it occupied during the social democratic era. Democracy can be rejuvenated. All is not lost. We are not yet at crisis point.

This kind of narrative is usually followed with a rather curt dismissal of unnecessary and counter-productive pessimism and a firm instruction to look on the bright side. It may be true to say that democracy can still be rejuvenated. The base populism and depressive hedonism of contemporary public culture might yet be transformed into ebullient and active citizenship. Our anxious and obsessive competitive individualism might yet yield to the politics of universality and a rational assessment of the benefits of solidarity. If that were to happen, we might then see our political parties propose a raft of new policies that would, one step at a time, curtail the worst excesses of capitalism's market expansionism, social disruption and cultural erosion. The democratic nations of the world might come together in stark recognition of the importance of global accord in our common struggle against the worst effects of climate change. All of this might happen, but, if liberal democracy is indeed technically capable of doing all of this, it's clear that it is no longer disposed to the task.

A growing assortment of academics from both the Left and the Right have now freed themselves from the liberal faith in incremental progress that has lingered on since the time of the Enlightenment. It's now possible to talk openly and honestly about the prospect of things getting decidedly worse for the majority of people across the West. This is not simply a matter of the ability of the financial elite to secure for itself a huge and growing proportion of our planet's wealth. It is not simply a matter of the tendency of abstract finance capitalism to disconnect itself from the real economy in which ordinary working men and women find their employment, income and security. And it is not simply a matter of growing anger at social injustice. As we have tried to stress, there are now compelling material pressures that demand to be taken seriously. We are already living through the first wave of problems caused by environmental change. We are already seeing the first signs of conflict over resources in resource-rich regions. We see the descent of workers into chronic insecurity in societies of widening divisions. Should we assume an imminent technological fix? Should we assume that our political leaders will take decisive action in the near future to ensure the survival and well-being of humanity? Should we assume that capitalism will magically rehabilitate itself? Will the elite voluntarily downsize to meet these new conditions? Should we assume that a self-aware electorate will voluntarily demand that their dreams are reconstructed and their consumer lifestyles are reduced in order to avoid the worst effects of climate change and place civil society on a more equal and secure footing? Can we identify among our leaders a growing willingness to take hard decisions and challenge vested interests, so that we might be better able to control capitalism, remoralise our societies and set them on a more sustainable footing? Should we really continue to have faith in the efficacy of piecemeal social reform?

We are not here to impose upon our readers our estimation of precisely how deep social reform should be. Our point is really quite straightforward. Popper and the other post-war establishment liberals did not open up society and liberate individuals; they closed down debate and placed the communication of truth and individuals' dreams in chains. It is now vital that we dispense with the powerful intellectual control mechanisms that have prevented us from asking searching questions about how we might significantly intervene in the present system to ensure that its destructive tendencies are curtailed. We must push past those who have worked very hard to prevent us from formulating plans that might enable each citizen to take on a socially valued role that can sustain a reasonably happy and productive life. We must recognise that liberalism's concern with individual freedom is ultimately useless unless it is understood in relation to other forms of social value. Freedom must be more than the freedom to amass huge wealth, the freedom to shop, the freedom to worship one's own god and the freedom to pursue hedonic fulfilment. It is time to reconsider the common good and to argue about what this common good might mean in our unique historical context.

The Left must take on the difficult task of dragging itself free from liberalism's normative yet negative conception of political freedom. We may believe that improving our democratic institutions will improve our experience of social life and encourage new forms of solidarity to grow, but this strategy underestimates the scale of the change needed to genuinely transform our current way of life. More elections and votes on a broader range of issues will not solve the problems that beset Western societies. As Marx was aware, freedom needs to be considered in its social as well as its political context. It is not just democratic institutions that need to be overhauled: we also need to revolutionise ostensibly 'apolitical' relations of production, exchange and communication. Of course, we do not vote on who *at source* will receive great wealth and who will be left to struggle at the very bottom and require welfare. Such things are regarded as organic and external to the sphere of the political. We must acknowledge that liberal democracy does not by itself threaten the continuity of powerfully destructive economic systems and the ascendancy of their oligarchic elites, and therefore we must acknowledge that democracy in its current state is part of the problem. For the moment, it seems, we remain attached to democracy and cannot conceive of positive change that does not also involve democracy in some form. But we cannot genuinely change our world by simply extending liberalism's form of parliamentary democracy. We must seek to change the nature of political economy, not simply the state's management of the economy.

We should now be able to talk freely about alternatives to the present system without being shut down by political elites and their influential representatives in academia and the mass media. The radicals of the Left are dismissed as unworldly utopians, but it is the defenders of the current order who are the real utopians. Their faith that we can simply carry on in the established pattern is deeply 'utopian': it eschews all rational and objective analyses of our current situation and systematically censors the 'speculative realism' that is a timeless aspect of human life – to speculate openly and honestly on the real consequences of our actions and how we might act differently (see Hall and Winlow, 2015). Of course, accepting that what exists will miraculously continue is much less demanding than addressing the far more problematic reality that is our present and future, the signs of which lie scattered around us for all to see. Ultimately, the continuation of global neo-liberalism in its current mode of operation might not, in the near future, lead to utter catastrophe, but it is most certainly leading to the gradual diminution of all that was positive and vital in post-war Western societies. This unthinking acceptance that neo-liberalism will continue indefinitely and all our problems will be overcome by technological innovation and the irrepressible nature of the market is ultimately a form of fetishistic disavowal: we know the truth, but the truth is so disturbing that we choose to banish it from consciousness and repress it into the unconscious, thus creating and maintaining our own unconscious with our own conscious choices that must be made every day. We choose to forget so that we can continue onwards without having to respond to the disavowed truth. Better to display an irrational faith in the ability of markets to find solutions for all of our problems than to suffer the pain of conscious realisation of how far things have degenerated, and just how many serious, large-scale problems lie before us.

Like it or not, we have some significant choices to make. These choices have actually loomed on our horizon for some time now, and parliamentary liberal capitalism has resolutely refused to address them. Of course, it is now increasingly difficult for the nation-state to hold capital to account. Global corporations are capable of moving money around the world in order to maximise returns and avoid taxes. Making a series of deep, structural interventions now that seek to make our world more just and sustainable for our children can no longer be dismissed as mere utopianism. When the juggernaut is heading towards the edge of a cliff, jumping in the driver's seat and trying to turn it around and point it in a different direction is not unworldly utopianism. It is simple pragmatism, but a form of pragmatism shaped by the truth of our current reality rather than pressed into the service of a liberal utopianism that reality has made historically redundant. The utopianism of parliamentary capitalism is to blindly carry on as normal and hope that all the evidence is wrong and that it'll all work out in the end.

In a similar vein, the liberal democratic Left must now realise that piecemeal reform isn't really helping the poor. Its attempt to cajole the neo-liberal state into doing good works simply isn't having any cumulative effect that benefits civil society. We must be honest enough to acknowledge that things are getting worse. If things are left unattended, they will get worse still. There will not be another industrial revolution in the West to provide younger generations with reasonably remunerative jobs. Workplace precariousness is now a structural imperative. All jobs, bar those at the very top, will come under increased pressure. The remnants of the welfare state in countries such as Britain look set to wear down even further. Pensions for old people, even at their current rate, look unsustainable. Carrying on as normal will ensure the gradual removal of those things that make social life meaningful. In the cultural sphere, carrying on as normal ensures the continued march of socially corrosive and politically regressive forms of competitive individualism, envy and competition.

We must keep in mind that, after the horrors of the Second World War, there were good reasons to build an expansive welfare state. The provisions of this welfare state were considered a timely and progressive social benefit that would reinvigorate civil society. Ensuring that a high standard of health care and education was free at the point of provision would, the politicians of the time believed, have a crucial integrative function that would carry us further away from the injustices of early capitalism towards a society that valued ordinary people. To remove these things from common ownership and place them in the hands of profit-orientated corporations is not pragmatism and it is not progress. Something of great value is being relinquished, and few of our politicians have anything much to say about it, save the usual platitudes about the social benefits of having a diverse and competitive private sector at the heart of our economy.

However, the post-war social democratic state, with its expansive welfare system and reasonably civilised labour laws, can't magically be brought back to life. The modern welfare state was constructed on the back of sustained economic growth in the real economy that provided productive work for millions across the West. Today, that growth is nowhere to be seen. Capital has already expanded into undeveloped markets. In material terms, there aren't too many more places left for it to work its magic. We have already picked the low-hanging fruit. Oil and gas deposits are harder to find, and those that remain are now hugely expensive to access and exploit. Actual production of a great many material goods has been shifted to low-wage economies in the east, and expansive fiscal and personal debt has been used to boost demand and keep the global flows of production, trade and consumption moving at a reasonable pace. Perhaps more to the point, the liberal democratic state appears incapable of securing reasonable tax revenues from staggeringly profitable global corporations and super-rich individuals. Even though, in historic terms, we live in a low-tax environment, a situation that results, at least in part, from the competition that exists between states to attract businesses and the very wealthy, we still fail to get the rich to cough up and pay their dues to the very societies from which they have profited. The super-wealthy now effectively choose whether or not to pay tax (see Neville and Treanor, 2012). Despite widespread knowledge and disgust, our politicians appear as yet unwilling to take decisive action. In this kind of situation, it is no surprise that funding the modern

welfare state is becoming increasingly problematic. If we add to this the precariousness of our labour markets, with their zero-hours contracts, and the constant
downward pressure on wages in all economic sectors, we can begin to see the
fundamental problem that lies at the heart of the neo-liberal economic model. If
what we have is to continue, the best possible scenario for Western workers is the
paradoxical one in which the exploited proletariat in the East will be squeezed still
further so that Western workers can maintain their consumer lifestyles by finding
better deals at our high-street retailers.

In this specific economic context, to even talk of a return to genuine social
democracy appears strangely utopian. As we have already stressed, the logic of
markets is accepted completely by the vast majority of Western political parties.
On both the political right and the political left, neo-liberalism is basic common
sense. We should also note that even one of the most radical and intriguing
democratic movements of recent times, SYRIZA in Greece, appears unable to go
much further than suggest the nation returns to the policies that were accepted by
a great many mainstream political parties during the post-war social democratic
period (see Chapter 8). To actually return to modern forms of welfare provision
and to accept the return of an economically interventionist state are unacceptable
to the markets and our nation's global trading partners. To do all this, and commit
to full employment, would be understood as something akin to a revolutionary
act by key institutions and actors in the global economy. Of course, returning to
social democracy could be done without discarding electoral democracy and
without dispensing with capitalism, but can we imagine such a series of events
actually coming to pass? Can we imagine the economic chaos that would result if
a major European state were to announce its intention to tax wealth, nationalise
key industries and commit to full employment?

The hope of the majority of those on the left these days is to see the return of
genuine social democracy, but to us this drive to return to the past seems both
naïve and strangely defeatist. This defeatism reflects the triumph of liberalism and
the absolute, unquestioned acceptance that liberal democracy is the best of all
available systems. It reflects a deep faith in capitalism's ability to bestow upon us
consumer items that, before their arrival, we didn't even know that we wanted.
All other economic systems seem irredeemably tarnished and unable to deliver to
us the forms of material excess that we now believe to be absolutely essential to
civilised social life.

In practical terms, it seems highly unlikely that we can return to welfarism.
Already, countries such as Britain and the USA are dependent upon foreign imports.
The products we use to sustain our lifestyles are produced in the surplus economies
of the East; these economies then lend money back to the Western industrialised
powers to continue to purchase the goods they produce. The USA in particular
is dependent upon this arrangement. To withdraw from it would be a huge shock
to our national economies and our consumer lifestyles. We would need a new
surge in economic growth to fund interventionist programmes, and it is very difficult

to see where that might come from. As we now know, reliance on the tax revenues of Wall Street is not a feasible option. Aside from the threats posed by endemic risk-taking, giving Wall Street additional leeway to expand its enterprises facilitates the continued movement of wealth from lower and middle social echelons to the super-rich. Of course, this would foment social antagonisms. And, as we have already noted, the abstract trading that is now central to life on Wall Street produces little or no work in the real economy for ordinary people. But, even if we could reproduce a political culture willing to take on the task of controlling capitalism, even if we could build new and potent checks and balances that would prevent capitalism's propensity to blindly destroy everything in pursuit of profit, haven't we now seen enough of capitalism to know its true nature? Can't we now see that capitalism will inevitably break its bonds and once again threaten our collective well-being? How long would it be before the libertarians of the Right were again calling for capital to be set free, and how long would it be before we succumbed to the seductive promise of greater wealth?

In this chapter, we have tried to identify one or two issues that have prevented us from openly discussing alternatives to liberal capitalism. If we appraise our situation with honesty, we must realise that it is stupid to console ourselves with the belief that we can turn things around at the next election, and that, with a small reform here and there, society's burning injustices can be extinguished. Mainstream politics seems entirely bereft of the capacity to address any of the problems we face. The frenetic activity of contemporary politics, played out on our news broadcasts every night, reflects a deeper inability to truly act, to genuinely begin to address the manifold problems of the present. It seems obvious that politics must now be re-energised. The first step is to return to the basic essence of politics. Politics is a field upon which we strive for the good, but it is not only that. It is also the field upon which we determine *what is good*. It is where we decide what kind of society we want to live in and then begin to work towards that end. It really is up to us to make decisions of huge magnitude and then fully accept the consequences that flow from those decisions. If we determine that we want to place equality at the very centre of a future society, we need to commit to that fully. We must be prepared to fight for it. Tinkering around the edges is getting us nowhere.

A sense of hope and a commitment to imagining a better world do not instantly transport us into the realm of totalitarianism. We must now move beyond the political catastrophism (see Hall, 2012a) that has hung like a dense fog over post-war Western politics. What sense does it make to assume that even the most abstract desire to make the world a better place disguises a deep-rooted ideological imperative to enslave and destroy? Isn't it stupid to stick resolutely to the belief that every plan that attempts to improve our world will inevitably make things worse? Isn't it now obvious that we do not live in the best of all possible worlds, and that we need more than piecemeal policy initiatives to rebuild a social and economic platform upon which possible community life can flourish?

In the hope of advancing this thesis and giving it some empirical foundation, we will in the coming chapters discuss the realities of contemporary oppositional politics in the West. In the next chapter, we try to consider what a return to genuine politics might look like.

4

THE RETURN OF POLITICS

The EDL in northern England

> Why does the Other remain the Other? What is the cause of our hatred of
> him, for our hatred of him in his very being? It is hatred of the enjoyment
> of the Other. This would be the most general formula of the modern racism
> we are witnessing today: a hatred of the particular way the Other enjoys
> . . . The question of tolerance or intolerance is not at all concerned with the
> subject of science and its human rights. It is located on the level of tolerance
> or intolerance toward the enjoyment of the Other, the Other as he who
> essentially steals my own enjoyment . . . The problem is apparently unsolvable
> as the Other is the Other of my interior. The root of racism is thus a hatred
> of my own enjoyment. There is no enjoyment but my own. If the Other
> is in me, occupying the place of extimacy, then the hatred is also my own.
> (Jacques-Allain Miller, quote in Žižek, 1995: 203)

In the quote above, Miller provides a reasonably succinct account of how Lacan's
analysis of enjoyment can illuminate our understanding of contemporary racism.
In this chapter, we extend this logic and seek to apply it to the politics of the
English Defence League (EDL).

Introduction

The attitudes, goals and orientation of the EDL reflect the strange ideological
contradictions of the contemporary political Right. Its members are drawn
overwhelmingly from Britain's old white working class. Some have found their
way to the movement through the field of organised football violence (Garland
and Treadwell, 2010; Treadwell and Garland, 2011). Others are veterans of right-
wing campaign groups such as the National Front and the British National Party
(Copsey, 2010). The majority, however, are simply disaffected, aggrieved and

forgotten young and middle-aged men who have witnessed, over the past thirty years, the disintegration of their communities, the disappearance of traditional forms of work and key changes in popular culture that have cast the white working class as entirely redundant, out of place and out of time, a troublesome memory from a time before capitalist universalism and its supposedly liberal and tolerant multicultural social order. Of course, to consider the white men of the EDL to be regressive and outdated is a significant oversimplification that misconstrues the reality of our politics and the politics of the men who make up the group. In the standard Hegelian sense, we must recognise that the dogma of liberal openness and acceptance carries with it its own inherent negation. Just as the old totalitarian societies of the East inevitably produced dissident movements that called for openness and liberalisation, the new liberal societies of the West that champion openness and liberalisation produce fundamentalisms that seek closure rather than openness, certainty rather than 'freedom', and a dependable symbolic order rather than the uncertainty and cynicism of postmodern liberal relativism. The forms of nationalism displayed by groups such as the EDL should, therefore, be considered an inevitable outcome of liberal capitalist universalism. The answer to this problem is not simply to challenge and overcome 'regressive' nationalism, but to challenge and overcome capitalist universalism itself.

Witnessing the men of the EDL move around the decaying post-industrial cities of northern England, it becomes obvious that their established place in the world has been withdrawn. The brave new world of 24-hour consumer urbanism wasn't really created with them in mind. Instead, they occupy parts of the city that appear cut off from the movement of history. However, unlike others who populate these same streets, these men have not yet lapsed into terminal dejection and withdrawal. Instead, they exhibit a form of proto-political engagement born of a deep and shared desire to rediscover the lost historical object of community and solidarity. They rally around a concern for the disappearance of traditional English culture and society and the threats posed to this culture by Islamic extremists and Sharia law. However, the traditional English culture they seek to defend is a myth. Like the melancholic in early psychoanalysis, the men of the EDL lament the loss of the thing that structured their enjoyment. They cannot let it go and they cannot come to terms with its non-existence. But the lost *thing*, the fully functional and unpolluted traditional culture, simply didn't exist in any real sense. It is the very act of losing the traditional culture that brings it into being, or, as Hegel put it, the lost thing 'only *comes to be* by being *left behind*' (2010: 348; emphasis in the original).

Their anger, if not their reaction, is fully justified. The English working class, which is of course made up of many ethnic groups, has been on the receiving end of neo-liberal reform for more than thirty years. The male members of the EDL are the sons of men who once contributed stable and socially valued forms of labour to the industrial economy. Some were indeed the *aristocrats of labour* (Hobsbawm, 1964; Lenin, 2010; Kautsky, 2014). Throughout their socialisation, they were encouraged to believe that they too could access stable and reasonably remunerative industrial work and achieve concomitant social status when they reached maturity.

Now, there is very little for them. They are forced to compete for insecure jobs that don't pay enough to raise a family. They live on residential estates that were, during the industrial period, reasonably civilised, organised and functional. The cultural life of these places was built upon industrial work rhythms, extended family networks and enduring social bonds. Families lived there for generations, and in many respects residents lived parallel lives that provided a degree of support and structure over the life-course. Boys who were also neighbours would go to school together, go to work together and experience many of the same life events in a similar social context (see Winlow and Hall, 2006, 2009). Work was often quite demanding, but it provided the money to support a family, with a little left over for leisure and consumerism. Group purity is a myth, but this history is not. The pissed-off white men who support the EDL know that it existed, and they are painfully aware that it is now gone.

Many of these men talk first about the problems they face in their immediate social environment. They talk of families moving out of the neighbourhood and strangers moving in. They talk about rising crime and endemic drug dealing. They talk about mess and decay and exhaustion, things falling apart, and a complete absence of any form of authority that might seek to put them back together again. They talk about the gangs of young men who get drunk and make life hell for the neighbourhood's older residents. They talk about effete metropolitan liberals who look down their noses at the likes of them. And, of course, they are also quite voluble when talking about the problems they face in finding and keeping a job. David is forty-two and lives in private rented accommodation on the edge of the estate on which he was born:

> When I left school I got a job straight away. It was no bother in them days. Straight into Johnston's Manufacturing, on the [production] line. It was great. I loved it. I mean, it was proper hard graft and fucking boring as shit but the money was great for a lad at that age. We had a laugh. I liked it . . . I lasted four years there. [The factory shut down]. I got some other factory work but by then everything was fucked. I went all over working short contracts. It wasn't too bad but nothing steady. Since I hit about thirty [years old] things have been fucking murder. I'm a good grafter but there's fuck all for me to do. You can get a job maybe in a call centre or in a shop but I can't do that . . . It's all short term. I need regular hours. I need to earn. I can't just sit waiting to get an hour here, an hour there . . . For Christ's sake, I'm not a kid anymore. I need a proper job.

David relies on private employment agencies to find him work as a security guard.

> It's the best I can do. There's fuck all else. I can do all right if I get a couple of months' steady work, but then you're fucking desperate to be kept on, or you're desperate to find something else straight away once you're finished. It's just shit work really. The pay is fuck all. I've got two kids for fuck's sake.

How the fuck do you pay for Christmas, birthdays? [. . .] I've never been any bother. Always tried to find work. The whole thing is just set up to take the piss out of people like me.

This kind of story is ubiquitous. Young Mike is twenty-two. He is locked in a cycle that moves him from low-paid work to welfare and back again. He now has a part-time job delivering pizzas.

I got a job working with our Tom [his uncle, a local builder] for a bit but he didn't have enough coming in to keep me on regular. I get a couple of days here and there but there's fuck all. My Dad was always on at me to get a job and I've tried. I've fucking tried. I worked in a sports shop for a bit. I've done some factory work but it's all short term: a week here, a week there.

David is also quite keen to talk about his neighbourhood. He is well known locally and he spent the first twenty-two years of his life living on the same estate. Since then, he has moved around a bit, but he returned to the neighbourhood around four years ago.

You know what it's like around here. I'm not pissing anyone off by telling you what's happened. When I was a boy the school was a good school. People had respect. You didn't see all the shit you do now. People worked. I could take you out that door right now and show you three, four drug dealers' houses. It's just the way it is. It's the way things have gone. You've got drugs all over the place and then you've got people thieving to get money [for drugs]. Nowt against them people [the drug dealers] but you never saw that when I was coming up. It's just all fucked.

David also sees problems in the younger generation who have no memory of the area's industrial past or its relatively organic cultural forms:

You always had lads getting pissed when I was young, but it's different now. It's just not the same. It's not like it was, honest. My Dad has had bother [trouble] outside of his house. The police are there all the time but nothing changes. And all the people what's moved in, people from all over the place. What does that say to the people that live around here? I bet they don't have straight-off-the-boat immigrants moving in where you live do they? [. . .] I talk to my Dad and he says the world's gone mad. He just can't make head nor tail of it.

David's friend, Paul, is also local to the area. He has fared rather better. He is a qualified gas fitter:

I was always told, get a trade. I knew I had to get a job and you had to have a proper trade behind you, even in them days. I done OK compared to a lot of others . . . [I've] been in work pretty regular. I've been full-time on the books, I've been out contracting, I've worked on the [building] sites. The work is there if you want it and you can graft. That's the problem with a lot of people around here. I agree with him [David], things are fucking hard and there's not a lot [of work] about, but I look at a lot of people around here and they're just fucking proper dirt-bags. He'll not say it but they need a proper kick up the arse. Some want to work and some don't. It's the fuckers that just expect everything for free that's the problem. It's them that end up with the kids in bother, dropping out of school. It's them that end up fucking torturing people with loud music and police calling at all hours . . . It's people what's come on to that estate, yes, but that's not the only thing. A lot of them people are proper fuck-ups. Some of the kids, I wouldn't want to tangle with them. It's not just there's no work.

David again:

It's immigration. We're just a small island for fuck's sake. I've got nothing against a lot of them. A lot of them are just trying to get a better life, but it just makes it that much harder to get work. There's more people. It's obvious. Some of them are working for less than minimum wage, I know they are, cash in hand. It's just mental. Why do we have to keep quiet about it? We're supposed to go along with it but it's not them fuckers who can't get a job.

Question: Who?

The rich cunts in the city. On the TV and talking in the newspapers, calling us racists. It's not their jobs on the line is it? It's not fucking loads of people moving in next to them is it? They [the immigrants] can't even speak the language. They've got nothing in common with the people. Why the fuck should we just fucking sit back and take it?

David, Paul and Young Mike all support the EDL, but they do not immediately conform to the popular image of racist thugs. All three are sure in their view that they are not anti-Muslim. As Young Mike says:

I don't give a fuck about none of that shit. It's just, why does it have to happen here? It [radical Islamism] is spreading all over the place, and they fucking hate us! Look at them protesting about the war and that. They fucking hate us.

David joins in:

> What's happened is just nuts. There's just been too many. There's not many of us left, and who gives a fuck about us? Get your fucking university people to get a petition going about that!

Question: 'So why support the EDL? Why not vote Tory or UKIP?'

> The EDL is about the working class. It's about local people. I don't want to vote for them cunts down south. It's about sticking up for our people. Everyone else does it, why can't we do it? The rich stick up for the rich. The Muslims stick up for the Muslims . . . The EDL, basically, is just a bunch of people who are sick of the way things are going.

Paul offers a different view:

> It's this Sharia law what bothers a lot of people. What's that got to do with our country? Why can't we just say, 'have it back home, but you can't have it here'? What's wrong with that?

Young Bren doesn't really care about politics. To him, the EDL is about sticking up for white people:

> It's just all the Pakis coming into the country, fucking everything up. What have they got to come here for? We don't want to be Muslims. We don't want none of that shit around here. Let them stay where they are. I'm not racist but there's just too many of them. And then you see them protesting against the war, you see them shouting at young lads who have gone off to fight, gone off to do their duty, you're got to be fucking kidding haven't you? This is our country. I don't care what anyone thinks. It's right what they're [the EDL] doing. It's just about saying, no, this is ours, fuck off.

Paul warms to the theme:

> You have a walk down Smith Road, have a walk down Saunders Crescent: there's Pakis everywhere. Me Nan lives down there. Everyone is trying to move out. All the shops have gone, everything's gone. Then you've got your Europeans. Are we living in fucking England or what?

David:

> You see them in flash cars and all that. Where the fuck do they get the money for that? And did you see on the box [the TV] about them grooming cases? . . . Gangs of Pakis picking up young white lasses and locking them up and

that . . . it makes me feel fucking sick. They want fucking hanging for that, and people's too scared to talk about it coz you get called a racist. People around here are fucking done with it. If we ever found out something like that happened around here the entire city would go up.

You've got to remember a lot of them is just coming over for the money. They can sign on, get a house, all the benefits. I saw on the box [the TV] that loads of them are just sending the cash straight back home. Not looking for work or anything. That's just fucking robbery that is. Why the fuck should I be paying money [in tax] and it ends up paying for someone over in Pakistan or Romania or wherever the fuck it is?

Question: 'Have you ever been on any of the EDL protests?'

Young Mike:

Aye, me and Bren went down with a bunch of others. Fucking coppers everywhere.

Young Bren:

It's a right good laugh as well. I like it. Fuck them cunts, you know what I mean? Send them all back, that's what I'd do. This is a Christian country.

Paul:

I've never had the time, but I would go. Fucking right I would. Why not? It's just showing people we're still here and we're not going to take any more shit. We're going to stand up for ourselves . . .

David finishes Paul's sentence:

And fuck anyone who says any different. Police, politicians, in the newspapers, who gives a fuck? They can all fuck off. We're not going nowhere.

Paul reflects on the changes in working-class politics:

My Dad was a shop steward down the pit [a union organiser in the coal-mining industry]. He wanted to stick up for people like us. He used to say that if we all stood up together no one could touch us. Everyone used to love me old man. He could hardly read and write but he was a smart bloke. That's what the EDL is doing now. It's about standing up for what you believe in. It's about looking after your own. It's saying we're not going to take any shit.

Question: 'What do you make of the left today?'

Paul:

> The left are a fucking disgrace. They've got nothing to do with looking after the working class. All they care about is looking after immigrants.

Like many others we spoke to, Young Mike assumes that the UAF (United Against Fascism) and other groups who form counter-demonstrations at EDL rallies represent the contemporary Left. He has no understanding of the historic connection between the working classes and the Labour movement in the north of England. He sees the far Right as the natural representatives of the working classes and the radical liberal Left as his opponents. For Young Mike, the political Left represent the urban, liberal middle classes who attempt to instruct the working classes how to live and what to believe in.

Young Mike:

> They're mostly Pakis. They come to the protest [as part of a counter-demonstration]. Not all of them. Calling us Fascists and hiding behind the police. Proper brave they were, shouting all sorts at us with fucking five hundred coppers behind them. Soft cunts.

'But the Left used to be about defending the working class . . .'

Paul:

> They're fucking against us mate, believe it. They fucking hate us. They've got no idea. They're soft as fuck. They've got fuck all to do with the working class. They're all immigrants and just look after their own.

Young Bren:

> Isn't it them [the left] that's trying to bring in gay marriage?

David:

> The left, you mean the Labour Party and that lot? What have they ever done for the people round here?

'You've had a Labour MP and a Labour council for years . . .'

Paul:

No wonder things are fucked. No one gives a fuck [about us], that's why people are going out protesting. For Christ sake, they're [radical Islamists] bombing us. They're taking our jobs. They're fucking things up all over the place. They want to change our country and turn it into something else and the politicians couldn't care less. The EDL is just saying enough is enough. We are going to fight it all the way.

Damien is twenty-two and lives in a different area. He was raised by a single mother on a notorious sink estate. After failing in education, he amassed a string of convictions for petty criminal offences before knuckling down in his late teens and attempting to find a regular job. He currently works intermittently in a warehouse for a leading supermarket chain. His wages are very low and barely cover the cost of food and heating:

There is nothing left for the likes of me, what chance have I got of a decent start? There is nothing here. Even if you do go college or whatever and get qualifications, it doesn't mean you're OK. Half the lads I work with in the warehouse have got the same contract as me, part-time, even with qualifications. I rely on a few extra hours, but they won't give me a full-time contract, just overtime, so they have you over a fucking barrel.

That's the thing, mate, see where I live [he rents a sparsely furnished studio flat in an impoverished part of the city, near to the estate where he grew up] it's all fucking Pakis with the businesses, the money. They own the takeaways, and where I am it's all takeaway shops, it's all cash businesses, so they aren't fucking paying in [paying tax] and they're all fucking fiddling the social too. You see them all cruise up in their fucking top of the range Audis and Mercs, all in fucking Armani and Boss gear, I see that every day and I have fuck all, what am I supposed to do? How can I get what they have on minimum wage part-time?

Richie is thirty-six and has supported the EDL for many years. He lives in a different city to David, quoted above, but the situation he describes seems exactly the same:

I remember growing up, we never had it easy. My old man [father] worked in a factory; Mam did a few hours in a shop once we were in school. Everyone knew everyone on the estate. It was poor and it had its problems, don't get me wrong, but not like now. There was a sense of community and hope, but that's gone now. Nobody really works; not decent jobs like in those days. Now it is all shop work, and the only shops local are big chain stores, loan places, fast food shops and bookies. It's bleak. There's no work, even labouring on a building site, it's all CSCS cards and massive competition, and if you get a start you are lucky if it lasts a couple of months. Jobs round here are all short-term contracts with no guarantees. Low wages, no certainty. It's no wonder that people feel angry about it.

Richie is angry. He talks of being left on the scrap heap and of the total, abject failure of the political class to address the disappearance of stable work and the disintegration of previously functional working-class communities. Richie believes that, in openly supporting the EDL, he is drawing attention to these issues and to the sense of anger and abandonment expressed by so many of his peers. Richie's support of the EDL has already brought him into contact with the police and the criminal justice system. Here he describes what drew him to the EDL:

> They can arrest me, lock me up, I don't give a fuck. The first demo I went to was in Manchester. It was great: it was on the news and we couldn't be ignored anymore. It was kicking off that got people to notice. The media and the politicians hate the working class like me . . . They don't say what we think about these fucking immigrants. No-one gives a fuck about the working class. This country was built on the back of people like us, hardworking working-class people, and no one is sticking up for us.
>
> I didn't like the BNP because I am not a racist, I don't buy into their views. I don't mind people with skills coming in, but I don't want an open door and I don't want to be told what I can and can't think and say. The EDL, when they started out, look at what they were against: fucking 'grooming' and paedophiles, Sharia Law in our fucking country and a fucking creeping multiculturalism that loved and welcomed anybody and everybody except the working class white, Protestant, straight man. Well fuck it, I didn't want to be silenced anymore, and if I have to have a row with some coppers and have a row to get my voice heard, then bring it on.

Jake is forty-five and has, for many years, been involved in the football hooligan scene in the North of England. He too is angry about the lack of reasonable employment prospects and the vacuity of contemporary politics. He is also quite worried about the prospects for his son:

> It's the youth I feel for, and our lad. He is fifteen now, so I have started taking him to [EDL] demos. It's him and our youth I fear for. I feel for them, I truly do. My old man was a steelworker. I have a trade, but how long can it last? I can probably manage to give him a start when he is old enough, but even then it's hard. There aren't the chances for the young ones like there used to be, and as if things aren't hard enough, the fucking pricks in government want to let a load of fucking Somalis and fucking Afghans in. [Mocking upper-class accent:] 'Yes, let the Roma in too while we are at it. Anyone else want in to free-ride England? We especially like you if you're a fucking dirty Muslim that can't speak the language. We've got a red carpet for you and it leads straight from the arrivals lounge to the front door of your free fucking council house [laughs]!'

We had immigration before, fair enough, but then we needed it for our industry. Where is our industry now? What have my lad and his mates got to look forward too? No fucking jobs, no prospects. It makes me fucking sick, mate.

Mikey is a man of significant reputation. He has been before the courts many times for violent offences and he is willing to use his capacity for violence to further the politics of the EDL. He has a particular hatred of anti-fascists and EDL counter-demonstrators, but he has also been known to attack the police and Asian men and women utilising public space. He has this to say about his support of the EDL:

Violence is basically the only way people take notice. How have the Muslims got to a position where they dominate, riots up North and fucking blowing stuff up? After they [Islamic terrorists] bombed the underground what did the government do? Pour money into their areas, set up clubs to stop radicalisation. What have white indigenous people got? Fuck all. They, the politicians, give it all to the fucking immigrant scum. I want the EDL to get more violent mate, I want it to go up, I want to see Muslims scared and put in their place, because it's only when we kick off that anyone says what we think.

Cosa Nostra

It's clear that our respondents fear further change, and that they are angry about the change that has already taken place. How can we best understand the combination of fear and anger in the ideology of the EDL?

We should start by reiterating a point we made earlier: the traditional culture and 'way of life' that the EDL seeks to defend did not exist. Its reality is a collective fantasy, restricted to a shared cultural belief in its existence. If, for example, members of the white working class believe that there exists a shared set of norms and values that bond their community together, then their culture, their particular 'way of life', has a not insubstantial utility that enables its members to access forms of enjoyment that relate to its various features. Understood in this way, culture is always a permanent regeneration project. It always has to be understood to be slipping away and in need of assistance to nurture it back to health and vitality.

For the male member of the EDL, the fundamental fear is that his relationship with the cultural 'way of life' will change or disappear, and, as a result, the individual will be denied access to the comfort and security provided by particular forms of encultured enjoyment. As Žižek (1995: 202) observes, 'the national Cause is ultimately nothing but the way subjects of a given ethnic community organize their enjoyment through national myths'. Here, understood through the lens of Lacanian psychoanalysis, culture gives life colour and structures our enjoyment. It enables us to take some pleasure from our particular cultural identity, secure in the knowledge that those around us also believe in and follow the rules and tastes associated with our shared 'way of life'. Fully committing to a culture enables the individual to enjoy its features and experience a certain ease of social engagement, a sense of rootedness and repose. We are free to enjoy particular forms of coarse humour, drunkenness, feasting, the elaborate systems and protocols that surround seeking out a mate, and so on. In our particular community, we know at once how to behave. We know all of the hidden rules of social interaction. We know which jokes to laugh at and which conversational topics are out of bounds. As long as we believe in the culture and the legitimacy of its rules, there exists a symbolic efficiency that gives the culture an internal integrity and order that shape and pattern our lives, identities and social experience.

The traditional culture and 'way of life' the EDL seeks to defend are, and have always been, structured in relation to external threat. If we strip away all of the gloss of postmodern liberal multiculturalism and investigate the reality of community composition, then we must conclude that, ultimately, all communities are organised in this way. The general belief that we can, these days, build a new 'open tribe' (see Goss, 2014), a tribe that is immediately inclusive and invites all to partake of its pleasures, is precisely the kind of baseless liberal utopianism that the Left needs to overcome. This is a Utopia of the cultural sphere rather than the political sphere, and so steadfastly ignores the brutal injustices and harms that are a natural outcome of global capitalism. Liberal cultural utopianism therefore acts to cover up the deep harms of the global market. It seeks to make us believe that these harms do not exist, or that they are of relative insignificance and should not in any way impact upon the composition of the tolerant and accepting liberal community. Are we to believe that a billionaire industrialist can be brought together peaceably with his own exploited sweatshop workers to form a mutually beneficial community in which each immediately accepts the others' interests and particularities? Why is it that so many on the liberal left these days believe that intolerance, rather than inequality and economic injustice, is the primary problem to be overcome? Is liberal multicultural society really so great if it tolerates systemic injustice on an epic scale?

It is possible to nurture new communities, built upon values and in which ethnic tensions are greatly reduced, but, in order to create such a community, we need the field of politics to be fully operative. This new and ethnically diverse community must seek to overlook or trivialise cultural particularities, rather than hoist them on high and worship them as an indicator of cultural vitality and progress. It is only when the individual is provided with a coherent system of political symbolism that cultural particularities can become relatively insignificant and take their rightful place in the organisation of community life. For example, if a white EDL supporter and a recently arrived Muslim immigrant are equipped with an overriding politics that unites them in a shared struggle, then the animosity that stems from their distinct cultural identities becomes far less important. Rather than fear and distrust characterising their relationship, or a closely monitored truce in which each group attempts to tolerate the other, the cultural Other is transformed into a genuine neighbour with whom we have shared values and goals. Of course, this substantial universal politics is precisely what the political Left should be constructing these days, but, in the liberal postmodernist era, of course, it is precisely what it has been destroying. Rather than instruct the white working class to tolerate the Muslim working class, and vice versa, the Left should diligently create and seek to popularise a political project for the entirety of the working class, and all ethnic and religious groups within it.

The contemporary discourse of tolerance, in which the mythical open tribe is composed of diverse ethnic and religious groups who are all tolerant of the particularities and eccentricities of each ethnic grouping, does not function to unite individuals in the pleasures of shared community life; rather, it creates a gap between the subject and its Other and compels politics to take on the role of policing it. The particularities of the Other will be tolerated only if they do not come too close, only if the cultural uniqueness of the Other doesn't impose itself too forcefully on my own idiosyncratic personal experience and fundamental cultural fantasy. The shared cause to which the subject and its Other are both resolutely committed dissolves cultural animosity in politics.

The dominant mode of patronising cultural education, in which the barbarians of the EDL are informed that all must be tolerant of all if they are to remain a part of the progressive liberal multicultural experience, overlooks clear conflicts of interest – which exist between all individuals and groups in capitalism's competitive socio-economic system – and creates the ground for its own inevitable failure. How can we become a tolerant liberal community when, in our economic life, we are all compelled to engage in aggressive competition? Isn't capitalism structured upon the principle of productive antagonism and surplus, in which the self seeks to take more from the other than they are willing to give in return? How can we expect the losers in capitalism's interminable competition to accept the outcome and their own painfully evidenced competitive inferiority (see Hall *et al.*, 2008)?

Because there is among the people no deep fidelity to the ideology of multi-cultural toleration, what we get is a situation in which all interest groups are forced to monitor the cultural freedoms of others relative to their own. Have the freedoms of one group become such that they are negatively impacting upon the freedoms of another? To what extent should we tolerate cultural traditions that are, in themselves, authentic, but demonstrably *intolerant* of difference? One cannot help but be struck by the fact that Western Europe's experiment with multicultural-ism, which no doubt began with the best intentions, has actively produced its own opposite. Ethnic tensions have not disappeared, but appear to be increasing across the continent. The lack of a clear political alternative to what currently exists has allowed rivulets of anger from East to West to flow into the established discourse of nation. Nationalism seeks to 'put things right', to contain and control those elements that disrupt the effective operation of the market. In this way, nationalism always exists as an imminent 'critique' of capitalist universalism, and its re-emergence references the failure of a true ideological opposite to challenge the hegemony of the market.

Matheme of castration

The specific traditional culture the EDL prizes and seeks to defend is not open to everyone. Like all traditional cultures, it is exclusive and only becomes 'real' for those who fully commit to its structures, rules and obligations. We get a sense of this when, for the first time, we experience an alien culture in which we have no direct understanding of the hidden rules of social interaction. To members of the host culture, the enjoyments that sustain the culture are obvious and immediately comprehensible, but to us they seem odd and rooted in illogicality and myth.

The culture's exclusivity encourages individuals to invest in its features. It bonds individuals together and encourages them to submit to a system of shared meanings. The culture is always *our thing*. Only we, its members, can fully understand and appreciate it. Others can never fully grasp what it is to be absorbed in our particular culture. It is only for us that its strange traditions and codes truly 'make sense'. They can be explained to others, but never fully understood. Despite this exclusionary element, members of cultures such as this usually understand their culture to be threatened by the presence of those external to it. In the discourse of the EDL, it is the growing proximity of the Muslim Other that elicits fears about the continuity of its supporters' way of life, but at the centre of this tangle of vague anxieties and material threats exists a deep and enduring dread that the individual may no longer be able to access the enjoyment that structures his own cultural experience as a member of the threatened community. In this way, within the terms of Lacanian psychoanalysis, it is the threat posed by the Muslim Other to the EDL supporter's own enjoyment that is the principal issue at stake.

The EDL supporter fears that the Muslim Other will seize his enjoyment and make it his own. The Muslim Other will supplant the member of the white working class, steal his employment and adopt his relatively comfortable consumer lifestyle. The EDL supporter is also disturbed by the Muslim Other's own excessive enjoyment and the way his enjoyment is organised in culture (see Žižek, 1995). He finds the Other's traditions strange and threatening: the religious festivals, the organisation of prayer, the music and the dancing, and the smells, sights and sounds of the culture, all appear radically at odds to one's own blessed community.

We can see elements of this in spoken accounts offered by EDL members. Of course, they routinely position the Muslim Other as a threat to the continuity of their employment or as a usurper of the employment entitlements of the white working class. They also often mobilise the imagery of the Muslim Other as welfare-dependent leech living off Britain's indulgent and skewed benefits system. Here, the EDL supporter often appears to believe that Britain's welfare system belongs to the 'indigenous' white population, and the welfare-dependent Muslim Other is literally stealing benefits that would otherwise be destined for himself and members of his own community. We can categorise these as practical or economic forms of 'theft', at least as they are understood by EDL supporters. There are also other forms of cultural theft that disturb supporters of the EDL. These tend to involve the misappropriation of cultural symbols that represent social status. We see this in the quotes on the preceding pages that contain elements of dissatisfaction and anger at the perceived economic successes of Muslim immigrants. Here, our respondents are angry that Muslim immigrants are able to access the forms of high-end consumerism that are out of reach of the precariously employed white working class. In these accounts, the Muslim Other is a cheat who avoids tax, aggressively pursues his own economic interests and, because of these endeavours, is able to afford exclusive consumer items lusted after by, but generally denied to, the white, working-class EDL supporter. In the discourse of the EDL, the Muslim Other's success in achieving ownership of such high-end consumer items is not simply a matter of revealing the relative economic failure of the white EDL supporter; the result of the interminable economic competition of consumer capitalism is transformed into an act of theft. The Muslim Other has effectively stolen what should belong to the self. Without the Muslim Other's intervention, the supporter of the EDL would be free to fully enjoy life and the various features of his culture.

The EDL supporter is also disturbed by the illogical pleasures of the Muslim Other. Here, for example, EDL supporters often poked fun at the Other's culture and often found aspects of it rather weird and unsettling. Many of our respondents were also quite vocal about recent criminal cases based on the 'grooming' of under-age girls and their systematic sexual exploitation by groups of Muslim men (see, for example, Laville, 2013). Our respondents often believed these cases revealed the rotten, corrupt and repulsive core of Islam and Muslim cultures more generally, even though there is nothing in Islamic texts that affirms sensual relations with minors. These cases appeared to confirm what EDL supporters already assumed to be the case about Muslim immigrant communities. Our respondents were, of course, horrified by these cases and angry to the point of violence. The fact that the offenders in these cases were Muslim men and the victims were young, white, working-class girls appeared to encourage the belief that the white working class was under attack by an illogical and barbarous intruder dedicated to the pursuit of forbidden and imponderably obscene pleasures.

Of course, the racism of our respondents enabled them to use such cases as tautological confirmation of the claim that the religion of Islam was polluting England, corrupting its youth and exploiting its most innocent citizens. For members of the EDL, the defendants in such cases were, first and foremost, Muslims who were sex offenders, rather than sex offenders who happened to be Muslim. In their spoken accounts, the crimes committed became inextricably bound to the religious faith of the offenders. Of course, white Christian paedophiles are similarly hated, but their religious background is considered completely irrelevant to the popular understanding of the crime itself. With Muslim sex offenders, the situation is reversed. EDL members treated these cases as a sign of things to come, if the flow of Islamic migrants to Britain is allowed to continue unchecked. It is almost as if our EDL-supporting respondents *expected* Muslim men to be involved in the sexual exploitation of young girls. The revelation that Muslim men have been involved in such crimes appeared to simply confirm their suspicions and reinforced their hatred and disgust.

As one might have expected, the image of the Islamic Other was poorly sketched out. For our respondents, it existed only as a *signifier of lack* (see Miller, 1977; Lacan, 2007). This absence of substance enabled our respondents to project almost anything negative on to its form. Child sexual abuse and mass murder were the worst things they could think of, and there was already evidence that Muslim men had been involved in such crimes. Why should they doubt the involvement of Muslim men is anything else that was harmful, disreputable or criminal? In our discussions, a very broad range of negative social behaviours were associated with Muslims, and it quickly became clear that their hatred of the Muslim Other tended to reference the fears and anxieties of contemporary post-crash social experience. We will come back to this in a moment.

Predictably enough, our respondents talked at length about Islamic terrorism and occasionally they pitched their anti-Islamism as a pragmatic response to this threat. Some believed their hatred of Muslims to be essentially reactive in nature, a pragmatic response to an objective threat. Some of our respondents talked in detail about various theatres of conflict in the Middle East and the rise of radical Islamism. Many of our respondents were aware of the perceived threats posed by the radicalisation of young British Muslims and they expected more terrorist attacks to occur on the British mainland in the coming years. Basically, they believed their aggression towards the Muslim Other was returned in kind, which hardened their position. Our respondents also talked at length about immigrants draining the benefits system and ruthlessly exploiting an indulgent welfare system that favoured immigrants and minority sexualities and punished the straight, white working class. Of course, our respondents were blind to the glaring contradiction in this narrative, in which they presented the Islamic immigrant as simultaneously a welfare-dependent idler and a hardworking competitor who threatened to steal British jobs. Although our respondents were keen to offer justifications for their hatred of Islam, they also talked at length about the hardships of the white working class. They talked of community dysfunction and the gradual disappearance of traditional English culture. The encroachment of immigrants merely served as a clear manifestation of a much deeper dissatisfaction with contemporary multiculturalism, the disintegration of community life and the loss of a previously stable relationship with the means of production.

All of these issues were important, but the issue that most animated and unified our respondents was their hatred of what now passes for politics and the political class. For some, their involvement in the EDL had only become necessary *directly because* of the failure of politicians. If politicians had been more attuned to the problems faced by the old working class, then these men would have happily remained disinterested in politics, attached to family and friendship networks and absorbed in the mundane rhythm of their previously stable work and leisure lives. For many of the EDL members we spoke to, it was not government policy that caused most consternation. In fact, they were disgusted by the entirety of politics as they understood it. Politicians of every stripe had abandoned them. They had presided over the destruction of the life-world of the old industrial working class and then ridiculed and disparaged those who had managed to clamber free from the wreckage. Politicians had privileged immigrants and minorities and forgotten about the indigenous population who had built Great Britain. They had been left to fend for themselves. They were entirely without political representatives willing to argue in defence of their interests and those of their community. Despite the

EDL's reactionary world-view, its members have, in their own very basic way, like the child who shouts out that the emperor is naked, recognised the crucial fact that we now live in a cynical and completely uncaring post-political era, and that is where they are right, and the supposedly educated liberal Left are wrong.

The EDL was, for our respondents, a basic, impromptu and quite haphazard response to their predicament. As the movement grew, it became obvious that there were many others who felt the same way, and this gave those involved in the movement from the outset a degree of courage and a modicum of ambition. In our interactions, they talked openly and expressed themselves forcefully, certain that the vast majority of their peers felt the same way. It is a mistake to assume that, in poor, white neighbourhoods, the voices of EDL members and sympathisers are in a considerable minority, and that, in time, and given sufficient exposure to the doctrines of liberal toleration, the problem of regressive nationalism will simply melt away. The thousands who turn up at EDL demonstrations are merely the tip of an iceberg that also feeds UKIP. The sheer scale of anger and dissatisfaction, and the almost total absence of any other oppositional discourse, suggests that English nationalism can grow quite considerably in the coming years.

It appears that, from its earliest beginnings, the EDL lacked a vanguardist elite capable of formulating strategy, agreeing policy and generally driving the movement forwards. The EDL is effectively leaderless and has no clear strategies to intervene in politics, either to take power or to have its concerns addressed by those already in power. Like other new political movements, attending demonstrations and connecting with like-minded others on the Internet appears to be as far as supporters can take it. There is no charismatic leader, no vanguard and no authority figure capable of inspiring fidelity to a clearly outlined political cause. Instead, these men talk of being pushed into a corner and having no other option but to strike out in self-defence. However, they have failed to identify their true enemy, and, as we will see later, a significant portion of the blame for this failure lies with the liberalised political Left.

Many of those whom we spoke to found the leaderless, fluid structure of the EDL quite appealing, but the absence of a charismatic leader is a major problem for the EDL if it hopes to grow and play a more active role in politics. Many seemed to believe that any leader would inevitably prove to be a let-down: he would capitulate to political pressure or abandon the principles of the organisation and its members. They hoped for, but could not imagine, an imposing leader who would take the protean EDL's core concerns and ideas to a broader constituency and, with intellectual creativity and powerful oratory, recruit others to its cause, sweep aside the political establishment and create a new one in its place dedicated to the improvement of the socio-economic conditions of the white, English working class. Ultimately, they wanted a leader capable of clarifying the group's message, broadening its remit, boosting recruitment and then, in time, carrying the concerns and interests of the nationalistic, white working class to the highest reaches of political power. However, they could not muster the faith to believe that such a thing was possible. Instead, they tended to focus on immediate social reaction to their protests and they took a degree of pleasure in upsetting the liberal mainstream.

Here, we can draw upon Lacan's analysis of the discourse of the Master (2000; see also Fink, 1995), by which he meant, not an arbitrarily powerful individual leader but a Master-signifier that can be represented by a selected individual. In this discourse, it is the Master who identifies a path forward, curbs the excesses of the social and economic system and sets matters straight. It is the Master who makes decisions and compels others to live by his rules. This figure of the Master is precisely what, for the moment at least, Britain's far Right needs but lacks. The one respect in which the liberal Left performs its political task effectively, for instance in the relentless demonisation of Nick Griffin, is the constant iconoclastic destruction of any potential representative of the far Right's Master-signifier.

We must recognise that many of the frustrations experienced by EDL members develop in relation to the inherent instabilities of capitalism. Unlike virtually any of history's economic systems one might care to mention, capitalism has no tendency to equilibrium. Rather, it is a self-revolutionising system that fully integrates flux, change and disruption into its structure and dynamic movement. Capitalism has no 'moral order', and moral subjects cannot regulate or control the mutating processes of production, consumption and exchange that drive the system forward. Furthermore, capitalism is entirely disconnected from the human costs of its activity. The harms of capitalism can to some extent be controlled, if there is the political will to constrain its activities – the social democratic era proved that – but, if its forces are fully unleashed, it will aggressively pursue its own growth and continuity, blindly unaware of and untroubled by the repercussions of its activities for human beings and the various support systems that sustain human life.

Members of the EDL, and other far right groups throughout Europe, are reacting blindly against the sociocultural disruptions caused by recent changes to dominant forms of capital accumulation. The EDL members are disgusted by the Left, which they believe to be dominated by politically correct liberals who care only about minorities and who despise the working-class, male heterosexual because of his supposed racism and sexism and because he refuses to accept the tutelage of the enlightened liberal elite. Our respondents were aware of at least some of the paradoxes of the standard liberal account of multiculturalism. They were angry that the enlightened left liberal elite – the subdominant faction of the general neo-liberal elite (see Hall and Winlow, 2015) – championed the earthy authenticity of immigrants but found the earthy authenticity of the white working class distasteful and regressive. They also bristled at what they believed was the smug sense of entitlement displayed by the left liberal elite and reacted angrily to their portrayal of the men of the EDL as idiotic racist brutes, too ignorant and lacking in reflexivity to understand why the liberal left faction of the middle-class moral majority found their discourse so repugnant. Are we to assume that the EDL simply misunderstands the contemporary Left, and that the men of the EDL have failed to grasp that the Left remains the principal representative of the working classes, or should we open ourselves up to the possibility that the Left itself has drifted further and further away from the life-world of the traditional working class, to the extent that it no longer represents their true interests? Our respondents' distaste for the contemporary political Left and their lack of interest in, and understanding of, its history and core principles mean that their naïve 'anti-capitalism' cannot take the form of a true opposite. Instead, in their vague proposals, we can identify a kind of national corporatism that fully accepts capitalism and instead chooses to place crucial emphasis upon British interests, both economic and cultural.

Of course, the men we spoke to did not talk about capitalism, neither did they express any great desire to move beyond it. Their primary economic concerns were to generate more jobs for white English workers and to ensure that white English workers were paid a reasonable wage for their labours. In this respect, the EDL is not unlike UKIP, the new British political party we discussed in Chapter 3. What both groups seek is a Master who will control capital's worst excesses, prevent its wild fluctuations and both save and restore a mythical traditional culture with which all Englishmen and women can engage fully. They want to retain capitalism – because they see capital as central to the nation's traditional culture and way of life – but they want to strip away this crucial aspect of its nature, this tendency towards incessant and socially harmful instability and change. In more practical terms, they want the new Master to remove those forces that have corrupted capitalism and created the manifold problems that beset the nation.

For UKIP, the authoritarian, bureaucratic structures of the EU are corrupting British capitalism and reducing its effectiveness as it tries to attend to the economic interests of its citizenry. UKIP appears to believe that there are no fundamental *national* economic antagonisms. The problems the country faces are essentially external problems, some of which have breached the national barrier to impair its economic development and contaminate its culture. The solution, then, becomes clear: politicians must address external pressures and impediments that are hampering economic development and seek to restore to health the country's labour markets and traditional culture. UKIP is, therefore, principally concerned with the return of sovereign powers and independence from the EU. This, it believes, will give the country the opportunity to prevent high numbers of economic migrants from the east coming into the country, and this will in turn cut unemployment and welfare dependency, boost the country's economic competitiveness and, of course, allow the beauty of the unsullied national culture to return to full bloom. If the country could be cleansed of pollutants, it appears to claim, capitalism in Britain will find a beautifully poised equilibrium that benefits all citizens. Essentially, UKIP wants a capitalism that has been neutered, deprived of its destructive energy, so that it can be more like its benign and beneficial 'true self'.

Much the same is true of the EDL, although, in truth, our respondents were not yet capable of identifying a clear political path forward that would improve or control capitalism's chaotic functioning. For them, immigration generally and Islamic immigration specifically were the crucial pollutants that corrupted English civil society and prevented the white majority from living life to the full. The sheer scale of Muslim migration to England and the supposed characteristics of Muslim culture were both eroding and contaminating the traditional English way of life and reducing the social experience of the 'indigenous' white working class. Muslims were leeching off the welfare state. Muslims were stealing their jobs. Muslims were willing to work informally at rates below the minimum wage. Muslims were making life unbearable for the white majority and, worse, they were becoming increasingly confident and assertive, keen to secure yet more privileges at the expense of the white working class.

In truth, the far Right in Britain does not need a new Master to identify a scapegoat it can blame for recent social and economic upheavals and the general instability of capitalist markets. There is already considerable anti-immigrant feeling dispersed throughout the country. The crucial role of the new Master is to clarify the anti-immigrant discourse and compel others to accept his diagnosis. Both UKIP and the EDL, in their different ways, identify the immigrant as the excessive character who disturbs what would otherwise be the stable cultural and economic life of the country. Here, of course, the contaminant, the thing that disrupts social harmony, is basically external to the nation, or at least never fully absorbed into its social fabric. In fascist Germany, it was 'the Jew' (see Žižek, 1995), with his supposed 'excessive' greed and profiteering, who was believed to cause economic problems and social disruption. Of course, greed and aggressive profiteering are proper to capitalism and integral to its functioning. There is no capitalism that is free from greed and profiteering, just as there is no capitalism free from structural economic antagonisms. The removal of the nation's perceived excess can produce no harmonious capitalist social order in which everyone is content to occupy their given place in the social hierarchy and free to enjoy a properly functioning national culture. In the discourse of the far Right, it is the Master's job to transpose the inherent imbalances of the capitalist market economy, and the social disruptions that inevitably result, on to the figure of the immigrant, identifying him as the root cause of the country's problems. Once the immigrant troublemaker is removed, the Master promises the return of a natural equilibrium to the nation and its economy. Everyone will return to their proper place, and all will be free to partake of the enjoyments of traditional culture.

The problem for radical politics, of both Right and Left, is that the time of the charismatic leader appears, for the time being at least, to be at an end. In recent years, we have passed through a period in which we appointed comical figures to lead us, figures whose buffoonery and man-of-the-people tastes appeared to render them endearing, and whose transgressions we are willing to forgive. Now we appear to be in a period in which grey bureaucrats have achieved political hegemony and institutional monopoly, pulling the strings to ensure that democracy doesn't intrude too much on the movement of capital. In both cases, capitalism has continued onwards unimpeded.

Lacan's point is that we always *subconsciously* desire a strong leader to stand in front of us and tell us how to live. The terror of symbolically inefficient, postmodern self-determination, in which all social institutions are subject to cynical deconstruction without any attempt to construct an improved replacement (Winlow and Hall, 2012a), inevitably produces political stasis. At once, we *unconsciously* solicit a new Master – because we are keen to live by his laws and relinquish subject-ive responsibility for determining our own being-in-the-world – but, lodged in a faithless postmodern era, we are also compelled to *consciously* dismiss the new Master. The 'truth' he offers cannot be truth as such, and we assume that beneath his discourse lie cynical self-interest and a manic desire for power. For the postmodern subject, the strident political leader is always only a flawed individual, no better than anyone else. The 'truth' that drives his analysis of the problems we face is simply an opinion with which we can either agree or disagree, but our support is never given to him entirely. For the moment, at least, the strident ideologue cannot make the ascent to the position of the Master.

As we have repeatedly tried to stress, ideology must be returned to politics if we are truthfully to come to terms with the problems we face. If ideology does return, our current batch of dull pragmatists might be replaced by a new band of forceful leaders, keen to reanimate politics and keen to assume the role of the Master. For our part, we hope for an intelligent and charismatic leader of the Left and fear an intelligent and charismatic leader of the Right, but to remain as we are, lodged in this depressive intervallic period – to do nothing and change nothing – is to risk destruction.

The scapegoat

We can, of course, identify a scapegoating mechanism in the spoken accounts of EDL members. When flailing around for an explanation for their present parlous situation, they came upon the traditional scapegoat discourse (see Girard, 1989), which seemed, in a very straightforward way, to explain all of life's frustrations and dissatisfactions. The Muslim immigrant was the disturbing excess that deprived them of what would otherwise be a peaceful and satisfying life. Can't get a job? Welfare benefits cut? Lifestyle reduced? Neighbourhood threatened by rising crime? Feel dissociated from your community? All sense of continuity and structure slipping away? Blame radical Islam and the endless waves of immigrants flooding into the country. These immigrants are determined to take everything of value from you, despoil your culture and ravage your country and its heritage.

Here, the righteous indignation EDL members feel about the radical ambiguity and instability of life in post-crash England cannot be discharged upon its true cause. Instead, righteous indignation is corrupted and dragged off course and identifies an Other who can be blamed and symbolically sacrificed in a national purge that seeks to restore a mythical, non-existent purity and balance.

When our respondents sought to identify those things that angered them and prompted their return to politics, they often talked of insipid, duplicitous politicians keen to destroy the country. They often conflated the politicians of Westminster with other metropolitan elites in the media, business, the academy and cultural production. The principal object of their hatred was the perceived instrumentalism of these elites, which, our respondents believed, existed behind a mask of progres-sive liberalism. As far as our respondents were concerned, these elites despised the white working class and were appalled by their perceived prejudices and cultural tastelessness. The EDL, therefore, is not just a new form of far-right radicalism structured by a hatred of Islam and mass immigration. The EDL also appears to be vehemently opposed to middle-class metropolitan liberalism and its domination of politics and culture. For some of our respondents, it was precisely this vaguely composed liberal metropolitan elite that inspired the most opprobrium. Our respondents could talk endlessly about immigration and radical Islam, but, for some at least, it was the self-righteousness of the liberal class and its obvious disdain for the supposedly uncivilised, working-class barbarian hordes that appeared to anger our respondents to the point of violence.

The EDL's hatred of the liberal class was such that we are almost willing to risk the thesis that its crude nationalism is structured in relation to an unconscious negation of the 'true interests' of the white working class. The EDL's desire to wrestle free from the benevolent guidance of the liberal elite is such that acting against its 'true interests' is the only way to reassert its autonomy. The traditional Left, which sought to move beyond capitalism – encouraging everyday men and women to see their problems in relation to the market – might provide at least some of the answers to the problems faced by England's white working class, but the EDL's hatred of the broad Left is such that it steadfastly refuses to borrow from the Left's discourse. For these working-class men, the Left has been irredeemably tarnished by metropolitan liberalism. In fact, the situation is even more extreme than that. These working-class men are firm in their conviction that this metropolitan liberalism represents the *entirety of the Left*, and the politics of the working class has no place within its borders. They have no conception of a Left concerned with egalitarianism and social justice. For them, the political Left is concerned with tolerance, multiculturalism and the rights of minorities. Its members are a bunch of sandal-wearing, latte-drinking, middle-class hippies who presume to instruct the working class on the path to liberation and social betterment. The politics of the EDL is a political creation of the contemporary white working class. It has successfully rid itself of all forms of liberal benevolentism. It is 'theirs', and it is entirely free from all interlopers who might seek to bestow their wisdom upon them. Unfortunately, the politics of the EDL is not the politics the white working class needs if it is to genuinely overcome the monumental obstacles to securing economic justice and reconstituting a functional community life it faces.

Modern versus postmodern racism

The members of the EDL we spoke to usually did not see themselves as racists, despite openly expressing hostility towards minorities in the crudest of terms. Their racism was of an uncomplicated and rather direct sort in which the hated Muslim Other was bestowed with a host of negative and often quite contradictory characteristics that were believed to justify aggressive denunciation and summary dismissal from the glorious English homeland. However, the EDL's hatred of liberal cosmopolitanism brings forward a different form of racism, integral to the ideology of liberal multiculturalism. Étienne Balibar (1991; see also Žižek, 1995) has called this a 'metaracism', a racism that can assume the form of its opposite. We can get some sense of this when British politicians line up to denounce the EDL before immediately moving on to argue that new barriers must be placed in front of prospective immigrants keen to move to Britain. In such cases, politicians would not dream of uttering the kinds of intemperate invective deployed by the EDL and instead identify the great benefits that migrants have brought to Britain in recent years. However, beneath this positive liberal gloss lies a more complex but deeply corrosive form of racism, the form of which is inspired by the ideology of multiculturalism itself. It is clear that most mainstream politicians in Britain and Europe are moving away from all prior commitments to multiculturalism, despite their verbal advocacy of cultural diversity. Our borders are now aggressively defended, and immigrants are often criminalised and subject to significant abuse (Aas, 2007). Perhaps more to the point, while using the language of toleration and mutual respect, these politicians also take the next step in suggesting that groups such as the EDL would not exist if earlier political leaders had been a little more cautious in mixing distinct ethnic groups. So, while talking of tolerance, mutual respect and non-violence, they in fact end up advocating the politics of nationalism, national purity and closed borders (see Žižek, 1995, 1997). Here, distinct ethic groups remain tolerant of each other, as long as they are not brought into contact with one another within the national space.

We can also see a form of racism that flows from a postmodern social order that survives by grudgingly tolerating, but never fully accepting, the presence of the Other. It is easy to condemn the EDL's direct racism, but can we also detect a form of racism within multiculturalism itself? Is there not a tendency in multiculturalism to reduce the Other to a range of shallow signifiers that deny the Other genuine Otherness? Is it not racist to seek to introduce a black couple to one's regular dinner party circle, or to attend a carnival specifically to momentarily immerse oneself in 'diversity', or to cultivate a friendship with an immigrant specifically because she is an immigrant? Does the liberal multiculturalist not take the position of the coloniser who patronises the colonised community by respecting it, by enjoying its cuisine and revelling in its vibrant cultural life, yet simultaneously arranges its incorporation and eventual demise? In the very act of respecting the surface signifiers of Otherness, does the multiculturalist not assert his superiority by positioning himself in a universal position above culture, free to look down and bestow his favour upon the Other's particularities?

Of course, our desire to identify the problems embedded in multiculturalism does not mean that we endorse the standard right-wing condemnation of it. It's clear that the EDL's racism is more corrosive than the inverted racism of liberal multiculturalism. Keeping up appearances and disguising our true attitudes and desires remain absolutely integral to the organisation of reasonably civilised social life. Our goal is instead to suggest that fundamentalism and multiculturalism are not opposites; they exist in tandem, and each is complicit in the other's continuity.

Below, Damien, twenty-two, expresses views common to our overall sample:

> I fucking don't really get politics mate, left and right. I am not a racist, I have mates who are black, I grew up with black people round me, but they fitted in with us, we got along together, in and out of each other's houses. It's not like that today. That community feeling, it's gone. I don't know, just like, I know everyone calls the EDL far right, so that is what I guess I am, fair enough. All I know is that I fucking hate those who oppose us, the fucking UAF and the fucking cultural Marxists. They are just queers, dirty spoilt whores who like ethnic cock, and middle-class pricks that don't know what life is really like when you live on a shitty fucking estate where everything is disappearing except the fucking foreign faces.

Jake, forty-five, continues with this theme:

> If you are working class, white and patriotic you are seen as scum. The people in power and the middle class are ashamed to call themselves English. If you listen to them, they expect you to self-identify as British, liberal and fucking tolerant. If you call yourself an English Nationalist, some people see that as a provocation and a badge you are racist and intolerant.

Question: What does that mean to you then, English Nationalist?

> I am English; I see England as my country, not Scotland . . . or Wales. I am pro-union, but I am not British like the fucking BNP. I would never vote for them because I'm not British, I'm English. I don't follow the British football team. I believe in keeping English jobs for English people first, and I am not a fucking liberal. I am fucking intolerant of some things, like fucking Sharia Law and fucking child brides. Those are fucking things I should be fucking intolerant of, and I don't fucking want them in my country. It's a bloody good job the previous generations were intolerant of some things too. If the previous generations were not intolerant of Nazism we would have the Swastika as a flag now.

Kenny is a proletarian entrepreneur. He occasionally works as a labourer in the building industry and sometimes as a part-time gardener. However, most of his income comes from trading in the illicit economy. He continues to sign on and claim various out-of-work benefits. He is doing reasonably well financially and he can afford occasional foreign holidays with his partner. Despite his continual low-level exploitation of the benefits system and his occasional involvement in crime, Kenny talks passionately about the exploitation of the welfare state by asylum seekers and illegal immigrants. He believes the system is now set up to privilege Muslims, while black and white Britons are marginalised:

It all started with the fucking politicians mate, I would shoot them with all the scum Muslims. The Conservatives never gave a fuck cos they know they don't have to live with dirty Muslims in their big London houses, but Labour, they're worse. I remember Labour sticking up for blacks, and that was fair enough because they [black people] came here and got on with it, they didn't rock the boat . . . but Labour didn't give a fuck when the Muslims came in and started taking the piss. They did nothing. They should have capped immigration, they should have protected the working class, but those cunts, they opened the floodgates. I don't like the BNP, I am not racist, but immigration now, it's Muslim immigration: Somalia, Iran, Iraq, Afghanistan, Pakistan, that is where they are coming from . . . The EDL basically, well, they are willing to tell these Muslims we have had enough of them, it's that, basically. If they can't live with us then get out, go back to wherever, you know?

Question: So what is it that gets you about Muslims?

Kenny:

> Where I live, they are the ones with the nice cars, the big houses, their kids running round like jack the lads in Mercs and beemers [Mercedes and BMW cars] that have been bought by ripping us off in their shops for a pint of milk while they look after their own.

Richard's account of the problems of contemporary Britain is also strewn with contradictions. Richard is a drug dealer, but he believes immigration to be the primary cause of his neighbourhood's disintegration:

> Tell you what, not all of us [in the EDL] are stupid, we know the score. We know we are being fucked over by the system and they do not give a fuck about us. It's dog eat dog. There's no other way. I actually see the Muslims and I see how underhandedly they look after each other. It's like the lies about moderate Muslims. I don't see moderates. I see more devious ones that secretly support their own. They might not say it but they do it. They might say they don't support terrorism, but every time there is an attack on the West anywhere, secretly they celebrate and nobody has the balls to point it out. They are like that because they stick together, because any Muslim, the most important thing to them is other Muslims. They are all one and the same. Where is that in my community? We have none of it, no fucking community. It's like everyone taking advantage and out for themselves, the politicians, the bankers, everyone just blinkered and only bothered by their own shit. That scares me, because while it's like that we're sleepwalking into a world where we could wake up under the fucking black flag of Islam. I can see that, that is why we need to get organised and fight back.

Our respondents often returned to this theme of Muslim communities 'looking after their own'. For some, this reflected a broader Muslim conspiracy to take over the country, whereas others utilised the lingua franca of liberal multiculturalism to argue that apparently functional, inward-looking communities were in fact pathological in some way and not in keeping with the cosmopolitan values of Britain. Here, of course, we encounter another contradiction, because, overwhelmingly, our respondents were keen to recreate and defend their own inward-looking, non-integrationist community, keen to 'look after its own'. It is not too difficult to see how this theme works in tandem with their concern for the disintegration of white working-class neighbourhoods. The EDL's melancholic brooding over its own mythical lost community prompted it to look on enviously at the enjoyment Muslims took from their own community life. Again, the EDL's narrative involves the Other's appropriation of cultural value. Muslim communities were believed to possess a cohesion and logic that were judged to be missing from their own white working-class neighbourhoods. However, jealousy is not the most pertinent issue here. Rather, the key emotional response, indeed the emotion that typifies the EDL's entire discourse, is anger. At root, the assumption is that Muslim communities possess the lost spirit of solidarity and brotherhood precisely because white working-class communities do not. And this in turn leads inevitably to the assumption that the spirit of solidarity and brotherhood – this lost thing that casts in shadow the entire experience of England's white working class – was in fact stolen from the white working class by the hated Other, who then flaunts his community's solidarity in front of the white working class, entirely disinterested in the envy and anger he inspires.

The politics of melancholia

It is worth expanding this point a little further. Freud (2001) famously identified the basic distinction between mourning and melancholy. Mourning involved accepting and rationally coming to terms with one's loss. Melancholy, on the other hand, results from an inability to truly accept loss. The melancholic remains pathologically attached to the lost object. The absence of the lost object transforms his social experience, and a heavy, depressive cloud descends that shadows the melancholic's social experience until the rehabilitative work of mourning can begin. It is now commonplace in post-Freudian psychoanalysis to attempt to rehabilitate melancholy. Doesn't the melancholic display an admirable fidelity to the lost object? How can one rationally come to terms with the loss of the object when the object itself, in all its complexity, cannot be fully understood?

As we have already claimed, the EDL displays an enduring attachment to the lost historical object of traditional white English proletarian culture. This culture, for those members of the EDL we spoke to, displayed a clear sense of solidarity and togetherness. Everyone who was a part of the culture understood and appreciated it (of course, if they did not, they were no longer considered to be part of it). If we imagine that this culture disappeared, or began to disappear, with the advent of neo-liberalism, then many of our respondents were too young to actually remember it. Of course, for them, this matters not at all. They too remember, or at least think they can remember, a semblance of something *else*, something that was not *this*, the actual (non-)existence of cultural life that appeared more stable, and in which people could be relied upon and appeared more content, open and supportive. This community, as it is experienced by its members, is always in a state of disintegration, and it was always this way, even during the heyday of the industrial working classes: eroding, breaking apart, slipping away, menaced by external forces keen to seize its positive substance.

Like the melancholic, the pissed-off white men of the EDL cannot accept and fully come to terms with the loss of their culture and traditional way of life. The politics of the EDL reflects a steadfast refusal to engage in the rehabilitative work of mourning. Its supporters do not want to come to terms with the non-existence of their imagined community. They want to defend what remains and begin a concerted attempt to re-appropriate and reconstruct what has been lost. For them, mourning the passing of their community would be a betrayal of biblical proportions. Where previous generations had successfully defended their community from manifold external threats, they would be the ones that allowed it to slip away. It is almost as if they believe that their social identities, indeed their own self-conception, would immediately disintegrate, as soon as they rationally accepted that the lost object of community was lost for good and could never be recovered.

Of course, the discourse of the melancholic acts to turn the subject away from social reality. Global capitalism, with every passing year, makes it progressively more difficult to retain the uniqueness of culture and the context in which it was intended to be experienced. The reality is that most unique cultures have been ripped apart by globalisation. The individuals who once formed such cultures have been thrust into the market and told to compete against those they once considered brothers and sisters and for whom they were once willing to die. The melancholic attachment to the lost object of community, in this sense, allows the instrumental market performer to pursue his own material benefit, while at the same time convincing himself that his heart remains with the lost object of the traditional community. And of course, we see the commodification and crass reproduction of 'traditional community' throughout global consumer culture. We can buy its artefacts, visit its ruins, watch individuals clad in traditional garb perform ceremonial dances and so on. The reality is that the community no longer exists, other than as a systematised form of identification that can be manipulated, commodified and exploited, and as a handy melancholic formula that enables the individual to retain the conceit that he has resisted the lure of mass consumer culture and remains the bearer of all the characteristics of the lost world.

The crucial Žižekian twist here is to counter the current trend to rehabilitate melancholy and argue forcefully for a return to the hard work of mourning. First, to reiterate, we must acknowledge that the lost object was never truly possessed in the first place. As Freud observed, the melancholic does not know precisely what he has lost when the lost object disappears. It simply didn't exist in the way it is perceived to have existed by the melancholic. Not only was it constituted by its own passing – that is, the object was only understood to have existed after its own disintegration – but our own assessment of its positive substance reflects a particular relationship between subject and object. Basically, the lost object was always, at least in part, constituted by our own subjective assessment of it. Our faith in the community and our submission to its traditions and rules are in fact fully constitutive of that community. Without our commitment to it, the 'object' simply doesn't exist.

We should also, very briefly, acknowledge the standard liberal assessment opened up by this line of analysis. Our understanding of the object of community reflects our own subjective position as much as it does the properties of the mythical object of community. Although our community structures the enjoyment of its members, the criteria for membership are both hidden and incredibly strict. One cannot simply apply to join it and immediately be taken to its bosom, and, of course, those born into the community who possessed personal characteristics that differed significantly from the norm were compelled to hide their individuality, leave the community or accept their position as a pariah, stuck forever on the outskirts.

Second, the enjoyments of community are not restricted to positive and ethical pastimes and traditions. In psychoanalysis, enjoyment is never fully rational. Enjoyment references the perversions of our own subjective fantasy space. The enjoyments of ethical individuals are not ethical enjoyments, because that is not how our subconscious works. We are, as Freud recognised, polymorphously perverse during our youth, and the arrival of a functional super-ego does not ethicise sexual fantasy, as any investigation of the Catholic Church will reveal. Furthermore, the community does not 'hold together' simply by enjoying the positivity of shared cultural life. The laws of the community also carry with them an obscene underside that sanctions ostensibly 'immoral' behaviours, enabling, indeed encouraging, members of the community to engage in harmful behaviours. For example, Žižek (2008, 2010) cites Klu Klux Klan lynchings and the beating, or fragging, of new recruits in the military as obscenities that reaffirm commitment to the community from which they arise.

If we return directly to the case of the EDL, we can see how a melancholic attachment to the lost object of community colours its politics and prompts the identification of an external Other responsible for its woes. Of course, there is nothing fundamentally wrong with constructing a utopian dream of a world it never truly possessed. In fact, the construction of a utopian dream of community can act as a sturdy platform upon which a dynamic and progressive politics can be built. What is problematic in the construction of the historical, non-existent Utopia is 'the way this dream is used to legitimise the actuality of its very opposite, of the full and unconstrained participation in global capitalism' (Žižek, 2000a: 659).

So, what would happen if the EDL were to break through its cloud of melancholy and engage in the hard work of mourning the lost object of community? Mourning the lost community and accepting a reality in which it is no longer present and cannot be rediscovered may well compel the EDL to cut its links to the perceived cultural vitality of modern, 'really existing' community life and appraise the cold hard world of post-crash capitalism and the faithless cynicism of postmodern experience. Of course, if we accept that the lost community is totally lost, then there is no need to defend it from those who are perceived to threaten it. We are forced to accept capitalist universalism and its mass culture, in which there are no exclusions and in which everyone is encouraged to engage. From here, we might imagine that it becomes possible to develop a very different politics, a politics that reflects and acknowledges the atomisation and instrumentality of our times and acts to close the gap between the subject and its Other, in order to manufacture a way of living together that is less hostile, less distant, less competitive, and from which new forms of mutual recognition might emerge. This acceptance opens up the possibility that the obscene reality of global capitalism can be identified as the true enemy of the working class, the true force that destabilises its reality. If a meaningful community life is to exist, it must be actively constituted in a way that reflects our present reality and develops in relation to a politics that looks anew at the problems we face. Rather than attempting to create a tentative balance – in which distinct communities grudgingly tolerate the Other until the Other is inevitably judged to have overstepped the hazy boundaries of mutually respectful conduct – the creation of a new *politics of universality*, a politics that cuts across the social field to create new forms of attachment, community and recognition, is the most productive path forward.

Every fascism bears witness to a failed revolution

The mere existence of the EDL clearly suggests that there is an abundance of dissatisfaction among England's white working class. However, the nature of the EDL's discourse bears witness to the failure of the Left to engage with the working class, symbolise its frustrations and capitalise upon the revolutionary potential that exists in marginalised neighbourhoods. Instead, in their desperate and uninformed attempt to understand their position, the pissed-off white men of the EDL grasp the regressive politics of ethnic hatred and, in so doing, ignore the fundamental causes of their grim circumstances.

Many of our respondents had encountered what they believed to be representatives of the Left at EDL demonstrations. These angry working-class men recounted tales of being deprecated, vilified and physically attacked by representatives of the political Left. How can we possibly understand this perverse situation in which the Left is now at war with elements of the traditional working class? Is this simply a traditional clash of ideologies, in which the egalitarian Left attack the fascists of the far Right? Can we not say that, when the Left denounces the EDL at its demonstrations, the Left is in fact appraising an inverted, mirror image of its own political failure? Does the mere fact that the EDL has grown so quickly, in a time of significant economic turmoil, reflect the failure of the Left to symbolise the anger and dissatisfaction of the traditional white working class and its failure to lead the working class towards an encounter with its true enemy?

5

THE CONSUMER RIOTS OF 2011

For four days in August 2011, England experienced its most destructive civil disorder for over a quarter of a century. The rioting began in Tottenham, a deprived area in the borough of Haringey, North London. The trigger for the riots was the killing of Mark Duggan, an alleged criminal, who was shot by Metropolitan Police officers.

In Tottenham, there is something of a tradition of marching to the local police station to express community discontent and anger at the use of excessive police force (see Muir, 2011). On this occasion, however, no senior police officer offered to speak to the crowd, and no representatives were invited inside to discuss their grievances. A peaceful and entirely legitimate protest against police violence and the killing of Mark Duggan sparked an outpouring of anger and discontent that quickly lost touch with these original grievances and spread throughout the capital and other metropolitan areas across the country. Those who took to the streets in Birmingham and Manchester had never heard of Mark Duggan, but their violence reflected the same sense of frustration and discontent felt by marginalised populations across Britain. Over 2,500 shops were looted, and the costs of the riots to the British taxpayer ran into the hundreds of millions of pounds (see Laville, 2011; Topping and Bawdon, 2011). Five lives were lost, and some 15,000 people were believed to have been involved in the disturbances (Bridges, 2012). As a disconcerted population watched the riots unfold in real time on 24-hour news channels and social media, they appeared to wonder how long the disturbances would last and how far they would spread. What did it all mean? What had become of the country?

Making sense of the riots is an important task. Many academics have assumed that the rioters were attempting to communicate something to the social mainstream – or to the political or financial elites that dominate our world – and so they busied themselves decoding the rioters' messages. This task necessarily involves recourse to ideology. Many supposedly objective empirical sociologists, especially those on the left, believe that they occupy a privileged position that enables them to identify the forces that drove the rioters to act as they did. This is not at all problematic. Forcefully debating issues of crucial importance should be positioned much more centrally in the social sciences. The problem comes with the assumption that the committed social researcher can effectively *talk for* the rioters, and that they alone can decode the rioters' messages on behalf of the public. Of course, the assumption that the rioters must have had a message to deliver is crucial. The truth is, however, that no messages could be clearly identified. The *riots* in themselves tell us much about our present reality, but to assume that the *rioters* must have been attempting to communicate some hidden truth to the world simply opens up the space for dogmatic ideological accounts that fill in the absence of a clear message with a message structured in relation to the supposedly objective academic's own political preferences.

In the resolute search for the rioters' positive message, these social researchers completely missed the riots' obviously negativistic aspect. The *total absence of a clear message* from the rioters is, quite clearly, a dominant feature of the riots. *The real 'message' is that there was no message.* Rather than retreating to safe academic ground – and mythologising the poor and their supposedly natural orientation to politics – it would have been far more productive for researchers to ask why, in an era of such profound cultural and economic turmoil and stark social inequality, the rioters had no clear message to deliver. Why, when those who rioted had so little to lose and so much to gain, did they have nothing to say? Why, during a historic crisis in the capitalist system, was the dominant characteristic of the riots the looting of consumer goods? Why, if they truly had the capacity to do so, did spokespeople not rise up among the rioters to articulate the source of their collective dissatisfaction in a reasonably clear way?

The total absence of articulate political opposition in the riots resonates with our central thesis. The rioters did not demand social justice (see Millington, 2013). They were not angered to the point of violence by political corruption and the vulgarity of corporate and banking elites (see Wain and Joyce, 2012). They did not loot shops in order to communicate their dissatisfaction at rising prices on the high street (see Harvie and Milburn, 2013). They were not disgusted at the commodification of urban space (Millington, 2013). To suggest that these things did mobilise the rioters simply transforms the rioters and the events of August 2011 into a blank screen on to which we can project our own yearnings and political preferences. The rioters' messages were not their own, but imputed to them by left liberal academics who were desperate to hear what they wanted to hear.

Our analysis (see Briggs, 2012; Hall, 2012d; Winlow and Hall, 2012b, 2012c; Hall and Winlow, 2013; Treadwell *et al.*, 2013) is a little more honest, not least because what we see in the riots is precisely what we do not want to see. There is absolutely no wishful thinking on our part. Where we see ideological incorporation and the absence of politics, we would very much like to see an articulate political opposition willing to take on the hard work of moving British society beyond neo-liberalism or even capitalism itself. Where we see the depressing triumph of consumerism set against a backdrop of atomisation, nihilism and negativity, we would very much like to see the blossoming of a new political community, with equality, solidarity and universality firmly in its sights. However, we will not allow our desire for these things to lead inevitably to the breathless proclamation that we have discovered them amid a distressing, apolitical and ahistorical outpouring of anger and frustration. We do not want to promulgate the common left liberal lie that suggests that the poor of the consumer era are a proto-political community, a political force-in-waiting disgusted by inequality and the immorality of the rich, who continue to periodically rise up to assert their will.

We want to talk honestly about how far things have fallen and how much work the Left has still to do if one day it is to create a world less scarred by injustice, insecurity and incessant competition. The political interests of the urban poor are best served by honest academic accounts willing to acknowledge that the rioters were incapable of expressing their anger in a productive and properly political way. To continue with the delusion that the poor today are magically able to separate themselves from the ruling ideology and oppose it with the altruism and solidarity that are still reproduced at the heart of their communities actively prevents an encounter with a truth that might spur genuine political action. Blind, apolitical violence that fails to identify its cause and present a viable alternative is not the first step on a journey that takes us to a better society.

For academics to represent apolitical violence as its opposite because it suits their political preferences actively prevents us from facing up to a much more disturbing reality, and it turns social science into pure fiction. *When politics is absent it needs to be created*, and this is something academics on the left must come to terms with. To assume that politics exists in abundance in marginalised neighbourhoods, even though it somehow never actually manages to materialise as new progressive political movements, covers up reality with institutionalised fantasy. It suggests a retreat into a world of make-believe where all poor people in the West are by nature proto-communists waiting for an opportune moment to set matters straight. By extension, it also suggests that the contemporary poor do not need any help identifying their true enemy, understanding their true social position or applying their rage to a productive purpose. Because so many on the academic Left imagine that politics remains dormant but nevertheless fully operative in its timeless organic form, and that it is only a matter of time before the new post-industrial citizenry rises up from the bottom to assert its will, we grant ourselves leave to remain seated in history's waiting room, sure that we will in time be proved right, and that a train will soon arrive to carry us into the future.

The train is not coming – at least, not by itself. It must be constructed, developed, set in motion and continually forced to move forwards. Its fuel will be intellectual honesty, hard work and personal sacrifice. If we sit waiting and fantasising about organic politics much longer, we will see everything around us decay and disintegrate. Life will get harder for the majority of people. Our environment will continue to deteriorate, natural resources will become scarce to the point that wars will be fought over them, and any hope we once had that our children will have it better will disappear.

The limits of research

Empirical evidence suggests quite clearly that the rioters themselves identified a range of factors that they believed to be the drivers behind their actions (see, for example, Prasad, 2011; Topping and Bawdon, 2011; Newburn and Prasad, 2012; Treadwell *et al.*, 2013). However, the limitations of these empirical studies are obvious: in most cases, subjects are entirely incapable of determining why they acted in the way that they did. Our years of ethnographic research with criminals and non-criminals have revealed this to us quite clearly. Asking a criminal why he did what he did elicits only an account, a narrative or a justification, *never* an unequivocal truth that can be presented as fact. It is the job of the academic to interpret such accounts by utilising theory, placing the criminal actor and their acts within a social, historical and economic context and thinking critically and imaginatively about what has been said and how it relates to what has occurred. If some rioters claim that they acted because the government's Education Maintenance Allowance – which granted young people a small income if they stayed in post-16 education – was withdrawn, and others claim that they acted to strike back at the police for the killing of Mark Duggan, and others still claim that they simply hoped to make some money by looting consumer goods from high-street stores, we should not conclude that the actual causes of the riot were varied and, thus, beyond our comprehension. Nor should we aggregate responses and assume that, if most rioters claim that they rioted because they were disgusted at rising consumer prices, this is the core truth that mobilised most of the participants. This is pure abstracted empiricism, and it is actively preventing the social sciences from moving forward. Abstracted empiricism rips data from their context and it refuses to engage in the kinds of theory construction that can drive forward our knowledge of the world.

We are not denying the value of empirical research. Accounts offered by research subjects can be illuminating. However, to believe that we can discover the truth of the riots by simply talking to those who took part in them is a profound mistake. It transforms the riotous subject into a pure Cartesian rationalist who never acts impulsively and who always understands perfectly the boundless variety of influences that shape her behaviour. Tim Newburn (2011), who headed up *The Guardian*/LSE rapid response investigation into the riots, has suggested that there needs to be a concerted effort to gather empirical data about the riots. We support him in this endeavour, but, without an associated theoretical effort, we will not move any closer to the truth.

Rather than thoughtlessly adopting the tired intellectual repertoires of the past, rather than relying on empirical research to reveal the truth, and rather than rushing quickly to defend the rioters from anything that might be construed as criticism or condemnation, might it not be reasonable to separate ourselves from the forces that compel us to find neat solutions and instead try to think in an original way about the riots and what they have to say about our society and the way we live now? For us, the riots appeared as a kind of desperate existential scream, issued by the excluded, that demanded nothing more than *attention and recognition*. Weren't the riots essentially a desperate cry, issued only in the hope that it might encourage the social mainstream to turn and acknowledge the continued presence of the forgotten and ignored?

It is vital that we also acknowledge that the urban poor who rioted are effectively the children of the consumer–capitalist 'good life' of unrestrained hedonism and perpetual indulgence. However, the commodity–objects of their desire remained frustratingly out of reach (Bauman, 2011; Tester, 2012). They had been promised that everything was available for those willing to apply a little effort, but their everyday experience told a different story. They were excluded de facto from the consumerised mainstream and cut adrift from the activities that signified social value and respectable forms of occupational and cultural inclusion. In the absence of an oppositional politics worthy of the name, frustration grew, and a sense of lack – an imprecise sense that something that should be in place was absent – established itself at the edge of consciousness.

The rioters were simply not equipped with an intellectual means of identifying the root cause of their frustration, and they could not access the forms of political symbolism that might enable them to imagine a world founded upon alternative sources of value. Immediately incorporated by the ideologies of contemporary capitalism, they hoped only to improve their circumstances within the existing capitalist system. They were angry that they could not access those things that appeared to signify individual value and relevance in a post-social world dominated by consumerism's sign-value system. Rather than joining with others to transform capitalism, they hoped only to transform themselves into a winner in capitalism's interminable competitive struggle. Blind anger grew in parallel with the frustration and anger of others suffering for similar reasons. Eventually, this anger reached such a high level that even a slight tear in the fabric of normality enabled it to spill out furiously on to the streets. The rioters' nihilistic acting out, born of deep frustration, aimed to communicate nothing more profound than *'we're still here you cunts!'*

So, our initial point is simply to say that the riots were not a poorly articulated call made by the poor for more and better welfare, for better jobs and a higher standard of living, for better educational opportunities or for the government to set about the task of reducing inequality. The material conditions in which the rioters found themselves inevitably set the context, but these conditions cannot reasonably be identified as the fundamental cause of the riots. We cannot realistically say that, because the rioters were 'socially excluded', they took to the streets because they wanted to be socially included, and we cannot say that the unemployed rioted because they were denied reasonably secure jobs.

Instead, the riots evidenced the almost total absence of genuine transformative or even regulatory politics within Western liberal capitalist societies and the debilitating cultural cynicism of our times. Liberal capitalism had just passed through an economic crash of historic proportions. Politicians had been revealed to be self-interested cynics. Inequality had reached a level not seen since the Great

Depression (Picketty, 2014), and the new financial elite, who had greatly contributed to the economic crash of 2008, were getting richer with every passing day. The time for politics and determined political opposition was at hand, but the angry and forgotten could not articulate an oppositional politics, even in a rudimentary form. There was no vanguard to lead them and no alternative ideology and collective symbolism to rally around. Instead, a hugely disruptive economic crisis revealed the complete triumph of capitalism and its ideological support systems. At its most unstable moment, there was simply no opponent able to take advantage of its weakened condition.

Anger and frustration existed in abundance but could not be directed at their fundamental cause. No dream of a better world existed. Capitalism remained an unchallengeable totality. Because of these things, although there may have been myriad individual grievances, private dreams and idiosyncratic notions of how the world works and how to fix it, the riots contained no core political message for us to decode. The attempts made by left liberals to fill the gap left by absent politics with their own anti-authoritarian message do the urban poor no favours at all. Depicting the rioters as inarticulate proto-revolutionaries – or even proto-Fabian reformers – motivated by a desperate desire to secure social justice is an intellectual and political error of epic proportions. The reality is much more disturbing, and addressing it with honesty reveals the true extent of the task that lies before the Left.

In continuation of our central thesis, much of what we have to say here addresses the absence of politics in the riots of 2011. Why were the rioters unable to transform their justifiable anger and frustration at social injustice into a political programme that sought to set matters straight? Where were the articulate representatives of the ex-working classes capable of stepping forward to identify their enemy and the cause of their frustration? It may, as Millington (2013) claims, appear quite naïve to ask these questions and to assume that it is indeed possible for the contemporary urban poor to organise themselves politically, but these questions and our supposed naïvety reflect only our awareness that it has, throughout our history, been possible for the poorest to *do precisely that*. By the same token, communities suffering under far worse material conditions than those experienced by the rioters of 2011 have, time after time, stepped forward to challenge – and occasionally topple – vested interests and seemingly immovable power elites. To point that out is neither cynical nor naïve, it is simply factual.

Our factually grounded analysis, then, addresses a specific historical epoch that is patently failing to equip marginalised populations with the intellectual and political capital that might allow them to grasp the utility – and the beauty – of political solidarity, universality and egalitarianism. We inhabit a conjuncture in which cynicism reigns, and faith that a political and economic alternative to our present way of life is possible has virtually disappeared; a conjuncture in which the incisive ideologies of the new capitalism have met with huge success in incorporating the majority into the system's project of continuity. Ultimately, the rioters said nothing when they had clear cause to speak up, because they had been stripped of any lexicon of political opposition that might have allowed them to identify their true enemy and a realistic alternative to contemporary liberal capitalism.

In a conjuncture in which genuine politics has been almost entirely expunged, in which the ideologies of contemporary capitalism are so triumphant, so expansive and so absorbent that they can incorporate and utilise almost all forms of cultural dissent, and in which anger and frustration continue to pile up in such abundance, there is no other route forwards. 'Meaningless' violence is the only language for the poor to draw upon. Ultimately, however, it communicates nothing other than rage in its raw form. There is no positivity in its message, because it remains detached from any form of clear and comprehensible political symbolism. Surrounded by the false-positive freedoms of consumerism and the negative freedoms of liberal democracy, fragmented by the dominant discourses of the sovereign individual and cultural pluralism, the poor are effectively denied an alternative discourse that might allow them to articulate their deeper *unfreedom* (Žižek, 2002). The freedom to shop, the freedom to vote, the freedom to choose one's own god, the freedom to aggressively pursue one's own interests, the freedom to separate oneself from all social obligations, the freedom to discard identities and recreate them at a whim: all of these things cover up a deeper unfreedom, an unfreedom that we believe was felt but not articulated by the rioters. The stripping away of alternative ideologies that might once have allowed us to grasp the reality of our situation, a process we discussed earlier in the book, is an incredibly powerful act of symbolic violence, and it is one that secures the continuity of capitalist universalism.

For us, the tone of much of the academic commentary on the riots reveals the inability or unwillingness of many on the academic left to move forward and develop new accounts of what contemporary parliamentary capitalism is capable of in the absence of a potent and coherent oppositional ideology, and what it threatens to do to human civilisation in the years ahead. In an attempt to offer alternatives to the standard conservative discourse of immorality and poor socialisation, some of the articles that addressed the riots identified tensions between the police and black residents (see King, 2013), whereas other articles lazily repeated the basic tenets of what we already know – the parlous objective conditions of the poor's existence, their stigmatisation and their reactive anger (see, for example, Cooper, 2012; Platts-Fowler, 2013). In this body of left liberal analysis, there is no account of ideology, no account of the consumer motivations that drove the looting and no account of the gradual erasure of coherent forms of collective politics and political repre-sentation. Obviously, neither is there any account of the deeper global economic transformations that have destroyed the productive economy and made Britain reliant upon low-grade service work and the tax revenues that trickle down from the financial services industry. Instead, David Cameron and his coalition government are identified as the evil-doers who have chosen to reduce the employment prospects of the poor, attack the welfare state and pursue vindictive criminal justice policies. If motivations are discussed at all, the reader is offered the image of a pragmatic-rationalist rioter who, when pushed too far by elites in government and their uniformed representatives in the police, responds with violence against the forces of oppression. Arguing from this position actively prevents interested readers from coming to terms with the forces that propelled Cameron and his government towards austerity and those that prevent the adoption of an alternative economic model that might actually be capable of providing people with reasonably rewarding jobs and curtailing the bitterness, fear, anger and enmity that hums away constantly in the background in England's poorest neighbourhoods.

Sticking rigidly to a one-dimensional critical account of the objective circumstances of the poor, while piously and unthinkingly chastising all who might seek to go beyond this account as closet Thatcherites and apologists for global capitalism (see especially Cooper, 2012; Platts-Fowler, 2013), suggests a deep fear of more complex and detailed accounts. The kernel of this fear is the truly terrifying possibility that talking honestly about the disintegration of ex-working-class neighbourhoods and community life, the decline of true working-class politics and the objectless frustration and blind apolitical anger that gave rise to the nihilistic acting out that we saw on the streets in August 2011 might reveal the ultimate intellectual and political exhaustion of the academic liberal Left. Its key constituencies, still trapped in the defunct discourses of nineteenth-century philanthropy and post-war hippy counter-culturalism, simply cannot come to terms with the reality of contemporary capitalism and the total inability of electoral democracy and its public services to prevent it from riding roughshod over what remains of the social and constantly disrupting the lives of millions. Instead, these things are considered off limits, as the academic liberal Left instead busily covers up reality and argues for new civil rights, more and better jobs, restored public services and increases to the minimum wage – without, of course, showing any detailed knowledge of the systemic adjustments necessary to make even these moderate concessions possible. Critique is good, it appears, but only when it is directed at their enemies on the political right and defends the myth of the noble and politicised 'working class' and the efficacy of the public services – such as youth work – to which some of these critics are professionally attached. Contemporary critical analysis of the actual socio-economic system in which we all live now seems beyond the remit of mainstream social science.

Buried under the endless skirmish between the liberal Left and liberal Right over the efficacy of their marginally different ways of managing capitalism's social problems is the real political problem of our times: the truly oppressive ideology that denies all alternatives a reasonable hearing is liberalism itself. Its dead democratic system, its promise of freedom without any consideration of what freedom is, what is being set free or where it might take us, its regressive ontological models that stress rationality and autonomy, its entirely unproductive obsession with the undialectical state–individual relation, the shrill bickering of its identity politics – all of these things, and a good deal more besides, create a pressing need for a renewed analysis of contemporary liberalism and its role in the reproduction of capitalism.

If the role of the liberal Left is to curtail the excesses of the liberal Right, and yet, generally speaking, miseries continue to pile up on top of each other, might it not be time to extricate ourselves from compulsory liberalism in order to think critically about its obvious limitations and how the interests of the people might be better served? Everywhere, liberals obsess about freedom. The answer to the problems of today appears to be obvious: equip individuals with more freedoms. The term 'freedom' is used with such abandon, but it is rarely understood. Might it not be time to free ourselves from the debilitating discourse of 'freedom'? Anyone with any connection to the real world and its troubles must now conclude that we need to build a world in which obligations to others, rather than freedoms for the self, are centrally positioned.

In a similar way, many left liberals chastise those who have identified consumer motivations among the rioters. These commentators position themselves as the oppressed outsider offering a radically different, deeply unfashionable, but absolutely necessary, intellectual corrective to the dominant narrative that has developed in the social sciences. This is pure mythology, a deliberate attempt to transform reality to better suit their intellectual agenda. In fact, the vast majority of academic articles in the social sciences that address the riots ignore capitalism, consumerism and anything else that might appear difficult and off the beaten track, to focus upon the social context of widening inequalities and falling job opportunities. Consumerism has been discussed in some detail (see, for example, Bauman, 2011; Moxon, 2011; Žižek, 2011; Tester, 2012; Miles, 2014), and this is reasonable enough, given the obvious consumer motivations of many of those who looted high-end retailers in London, Birmingham and Manchester city centres, but it is absurd to suggest that accounts of consumerism have achieved some kind of hegemony in academic explanations for the riots. Rather, there has been a notice-able rush on the liberal left to simplify and dismiss any account of consumerism, in order to leave a pathway open to defend the rioters from the predatory right-wing media and identify the usual suspects of inequality and declining job opportunities. Many left liberals have displayed a strong desire to continue the entirely unproductive slanging match with a virtually non-existent academic right wing. This mythical Goliath magically becomes the oppressive majority, and so the real oppressive majority – the liberal Left who control all the key positions in the system – can continue to play their customary but now completely reversed role of the oppressed minority waging a heroic and interminable against-the-odds struggle. Rather than analyse the reality of our times, the liberal left social scientific establishment is content to cry freedom and continue its war with the *Daily Mail*.

To suggest that those who looted stores during the riots were motivated in some way by the hypnotic power of consumerism is not the same as suggesting that they are morally deficient or too weak to pursue a nobler political calling. There is no direct critique of the rioters in these accounts at all (ibid.), and it is ridiculous to respond as if that were so. Rather, it is to identify the ubiquity and power of consumerism's sign-value system and position this in relation to the *absence of anything else* that might have occupied the rioters at the very moment when the police had retreated and left the rioters in almost total control of the streets. Consumerism, for the rioters, is not an absolute, unrivalled Good that dominates every waking moment. Rather, the power of consumerism to mediate relationships and transform the image that bounces back at the individual from the social mirror must be set against a background of stark negativity. Consumerism characterised the riots and appeared to exist as a positivity for the rioters precisely because there was nothing else that might win their hearts, and precisely because it existed against this background of stark negativity, cynicism, individualism and lack. At the very moment of their carnivalesque triumph, with the police on the back foot and with control of the streets, what did they do with their new-found raw freedom?

If we review the literature that talks about consumerism in relation to the riots, and if we do this honestly, instead of constructing a standard 'straw target' argument, we can see that these authors are actually attempting to draw our attention to the incisive nature of liberal capitalist ideology. When left liberals choose to read this critique as a critique of the rioters rather than capitalism's sign-value system, we gain some insight into their own restrictive intellectual commitments. For them, of course, the subject is always rational and calculative and simply cannot have the wool pulled over its eyes by capitalist ideology, or anything else. There is no ideology that pushes and pulls the subject and intrudes upon its extimacy to reshape drive and desire and bond the subject to the reproduction of the present. Instead, we get a kind of inverted neo-liberal analysis in which the individual is a fully self-creating agent, understands immediately the forces that surround him and acts with careful forethought as he plots out alternative behavioural paths. The economic freedom of the liberal Right is displaced by the sociocultural freedom of the liberal Left, but beyond that there is not a great deal to distinguish the two approaches. In the standard left liberal account, the rioter, in full communion with his fellows, was so disgusted that his freedom had been curtailed by government, corporations and the police that he struck out in self-defence to re-establish the boundary over which oppression and exploitation may not pass.

All of this suggests to us the limitations of the left liberal social scientific project and the inability of its adherents to drive new research agendas that reflect the reality of the world in which we live. They do an efficient, if rather repetitive, job of identifying complex shades of intersectional injustice and waging their war of constant iconoclasm, but they have been noticeably silent on actually offering productive intellectual or political routes forward. They often express their disgust at the injustices of capitalism, but they are not so disgusted that they are willing openly to advocate an alternative to it. Instead, they hope that democracy will magically heal itself, and a plucky band of social liberals will find their way into office with a mandate to curb capitalism's excessively destructive aspects. One imagines that they hope to achieve an unlikely homeostatic balance between all the various interest groups that comprise the postmodern liberal multitude, where each group is satisfied with its freedoms and not yet angry about the comparative freedoms achieved by other interest groups. For them, however, there is little or no desire to move beyond parliamentary capitalism, and we must imagine that this is because they subscribe to the liberal belief that everything that is not parliamentary capitalism will inevitably prove to be a good deal worse.

For them, the answer to structural injustice is to increase structural justice, which is rather like saying that the answer to an overly cold room is to increase the temperature, but quite how this is to be achieved remains a mystery. The answer to declining job opportunities and increasing workplace precariousness is for government to provide more and better jobs, but again they don't tell us how this can be done in a recently reversed global economy that has been reconfigured to ensure that Western nations consume and poor Eastern nations produce, so that the circulation of capital can be accelerated and continue to make business oligarchs very rich. Let's face facts: It is so easy to demand more social justice. It is dead simple to win friends by suggesting that more should be done to help the poor. We can go on indefinitely identifying particular interest groups for whom we need to do more. Proposing that the power elite curtail socially and ecologically harmful practices is a breeze. Who in the contemporary social sciences could be against such things? Talking in impassioned tones about those things we are against and demanding that myriad technical changes in social policy and the welfare system should be made, in order to do what our currently limited political will and resources will allow to be done about them, are, ultimately, a cinch. Moving beyond this to identify a positive route forwards is a far more demanding intellectual and political task. However, it is absolutely imperative that we take on this task, if we are to rejuvenate the increasingly formulaic social sciences. And, far more importantly, it is vital that we produce and popularise a positive and comprehensible account of what a post-capitalist society might look like, if we are to avoid the gradual exhaustion of the spirit and the disintegration of what currently exists.

Politics on our own terms

In an article in which he portrays the rioters of 2011 as latter-day revolutionaries driven by a sense of unity and common cause, Gareth Millington (2013) suggests that the cynics of the far Left who have proclaimed our entry into a post-political era are totally wrong. If they were to broaden their conception of politics, they would be able to see a far more positive picture of a brand new form of mass politicisation that bodes well for the political Left. For Millington, and many others on the liberal left, politics is alive and well and plays an active part in the communal life of England's marginalised populations.

We have already countered this dead position elsewhere in the book, and so there is little sense in repetition. Instead, before moving on with our own account of the riots, we will simply recapitulate the main point that the systematic broadening of the field of politics, a technique that was central to post-1960s cultural studies, fragmented and incapacitated the political Left in a way that made a major contribution to its heavy defeat in the 1980s. The act of broadening the field of politics allowed the Left to accept the continuing triumph of global capitalism as it celebrated its myriad small victories on the field of culture and identity politics. No victory had been forthcoming on the field of traditional politics, and so the liberal radicals of the 1960s appear to have taken the decision to broaden the field of politics to the extent that it subsumed the entire field of culture and all the mundane and apolitical activity that transpires on it. From then on, the most inconsequential of cultural activities could be reinterpreted to identify some micro-structure of oppression, domination and resistance. Put simply, politics invited into its domain the whole constellation of specific and often separatist cultural issues that would eventually colonise and destroy it. Politically disabling cultural separatism was the destination at which cultural pluralism would inevitably arrive. Whether this was simply an unfortunate accident or a contingency known to post-war liberalism is a moot point.

A huge amount of intellectual effort has been applied to charting cultural opposition to authoritarianism and oppressive social structures. Indeed, whole libraries have been written about myriad forms of cultural insubordination, subversion and resistance. Strangely enough, though, despite the huge effort, all this counter-hegemonic cultural activity hasn't borne a great deal of fruit on the political stage. It is certainly difficult to maintain that we are now, in the year 2014, fundamentally and in all dimensions better off as a society than we were in the 1950s and 1960s. This is not to say that there have been no significant and very welcome advances in some areas, but things have certainly got a good deal worse in others. The juggernaut of capitalism remains with us. Indeed, in many respects it appears more secure in its position and destructive in its relentless expansion and colonisation than it has ever been.

The broadening of the field of politics that occurred during the 1960s, the effects of which remain with us still, should be understood quite simply as what it is: capitulation to the restoration of a pure form of capitalism in the wake of the failure of state socialism and communism and the retraction of the political and economic concessions that made post-war social democracy possible. It represented an acceptance that capitalism could not be vanquished. This wrong move meant that the political Left lost touch with its core principles, principles that must now be returned to the centre if it is to have any chance of moving forward. Ultimately, the reconceptualisation of politics that occurred during the 1960s and reached its apogee during the postmodernism of the 1980s and early 1990s – and remains with us today in the work of Millington and many others – is an admission by the liberal Left that it can achieve no victory and no supremacy on the field of political economy. In the absence of politics, the ideology of the market continues to be transformed into the everyday logic of economics. The field of economic practice is thus depoliticised and allowed to present itself to the world as an objective science. The Left concedes defeat on this field, and so concedes defeat on the only battleground on which it is possible to create genuine equality, and instead shifts its focus entirely to culture and the battle against biological predestination and oppressive social conventions. The chasm between economics and politics/culture, which was initially excavated by right-wing classical liberals in the eighteenth century, has been maintained and widened – after social democracy built a few fragile bridges in the mid twentieth century – with the active collusion of the liberal Left from the 1960s. The class struggle was dismissed as an old and restrictive discourse that could be quietly forgotten, and the era of liberal identity politics moved centre stage. Identity politics continues to dominate the Left, which, generally, fights for the rights of interest groups but steadfastly refuses to engage in universalist accounts of class struggle. However, as we saw with the rise of the Occupy movement, which by comparison made the established liberal Left look like the ashen-faced zombie that it is, things are slowly and sporadically beginning to change, although perhaps not quite with the momentum we need.

In the post-political climate created by late-modern liberalism, the suggestion that the rioters of 2011 were animated by a drive for equality and unity is pure wishful thinking. It represents a turning away from a bleak post-political reality to live in a dream world, in which an organic drive for equality magically flourishes on the barren wastelands of the neo-liberal revanchist city. This tendency to project one's own political yearnings on to marginalised and depoliticised subjectivities reaches its intellectual pinnacle in the work of Akram (2014), who provides the most complex account of oppositional politics in the riots of 2011. Central to Akram's work is the claim that the riotous subject carries with it a 'preconscious' commitment to progressive politics. She admits that politics were not articulated or practised by those who rioted in England in 2011, and she implicitly concedes that the rioters had no conscious grasp of the politics that she claims drove them to act as they did. However, she maintains that politics is in there somewhere, working its magic behind the scenes, a fundamental, irrefutable and essentially organic political orientation that shapes the subject and its social identity and foments opposition to the injustices of capitalism. The subject has no conscious access to this raw form of politics, and so it cannot be articulated, and no evidence can be provided to indicate that it does in fact exist. Akram draws on the work of Pierre Bourdieu (1990), but she fundamentally misunderstands, or deliberately misinterprets, his central concept of habitus. Habitus, as Bourdieu understood it, is an internalised guide to the *dominant external logic of practice*, not a site for reflexive thought, and nor is it an internal source of oppositional pre-political impulses to be stirred into action as the individual is exposed to inequality and structural injustice.

This convenient misunderstanding allowed Akram to project her preferred politics on to the 'preconsciousness' of entirely depoliticised, postmodern subjectivities. For her, politics existed in abundance in a historical epoch characterised by the absolute, unchallenged supremacy of capitalism in the West. The absorption of potentially political young people into the depoliticising surrogate social order of consumer culture appears obvious to us, but Akram refuses to look this painful reality full in the face. Instead, she creates a fantastic intellectual framework that gives the liberal Left a welcome boost of energy and another opportunity to deny the systematic depoliticisation and ideological neutralisation of the ex-working classes. This framework enables her audience to keep on believing that oppositional politics reproduces itself organically in our most marginalised neighbourhoods. For the liberal Left, the subject who inhabits these spaces dreams of changing the world to fit in with their ethical preferences, rather than dreaming of changing themselves into a winner within the existing capitalist system. Why did the rioters choose to do harm to each other and their environment, if they were indeed equipped with the 'preconscious' motivation to advance a political response to their parlous social and economic circumstances? Why did they loot stores that sold valued consumer items, when they could have pressed a case for equality and social justice? The absolute failure of the liberal Left to engage with the reality of the riots and its dogged refusal to engage in reflexive self-criticism around its core domain assumptions leave the road open for the political Right to push its account of subjective and familial pathology deeper into the popular consciousness.

The context of consumer culture

Millington (2013) also tells post-political pessimists that one only has to listen to the voices of the rioters to discover a much more positive truth. We did, and in previous work (see Treadwell *et al.*, 2013) these voices were unanimous in expressing consumer motivations for joining the riots. No awareness of their structural position in the world was apparent, only a vague, objectless and directionless anger. Even in those accounts where rioters have talked of falling employment opportunities and their hatred of the police, they do not present these things in political terms. Instead, researchers have endeavoured to broaden the definition of politics so that these things can be presented as inherently 'political'. If the rioter is angry that she cannot get a job, or because she cannot access reasonably supportive welfare systems, why should we immediately assume that this anger reflects a general orientation to oppositional politics or even a desire to regulate and humanise liberal capitalism? Why should we not assume that her anger springs from a thwarted desire to get ahead within capitalism? Why do we imagine that the rioter is kicking against capitalism, rather than at her perceived failure within it?

The tendency to reduce politics to anger and thus inappropriately conflate the two concepts is displayed in much of the left-of-centre literature that addresses the riots. To us, this reveals the depressing extent of the liberal Left's failure and its general unwillingness to re-engage its opponent on the field of political economy. It also suggests that the cultural turn was a monumental mistake that has denied younger leftists the edification of more challenging intellectual accounts of what political struggle is and what it entails. The sociological and criminological Left should be engaging in a stringent ideology critique that treats capitalism as a worthy and powerful opponent, currently in complete dominance and completely dedicated to its own continuity. To believe that we are subverting its rule by playing around with the social symbolism of music and clothes and breaking into high-street shops is madness. Anger without accompanying political symbolism is just anger. Unless we can identify a destination, a world we want to live in and one we are willing to fight to create, anger will continue simply to be acted out in an unproductive and politically blind manner. It is only when we equip those who took to the streets in August 2011 with a persuasive and coherent account of what is and what something better might look like that we will begin to see genuine movement.

Of course, constructing such an account is a hugely challenging task. Telling the West's consumerised populations that, in all likelihood, they will have to get by with less is a very difficult sell. Ultimately, if we are to avoid catastrophe, we need to change our dreams, not simply get angry about our inability to realise them.

6

WHAT WAS OCCUPY?

The Occupy movement came to prominence in 2011, three years into a global economic crisis that began with the collapse of Lehman Brothers, the fourth largest investment bank in the United States (see Horsley, 2014, for an overview). Unemployment, underemployment, home repossessions and falling wages were severely affecting the lifestyles of many millions of people across the country. The US government had spent hundreds of billions of dollars bailing out corporations, banks and other financial institutions (see Barofsky, 2013), and its quantitative easing programme, which ran from 2009 to 2013, appeared to be yet another measure geared towards safeguarding the financial security of the richest (see Harvey, 2014). Inequality had risen to levels not seen since the Great Depression (Picketty, 2014), and there was widespread popular anger at the injustice of it all.

The movement began in Zuccotti Park in New York, close to the Wall Street institutions believed by most to bear the bulk of the responsibility for the crisis. It quickly spread across the United States and to other countries around the world. For a year or more, the West had looked on as the Arab Spring unfolded, and, in the early news broadcasts covering the protest, there seemed to be a sense of anxiety – and perhaps, in quarters, anticipation and hope – that the Occupy movement might signal the dawning of a new revolutionary age in the West. In this chapter, we want to investigate the nature of the Occupy movement and think through what the movement can tell us about contemporary political protest.

Before we begin, we should first of all acknowledge our support for the people who protested. Even though, in general terms, the number of protestors present at Occupy sites was often quite small, and despite the mainstream media's tendency to deride the protestors as a bunch of dreadlocked middle-class hippies, totally divorced from the pressures of the real world (see, for example, Wilkes *et al.*, 2011), those who took to the streets in 2011 really did stand for the 99 per cent. Their ultimate failure to change the world – or even fulfil the more modest task of compelling democratically elected leaders to curtail policies that further enriched the corporate and financial elites – tells us much about our predicament today. They could not re-engage the great mass of depoliticised consumers across the West who had so much to gain from Occupy's ultimate aim of holding the anti-social rich to account, nor could they construct and popularise a comprehensible alternative to the present capitalist system. The rise of the Occupy movement is, nonetheless, important. Its partial successes can be built upon, and, one hopes, future leftist political movements can learn from its mistakes.

The return of universalism

Occupy did a reasonable job of identifying the ultimate cause of the pressures and frustrations that were bearing down upon so many ordinary Americans, but, for us, one of the most appealing aspects of Occupy's discourse was what was missing, what it did not say. Occupy transcended the debilitating logic of identity politics, which had bogged down the Left since the 1960s, and once again sought to problematise the capitalist system itself. The success of its core slogans – 'We are the 99 percent' and 'Justice for the 99 percent' – had an appealing air of class antagonism. Occupy had broken free from the restraints imposed upon leftist politics to identify its true enemy. It was not calling for a particular interest group to get a better deal out of capitalism, nor was it calling for a particular interest group to be first in line when it came time for governments to allocate resources. Instead, the protesters appeared to construct a simple, universal project that ignored cultural particularities in a way that brought together the 99 per cent and identified their shared interests: not more justice for women, ethnic minorities, minority sexualities, welfare recipients, illegal immigrants, prisoners and so on, but *justice for everyone*, irrespective of gender, skin colour, religion, sexual orientation or the region of birth. This is the key issue that prevents us from cynically dismissing those involved as latter-day hippies keen to encourage those at the top of our political and economic systems to be a little nicer to society's victims. This is the reason why we can't suggest that the movement was immediately incorporated by the ruling ideology. The rediscovery of political universalism is, without doubt, a significant development for the Left.

Crucial to the construction of this new political universalism was the identification of the absent 1 per cent as the source of post-crash social disruption and the true enemy of the people. Occupy pushed past the ideological injunction to respect the talents and achievements of the super-rich. It disregarded the absurd political claim that our economies and the livelihoods of ordinary men and women are dependent upon the boundless talents and calculated risk-taking of the corporate and financial elite. Instead, the super-rich were portrayed as parasites sucking the blood out of our society and economy. The super-rich had become so by appropriating the commons, by claiming for themselves what should be owned and enjoyed by all. The financial elites of Wall Street, ensconced in their skyscrapers just a short distance away, had enriched themselves enormously during the boom times and, when their reckless gambling failed to pay off, they had walked away from their debts, leaving the ordinary taxpayer, working in the real economy, to pick up the tab. It is this fundamental change, this rediscovery of the language of class struggle, that sets the Occupy movement apart. Of course, it is also absolutely true that the Occupy movement failed to take the crucial next step. The carnival of the protest and the pleasures that accompany the formation of a political community could not be carried forward into the phase that must follow, the phase in which the hard work of organisation begins. Instead, the energy of the initial protests dissipated, and the possibilities presented by the initial event were closed off before they could be fully acknowledged and acted upon.

Aggressively self-interested elite, reform thyself

So, what else can we say about the successes and failures of Occupy? How can we reach a reasonably objective judgement about its discourse and its challenge to our political and financial elites? How did the people respond to its message, and why did the movement ultimately run out of steam and disappear from the political scene almost entirely?

The Occupy movement did not produce a leader, and, although some spokespeople did step forward, no unequivocal statement of aims and principles was forthcoming. Its message tended to trickle through to the people on news broadcasts and in newspaper articles, blogs and other forms of electronic communication. Of course, the absence of an established leadership was attractive to many of those involved in the movement (Graeber, 2011), and this distrust of formalism and hierarchy appeared to reflect a certain anarchistic sensibility at the movement's core.

Occupy's refusal to construct a clear statement of aims and principles, concrete policy proposals or a blueprint for a better world has similarly been identified as a great strength of the movement, rather than a weakness. Instead of capitulating to the incessant demands of the consumerised media to utilise the tools provided by the established political discourse, Occupy stuck to its guns and, in so doing, opened up a space beyond liberal democracy into which a broad range of popular dissatisfactions might flow. Constructing clear policy suggestions would have blunted the movement's radical edge and forced it into the sphere of the ruling ideology. A demand for genuine historic change would have inevitably become a request for social democratic reform. At least initially, it seemed that Occupy's strident critique of social injustice would not succumb to the insistent call to talk in the language of parliamentary capitalism.

This is an interesting enough argument, but, to truly understand the implications of the absence of any policy, clear ideological affiliation and an initial blueprint for a post-capitalist society, we must address the cultural field that Occupy hoped to address. We must consider the expectations of those sitting at home and those who could have been recruited to the cause. We must also consider the present reality of our political system and the way it is understood by the majority of people.

The people at home, watching events unfold on their TVs, appeared to want an articulate representative to emerge who could distil the movement's goals into soundbites that could fit neatly into evening news broadcasts. They wanted political advertisements informing viewers precisely how the Occupy movement would boost their income, safeguard their economic position and protect them from threats to their security. It is certainly possible to imagine that the people at home wanted a political movement that aggressively represented their interests, but they also appeared to want one that would slot neatly into the established political framework and ask nothing in return except an appropriately placed cross on a ballot paper. Democracy and the electoral process, of course, had emerged relatively unscathed from the 2008 crash. People were aware that elections failed to change things, but they still could not see a more appealing alternative, and Occupy could not bring such a thing into view. The people seemed sure that all of politics needed to take place on the field of electoral democracy. Only barbarism and totalitarianism existed beyond it.

Before we go any further, we should also note that a fundamental issue, the truly titanic challenge facing the entirety of the Left, appeared to hang over events like a cloud. Occupy's failure to address this issue in a way deemed appropriate by the media and the citizenry caused many to lose patience with the protestors before eventually dismissing them as a political irrelevance. For the viewing public, the Occupy movement was momentarily distracting, but it was ultimately incapable of dragging them away from the lures of the ruling ideology and towards a comprehensive, powerful and attractive opposite.

This 'titanic challenge' is the demand that the Left must identify a solution, politicise the masses and hopefully be the vehicle for the solution's ultimate realisation. That challenge is to provide a clear and compelling answer to the fundamental question: If not this, then what?

Democracy in America

A leader capable of identifying a productive route forwards might have changed things for Occupy. The Left today could certainly use a forceful political figurehead, driven by resolute ideological commitment, who inspires political allegiance and who is capable of establishing herself as a just authority figure in the eyes of the disengaged consuming public. The absence of hierarchy may have been appealing to many of the protestors who gave life to the movement and propelled it into the public consciousness, and to the Left's intellectual elite who supported from the side-lines, but this absence did little to persuade others that something new and powerful had developed, something capable of actually intervening in political life to address some of the diverse frustrations of ordinary Americans.

A leaderless Occupy did a reasonable job of drawing attention to those things that it was against, and to those things that were damaging the lifestyles of ordinary working people. Wall Street and its financial institutions were positioned as the enemy. For the first time in decades, a leftist political movement had made a spectacular appearance in the public's line of vision by identifying the capitalist system itself as the ultimate cause of disruption, the ultimate problem to be addressed and overcome. However, it could not identify an alternative to liberal capitalism that could be named and immediately understood. It failed to endorse an alternative politics that moved beyond vague platitudes about equality and fairness. In truth, these failures reflect deep historical trends that have dulled our capacity to believe that anything can be constructed that would improve upon parliamentary capitalism. These are not the failures of Occupy as such. Rather, they reflect the failure of our times to equip liberal capitalism's vocal antagonists with the symbolic weapons necessary to take on a powerful, skilled and deeply entrenched opponent. Inspiring and transforming an individualised, consumerised and depoliticised public into a new political community, united in its shared faith in a better world, was beyond Occupy. For the moment at least, the creation of such a community remains the stuff of dreams.

The people watching events unfold at home on their TVs wanted a political alternative presented to them gift-wrapped, in the standard post-political democratic form. They didn't want to become involved in an active protest movement, with all of the associated sacrifices and risks. Despite its obvious flaws, democracy asks only that concerned citizens take a few minutes to cast a vote every five years or so. Here, a deeper and more arduous political commitment appeared to be necessary. A significant portion of the people were angry, but were they angry enough to get off the sofa and head out on to the streets? Were they angry enough to risk state violence and arrest, or did they hope that others would express their anger and enact their opposition on their behalf?

Unfortunately, for the moment at least, it seems impossible for these critics to take the next step and see that the democratic system itself is preventing progressive change. Of course, everyone is entitled to vote, and anyone can run for office (at least formally). If one is elected and enjoys popular support, it is possible for real change to occur. But in practice all of this is nonsense. It is difficult to imagine what progressive change can now emerge from the USA's democratic system. Those dissatisfied with life are instructed to get involved in the existing democratic apparatus and, in so doing, reform government and drive the country forwards, but the ideological content of this instruction is patently obvious. Electoral democracy militates against genuine social change and enforces a horizon of the possible. Only piecemeal reform can take place, and, as we can see with Obama's presidency, everything appears set up to ensure that even small-scale reform cannot take place unless it paradoxically acts to further free the individual from overbearing government, which of course frees the rich far more than the poor. The perceived openness and fairness of the system is a mirage, a particularly effective ideological screen that disguises the reality of the system and ensures the reproduction of what currently exists. The ideology of progressive electoral democracy acts to convince the public that genuine change, when it is the will of the people, remains entirely possible. In this way, the purity of the democratic ideal remains in place. Electoral democracy is still considered the best possible means of organising a free society.

Despite the fact that there exists considerable criticism of democracy-in-action, democracy itself remains entirely legitimate, and a better system simply cannot be imagined. Liberalism's drive to stem the free flow of the utopian imagination has prevented any open discussion of what might exist beyond the borders of contemporary parliamentary capitalism. Instead, we are instructed to accept that there are only two options available to us: we can stick with democracy, or we can abandon it and return to the dark ages of totalitarianism and dictatorship.

Of course, a significant proportion of the overall population was angry about economic insecurity and unemployment, and much else besides, but Occupy could not reach out to the broader population to capitalise on this anger. It couldn't bond those struggling and dissatisfied with their lot under liberal capitalism to the core goals of the Occupy movement. Occupy lacked the structures, networks and community organisations that might have been used to encourage ordinary people to connect their personal troubles to those experienced by many others throughout the class system. Some will no doubt claim that things had not quite descended far enough for a significant number of citizens to support a radical political break of the type suggested by Occupy. Poverty needed to advance still further, unemployment needed to rise, more empirical evidence needed to emerge of the inherent injustices of capitalism and its tendency to concentrate wealth in the hands of the few.

There is an element of truth in all of this, but, as we have tried to emphasise, anger, deprivation and knowledge of corruption do not immediately produce a drive for social justice and political transformation. People can remain angry and impoverished for decades, centuries even, without setting out to engineer political change. Basic ideological precepts capable of transforming the way the individual understands his relationship to the socio-economic system need to be in place. The ultimate source of one's anger and hardship needs to be identified, and then one must acknowledge that others experience similar hardships as *concrete universals*, various real, experienced effects of the same objective, systemic cause. Then, crucially, there needs to be hope and belief that, when the cause of one's dissatisfaction is neutralised, something else, something positive and appealing, might be constructed that sets matters straight and acts to prevent the rise of an equivalent disruptive cause. A significant part of politics, properly understood, should revolve around the clear identification of this 'something else', this other world that might be brought into existence. Only then will we be able to see clearly what we are protesting *for* in addition to what we are protesting *against*.

Because Occupy could not symbolically close the distance between itself and those watching the protest at home, it could not persuade enough hard-pressed individuals to re-evaluate their personal struggles in light of Occupy's account of capitalism's inevitable negative outcomes. The concrete universal became more concrete, but could not become universal. And, of course, as several commentators have observed, Occupy appeared to possess a habitus slightly at odds with that displayed by the ex-working class watching at home, the population who must be recruited to the cause if it is to have any chance of success. The protesters were often presented as the educated, liberal middle class, and so they were, by implication, actual beneficiaries of the system they were attempting to call to account. Who were they to complain, when so many others had it tougher? Numerous newspaper articles poured scorn on the radical credentials of the protesters and portrayed them as spoiled brats who should get a job and stop complaining. Much of this hostile media commentary was a standard ideological strategy that sought to transform Occupy into a joke, in order to prevent the working classes from connecting to its discourse, but the huge material and cultural gap that existed between the potentially vanguardist Occupy movement and the ex-working classes was nonetheless important in alienating populations and determining the outcome of the protests.

For Occupy to really follow through on its initial promise, it needed to traverse this huge chasm that divided its reasonably informed protestors from the great mass of ordinary workers who were struggling to make ends meet. Of course, for the majority of debt-ridden workers in the real economy, the great hope is not to step into some radically indeterminate future of shifting polymorphous subjectivities, but to secure reasonably stable exploitation in the form of a steady job with regular income. For most workers, the importance of staying employed pushes all other considerations to the margins. Politics, the economy, interest rates, bailouts, quantitative easing, Wall Street: what did these things matter, when one had to focus on getting and keeping a job, paying the rent and feeding one's family?

In contemporary consumer culture, it is almost impossible for the individual worker to fully comprehend the complex factors that have turned the battle to remain socially and economically included into a perilous tightrope walk across a gaping chasm, at the bottom of which lie exclusion, penury and the psychological punishment of feeling worthless and forgotten. This is why community and workplace organisation and the party form, where people can learn to trust and rely on each other in real situations, remain so important for leftist politics (see Dejours, 2003). An appreciation of equality and solidarity does not develop organically. It is not a natural outcome of living 'together' under the capitalist system as isolated monads, connected only by the electronic communications apparatus. It has to be actively created and nurtured in real life and real time. People must be equipped with an ideological means of grasping the reality of their position and encouraged to imagine something better. Enabling workers to see that they suffer the same frustrations for the same reasons can lead to an acknowledgement of shared interests that can be advanced as well as defended. Constructing a clear political programme that centres on core principles is crucial. Political ideology can enable individuals to understand their own debilitating anger and frustration in a new way, and, to some extent at least, politics allows the individual to deposit his anger in a broader political narrative that promises a future reckoning in which all of life's perceived injustices are set straight (see Žižek, 2008; Sloterdijk, 2012).

As the Occupy movement got under way, the political Left in America appeared to be in such a parlous, fragmented condition that the institutions and organisations that might have once enabled a politicised vanguard to reach out to ordinary workers were no longer operative. Many on the left believe the Internet can fill the gaps left by the disintegration of modern political organisations, but online discussion forums and the like simply do not work in the same way. This is not to say that new forms of medium cannot assist political resistance, especially in communicating very quickly repressive political practices that appear to demand an immediate response, but it is hard to imagine how they might compensate for the immediate social engagement that accompanied, for example, the establishment of labour unions and workers' associations. Internet forums cannot reach out to the disinterested or the antagonistic and, over a prolonged period of time, seek to educate, persuade and establish trust and a shared vision. They cannot encourage the disengaged to become attuned to the attractions of progressive politics by interacting daily in bodily proximity with others keen to connect their shared situation to forces beyond their immediate comprehension. In the absence of everyday mass encounters in exploitative work situations, the task of building the kinds of organisation that might politicise the depoliticised is huge. The atomisation, withdrawal and possessive individualism that characterise consumer culture act as a mediatory bulwark against the formation of new political communities keen to move beyond capitalism (Baudrillard, 2007; Winlow and Hall, 2013). Still, this is work that needs to be done. Leftist political movements and the individuals who comprise them must display a fidelity to the event if they are to progress their cause.

The event of Occupy

Understandably enough, some critics have argued that the Occupy movement was essentially 'post-ideological'. As time wore on, prominent members of the movement appeared to recognise the value in giving their audience principled policy suggestions, and these, almost inevitably, tended to focus on the negative ambition of curtailing the worst excesses of liberal capitalism. Even a radical protest movement such as Occupy – which, in its strategies, tone and ambition, represented a major departure from the established pattern of leftist political engagement – appeared to display reformist tendencies. Occupy London (see occupylondon. org.uk), for example, identified its commitment to the improved regulation of business in its initial statement and clearly remained dedicated to the democratic ideal. It also displayed a strangely naïve faith in the justice system, fighting an eviction notice through the courts, and much of the material on its website – encouraging visitors to sign petitions, passing on information about the extent of corporate tax avoidance and so on – appears liberal, reformist and entirely restricted to constant communicative interaction in a general Habermasian sense, an abstract negativity strangely at odds with the initial radicalism, universality and promise of the 99 percent movement. Automatically, it would seem, as if it knew no other way to go, Occupy busied itself with the negation of its own promise of negation.

Even amid the tumult of a radical political event, the choice to abandon the promise of the new and instead attempt to reform and revitalise what exists remains a beguiling prospect. These significant moments, roughly equivalent to Lacanian

(2007) quilting points, are scattered through social reality. They condense the present into moments of concrete universality pregnant with the potential to launch our lives, cultures and societies in a radically different direction. If we have the fortitude to carry them forward and see them through, to negate the system and create the space for positive displacements, we find our reality transformed in ways that would have been hard to imagine before the event began.

But these events are not magically imbued with transformative power in and of themselves. They are animated by human subjects, who, of course, interpret and respond differently to the event's symbolism. The individual can be transformed and see life anew in light of what has transpired. Some might immediately abandon their established priorities, dismissing them as an irrelevance in comparison with the possibilities revealed by the event. Alternatively, the individual can dismiss these moments as frivolous or unimportant, or polluted by pointless and risky idealism. They can reject the potential of the event or reduce it to an illusion, or mere wishful thinking. It is easier to return to the normal rhythm of our lives than to confront the event head on. It is easier to dismiss the substance of the event as a pipe dream than it is to reconstruct the self in an act of fidelity to the event's potential, and it is easier to snatch at a small victory when, with effort, resilience and determination, a much greater one might have been achieved.

So it is with political events that develop as a response to the injustices of contemporary liberal capitalism. We can dismiss the utopian imagination as misguided and focus on attempting to secure small concessions from incumbent power. We can continue to complain in isolation and believe that every opposition movement is corrupted in some way and ultimately doomed to failure. We can quickly proclaim victory and head home – thus avoiding the conflict that must come – when no victory of any consequence has been achieved. Or, we can recognise and accept the hard work and personal sacrifice needed to generate the momentum that might carry us into a new historical epoch, less scarred by inequality, injustice, envy and isolation. The development of the Occupy movement could have been an event of genuine historical significance. Indeed, it might still prove to have been so; maybe it is too soon to tell. However, as we write these words, the potential of the movement appears to have ebbed away, and the opportunity to change history has been lost.

Ideology and post-ideology

The refusal of the protestors to name an ideology that could be placed in opposition to parliamentary liberal capitalism is more significant than it might appear. The act of enunciation concentrates political energies and opens up a space in which ideas can evolve. It is only when the idea is spoken that it is fully brought into being and becomes capable of eliciting commitment and affecting social reality. Rather than pursue this course, the protestors withheld clear ideological identification, preferring instead to reassert the movement's broad scope and universalism. There were to be no exclusions, be they ideological or otherwise, in the 99 percent movement.

The absence of a named ideological position is associated with broader forces that have eroded our capacity to consciously believe, forces that encourage us to presuppose a rational subject capable of mixing policies to maximise beneficial outcomes, and forces that impose a horizon of the possible upon politics and society. Even in these times of deep and enduring crisis, it seems that pragmatism rules and conscious ideological commitment alienates.

If a disavowed ideology was present at the heart of the movement, it's quite difficult to identify precisely what it was. The group was committed to equality, and elements of modern socialism and communism can be identified in its general discourse. It was a form of pacifist anarchism, however, that seemed to be most in evidence. The group's declaration of occupation (see occupywallst.org) was admirably radical and rooted in a materialist assessment of economic and social justice, but, as we have already noted, no real leadership emerged, and a great deal of emphasis was placed upon consensus building. The movement was also pacifist from the outset. Its violence was restricted to its desire to break from the present in the hope of producing a new egalitarian future. Its supporters established their camp, but did little else to provoke the forces of law and order. They appear not to have thought too far ahead about what they hoped to achieve. Instead, they appeared keen to simply register their disgust and dissatisfaction with liberal capitalism and hope to draw others to their cause. Where it would all lead, no one seemed to know. The initial occupation in Manhattan began with minimal planning, and parallel protests across the West quickly developed, as news spread of a new, leftist political movement. There was no organisation behind Occupy pulling the strings, and there was little in the way of established strategy. The movement developed and grew in a haphazard and unpredictable way. Would adjustments to various economic and social policies count as a victory, or did the protesters hope that they had kick-started a series of events that would lead to a non-violent revolution and the eventual establishment of a new society? There was no clear answer.

The refusal of the Occupy movement to identify itself with a named ideology was no doubt, at least in part, a pragmatic decision geared towards ensuring that the maximum number of people could find some utility in its message. But this, of course, returns us to an analysis of our 'post-ideological' times.

Badiou (2010a) maintains that communism is an eternal idea that can never be fully extinguished. It returns in each epoch to have its basic elements considered anew. These basic elements – especially communism's commitment to panoramic egalitarianism – can be put forward as answers to problems encountered as history unfolds. Communism, for Badiou, is always there, in the background, ready to be drawn upon as people appraise the problems, frustrations and injustices of social life in any given epoch. The core elements of communism endure, but other aspects of communism are entirely mutable and can present themselves in radically different forms, in different historical, social, cultural or geographical contexts. The communism of the past is not the communism of the future, and the communism of a small community is not the communism of a huge and diverse post-industrial society, save for the core elements that remain unchanged.

Ultimately, communism tells us that another world is possible, that individuals need not be ruthless competitors over their economic livelihoods, that society and economy can be reorganised, that the great benefits of our society and physical production system can be shared and used to enrich the lives of all, and that equality can become the central principle of a better way of life. It tells us of the benefits of mutuality and committing to the well-being of the collective, and in so doing it encourages us to look back at capitalism and conclude that it doesn't have to be this way; we do not have to be alienated from one another; we do not have to raise the acquisition of wealth above all other social considerations; we do not need to incite the envy of others. We can do better.

All of this was swirling around in Occupy's fragmented discourse, although it often tended to be expressed in the opposite form: not as a positive endorsement of these things, but as a negation of their opposite. For example, the endorsement of equality was expressed as a critique of inequality, and an endorsement of common ownership was expressed as a critique of private accumulation. It would, of course, have been self-defeating for Occupy protestors to identify themselves as 'communist', or indeed clearly align themselves with any of the ideologies on the broad left, not because there is necessarily a popular antagonism towards the principle of equality – although one of the great accomplishments of liberalism has been to gradually reform popular attitudes, to the extent that many individuals believe the experience of equality would negate established freedoms and act against the raw beauty of their own individual uniqueness – but because, in America, there is a long-running popular animosity towards ideology as such, and communism and socialism in particular. The terms have been systematically and thoroughly discredited throughout the country's modern history, even before the Stalinist disasters in the East.

Liberalism and conservativism have, since the end of the Second World War, come to work hand in hand. In the United States, 'liberalism' has evolved to the extent that it now means social liberalism, and 'conservatism' generally means right-wing liberalism, with an added and strangely postmodern touch of god-fearing Christianity, just to stop things going too far. Both right- and left-wing liberals appear dedicated to the democratic ideal, although it is becoming increasingly clear that, as the market moves on to its next phase, democratic oversight of the political apparatus may well be seen as a significant hindrance to capital accumulation and may be reduced, or sacrificed entirely, to ensure the continuity of markets.

Liberalism itself is widely disparaged, at least partly because so many people do not fully understand it, and in disparaging it they appear to be disparaging something else. However, whether the majority knows it or not, in the reality of everyday political economy liberalism is, quite clearly, the ideology that won. Its discourse shapes the politics of Left and Right in America, and its basic principles – from the unleashed forces of the market and the limited state to the sovereignty of the individual – have become the basic common sense that everyone takes for granted and that needs no longer to be discussed, because everyone is already in agreement. Liberalism has expanded its borders to such an extent that it has become increasingly possible for all individuals, no matter where they place themselves on the political spectrum, to identify themselves as in some way 'liberal'. This should encourage us to acknowledge the close connection between liberalism and the ruling ideology, or rather the place of contemporary liberalism within the ruling ideology. Liberalism defines huge swathes of mainstream politics, and, for many citizens, its core elements exist as pure *doxa* and are, therefore, beyond critical consideration.

In America, one might openly identify oneself as a conservative or a liberal, but this is a red herring, because the proper philosophical and ideological background to these things is quite separate from the way they are used in popular conversation and in mainstream political debate. All other ideologies are off the table. To identify oneself as a communist or a socialist is, in the eyes of a great many Americans, to say that one is against the democratic ideal and resolutely in favour of massively diminished civic freedoms, totalitarianism, dictatorship, the brutal treatment of minorities, the immiseration of the people by the oppressive state and much else besides. You may say that you believe that there should be a greater degree of equality than presently exists, and you may say the state should do more to assist the poor, but you may not say that you are a communist, at least not if you want to be taken seriously and remain safe. You may say that democracy needs to be overhauled, and that corporate power is corrupting American political life, but you may not say that democracy is an illusion that needs to be dispensed with so that the nation can continue its pursuit of freedom.

If you are asked, while in America, whether or not you are a communist, it is a mistake to offer an immediate and unequivocal answer. If you are open and honest and happy to take on the risks of discussing such matters in a nation in which there are well over 200 million privately owned guns, you must immediately respond, 'it depends what you mean by "communist"', because, in all likelihood, the person who is posing the question is incapable of distinguishing communism as an Idea, in the Badiouian sense, from the dictatorships of Stalin, Mao and Pol Pot. For most citizens across the West, communism advocates brutality and oppression and the removal of everything we judge to be positive about our daily lives. To answer that you are a communist, in the sense that you are committed to equality and to the rejuvenation of the commons, is likely to lead to the accusation that these things only exist to camouflage a commitment to dictatorship and oppression, and that one is secretly committed to returning society to the Dark Ages, or possibly the mass extermination of minorities and political opponents. Given this climate, it made absolute sense for Occupy to withhold clear ideological identification. To identify as a communist or even socialist or anarchist movement would have defeated the movement just as it began to get under way.

Of course, the name 'communism' is really not so important. What is important is the clear communication of a commitment to the core principles of the communist Idea. If these principles are grouped together and called something else, it matters little. What matters is that they are again operative in a political context, that they are no longer simply philosophical considerations, and that they are reintroduced to the people in a way that corresponds to their concrete experiences of social reality. Because communism remains tainted by the symbols of absolute evil (see Badiou, 2002; Hall, 2012a), it makes sense that those at the forefront of the Occupy movement refused to speak of it. For the moment at least, and certainly into the near future, communism cannot be rehabilitated in the eyes of the American people. However, its core principles can still attract politicised and depoliticised individuals and communities, especially if they are articulated under an alternative ideological banner. However, we must note that, in continuation of our earlier point, no new name was forthcoming. The core message of Occupy, when we boil it right down to basics, was negative rather than positive. It was *against* capitalism rather than *for* something else. The positive Idea could not be enunciated, and this appeared to ensure that Occupy's discourse lacked the purchase that might have enabled it to openly discuss alternatives to capitalism, without being dismissed out of hand. As it was, the core principles of the communist Idea existed only to structure a critique of liberal capitalism. They did not coalesce into a new and clearly identifiable ideology that could be positioned as a genuine alternative to it. The 'better future' is now a fragmented cluster of private visions that dare not speak its own collective name, or, for that matter, any existing collective name at all.

It is, however, wrong to suggest that withholding a commitment to communism was a purely pragmatic gesture or a calculated strategy geared to maximise the reach of the movement. We venture that, if we had talked to those protesting in Zuccotti Park, many would not have advocated communism, socialism or anarchism, even privately. So despoiled and discredited are these ideologies in the popular imagination that even their unconscious adherents openly disavow them. Instead, they are simply 'against that which is' (Marcuse, 2002: 66). They are against the inequalities and injustices of the present, but they cannot identify a progressive alternative. Burgum (forthcoming) has noted that many of those connected to the Occupy movement in London fail even to align themselves with the political Left and instead see themselves as ethical objectors to both the totality of capitalism and specific aspects of its governance. Their critique is an ethico-cultural critique rather than a political one, and Burgum's outstanding empirical research reveals quite clearly that many of those involved preferred to reform the system rather than abandon it in favour of something else. Much of Burgum's analysis focuses on the enculturation of political opposition and contemporary capitalism's capacity to co-opt symbols of political resistance, but he also claims that some of those present during the protest and its aftermath had little, if any, connection to progressive politics and instead used events to engage with like-minded peers, take drugs and generally have a good time.

Despite these important observations, the protestors and the general public at home appeared to want *something else*, something that was unequivocally *not this*. They could see little attraction in any established ideology. They were suffering under free-market capitalism, and communism and socialism were too tarnished to attract vocal support. Both the protestors and the people appeared to want change as such, change without its downside, change that led to something better, something quite similar to the present but with less inequality, injustice, corruption and so on. This something else could not be named, or even expressed in a way that moved beyond the attenuation of the pressures and frustrations that characterise the present. Equality, a commitment to common ownership and some of the other core principles we discussed above were present in the discourse of Occupy, but they were not drawn together in a way that identified a clear and productive route forwards.

In popular culture more broadly, there seems to be a vague desire for this vague *something else*. People want to experience the shock of the new. They hope to encounter something that will jolt them out of their lethargy and cynicism. They yearn for some authority that will force them to believe. Even the politically engaged activists of Occupy hoped for a series of events that would clarify matters and identify precisely what needs to be done to reconstitute civil society on a more equitable footing. The people continue to display a passion for the Real (Badiou, 2007), but the true object of their desire can be neither accessed nor identified. The subject is instead condemned to search dejectedly through a consumerised and depoliticised landscape in search of something that might act as a substitute.

Despite wanting to end capitalism, the protestors could not bring themselves to set out on a journey that led to this destination. Doesn't this find some kind of literal expression in the strategy of actually Occupying, in actually sitting down and telling the world's media that you intend to remain there until some substantial but unspecified change is forthcoming? Did the protestors not secretly hope that some external authority would enact change on their behalf? Can we tentatively suggest that the protests, at least in part, represented a collective desire to register dissatisfaction, to have that dissatisfaction affirmed by others, to effectively pull on the coat-tails of power until power turned to acknowledge the existence of this dissatisfaction? If there is any truth in this, can we then take the next step and suggest that speaking truth to power is ultimately ineffective? Doesn't power already know that dissatisfaction exists in abundance? Should we really cling to the fantasy that political and financial elites will rehabilitate themselves when presented with the shocking evidence of the true extent of inequality, social harm and political disaffection? Isn't the act of protesting to register our dissatisfaction immediately absorbed into the purview of democratic politics? Don't our politicians instruct us to be grateful that we live in a democratic society that allows protest to take place?

It is imperative, when faced with such protests, to ask: what has changed as a result? Has government policy altered? Have elites been shamed into adopting a more pro-social bearing? If the remaining logic is simply that the protest enables pissed-off individuals to cathartically release their pent-up frustration and momentarily draw strength from being around others who feel the same way, before returning to their lives to again be subject to the same objective causes of their frustration, then we can begin to see the limitations that have been imposed upon democratic political protest.

In this context, wouldn't the truly political act, indicative of a genuine return to history, have been to present Occupy as a power capable of enacting its own change, a power capable of standing in opposition to domesticated democratic politics? Wouldn't this have enabled the public to identify in Occupy a potential for genuine change? Wouldn't this have encouraged the public to choose whose side they were on, and wouldn't Occupy have then been able to position itself as a political organisation capable of representing the interests and addressing the frustrations of ordinary Americans?

As we have already argued, this impasse reflects the ideological triumph of liberal capitalism, and it also reflects the rise of postmodernity, with its incredulity towards metanarratives and its suspension of the category of truth, and the decline of symbolic efficiency that follows (see Žižek, 2000b; Hall, 2012a, 2012c; Taylor, 2013; Winlow and Hall, 2013: 151–64). It's not necessary to fully elucidate this point here, especially as we have already discussed it at length in the works cited above and elsewhere in this book, but we can say again here that the postmodern subject is encouraged to distrust ideology and believe itself to be too rational and level-headed to completely submit to an established belief system. Why commit to any one ideology, when it is possible to dip into the history of political ideas and mix together those things that seem appealing? The pure subject of belief is dismissed as a relic, closed-minded, and probably someone suffering from a personality disorder of some sort, too weak to face up to a reality of pure self-creation and self-determination, unnerved by the prospect that there is no sure means of determining what is right and what is wrong, and anxiously clinging on to a rigid belief system in the hope that it will protect him from the turbulence of freedom.

Instead of following the injunction to remain faithful to faithlessness and to display unswerving belief in our own non-belief, it makes far more sense to acknowledge the role of ideology in shaping our understanding of social reality. It is wrong to reduce ideology to a distortion of what would otherwise be a rational and immediately comprehensible social vista. Rather, ideology as systematised belief allows us to interpret what would otherwise be disconnected and incomprehensible social phenomena. Ideology allows us to leave behind a state of nature and enter a state of culture, a journey that enables us to draw upon the newly created meaning that lies therein. In the political sense, faith in ideas enables people to construct far-sighted visions of the new and drive history forwards. Rather than blind us to an otherwise rational and logical social reality, ideology inevitably shapes our interpretation of that reality. At the very moment we believe ourselves to have wrestled free from the corrupting influence of ideology to inhabit a new environment in which phenomena can be addressed logically and without ideological lures and distortions, we are more deeply embedded in ideology than ever. It exists around us all of the time.

Belief enables people to overcome the cynicism, resignation and possessive individualism of our times. It enables the individual to transform herself into an agent of her belief, dedicated to ensuring that it has some purchase in the real world. For decades, the liberal class has instructed us that it is wrong, and potentially dangerous, to believe too strongly, that we should instead act as reflexive rational agents, capable of objectively appraising truth claims, and that we should face up to the prospect that our system of belief acts to draw us away from reality. Disabusing the people of their passionate commitment to belief has been one of the major social and political goals and outcomes of postmodern liberalism. This message, of course, has made a significant contribution to the political stasis we have experienced for two decades or more. Belief and commitment have been jettisoned from politics, and a dispassionate administrative sensibility has taken their place.

The entire framework of 'post-ideological' social and political analysis too often omits this crucial insight. It is certainly true to suggest that the politics of the first two-thirds of the twentieth century displayed a much greater degree of passionate ideological engagement than the politics of today. It is true to suggest that, as neo-liberalism became the dominant global economic system, and as communism crashed to leave capitalism triumphant, mainstream politicians of both Left and Right tended to agree on key aspects of economic management. It is also true to suggest that politicians these days tend not to express clear ideological commitments and suggest that they take a pragmatic approach in the formulation of policy. And it is also true to suggest that bland administrators, who care only about the continuation of the present, now play a much more central role in the organisation of Western politics than they have in the past.

However, it is difficult to argue that there is not an ideological dimension to contemporary Western politics. The ruling ideology and its neo-liberal economic model continue to shape both our economic and cultural lives. Can we not see ideology at work in the various austerity programmes under way across the West? Despite the fact that most of our economic problems stem from the collapse of poorly regulated financial markets, politicians of both Right and Left identify the neo-liberal solution and argue that cutting welfare and spending is the only logical course available if the state is to get itself back on an even keel. The answer to the state's structural deficit is then to go still further along the neo-liberal path and scale back the welfare state still further. Isn't this a clear example of the continued influence of ideology upon politics?

The successes of neo-liberalism have been truly dazzling. In the absence of a worthwhile ideological opponent, neo-liberalism has established itself as political common sense across most of the developed world. The phrase 'post-ideology' is, then, something of a misnomer. After the supposed purity of properly ideological modern politics comes, not a post-ideological, postmodern politics, but a politics in which deep ideological commitment is disavowed and cast into the unconscious, where, of course, it is a far more powerful and less reflexive drive to everyday conformist action. Ideology is still, quite clearly, operative on the field of politics. Now, however, it works its magic behind the scenes. It lies behind the politics of pragmatism. When politicians tell us that they are pragmatists dedicated to boosting the consumer lifestyles of citizens, we should not take them at their word. We should ask them about those things that, in their view, appear common sense and thus structure their assessment of what is and what is not 'pragmatic'. Consciously, they may believe themselves to be pragmatists, but their idea of pragmatic social and economic management is inevitably shaped by the dominant ideology. The ruling ideology speaks through the politician who tells us that the only way to improve the lifestyles of the majority is to scale back the welfare state and offer tax cuts to the rich, in the hope that their boundless talent and creativity might drive the entire economy back to growth. The political pragmatist, by utilising the moves outlined in the standard neo-liberal playbook, is inevitably captured by an unconscious ideological commitment that demands that the politician fight hard for the continuity of liberal capitalism. Even in the apparently logical drive to boost the lifestyles of citizens, we see a parallel drive to reproduce liberal consumer capitalism. The politics of pragmatic economic management is pure ideology and nothing else.

The dismissal of the ideologue as a dangerous and closed-minded maverick and the presentation of the neo-liberal administrator as a level-headed pragmatist who weighs up the available evidence before determining his political course form a thoroughly ideological operation. In fact, we draw closer to the truth if we reverse things. It is the neo-liberal administrator who is committed to dangerous ideas. It is the neo-liberal administrator who refuses to countenance the available evidence. The committed ideologue who argues that we need radical change is, by comparison, a level-headed pragmatist who takes stock of the position we are in and takes a speculative-realist glance at the likely shape of the future, based on a cold, hard look at the trajectory of the present, before concluding that the only pragmatic response to our situation and its likely outcomes is to radically change.

Post-ideological ideology

An analysis of ideology, then, has much to tell us about the politics of the present. Describing the present as post-ideology is correct, but only up to a point. In the same way, the discourse developed by the Occupy movement can be described as post-ideological, but only up to a point. The statements made by Occupy were understandably inchoate, but they were also strident, unequivocal and idealistic (see, for example, occupywallst.org). At least in the first instance, Occupy's discourse did not display any obvious suggestion of meek reformism. This seemed to creep in later. There were also points at which it appeared to want more than to force its way to the bargaining table, or to simply register its dissatisfaction with government policy in front of the world's media. It is certainly true that we can see in Occupy a willingness to reform what exists, but the reforms that Occupy suggested were precisely the kind of deep reforms that cannot take place within the framework of parliamentary capitalism. On the surface of things, liberal democracy is capable of enacting even the most significant and far-reaching social and economic reform, but this is, of course, just a surface image that betrays the ultimate impossibility of the system itself radically changing. Of course, a government could come to power with plans to tax and redistribute wealth, nationalise key industries and provide all with rewarding, socially productive labour and guaranteed incomes, but can we actually imagine such an event coming to pass within our present framework?

As Žižek has noted, there is a powerful disruptive potential in the act of requesting apparently small reforms that we know simply cannot be realised. The failure of power to give the people what they have politely and reasonably requested makes clear the disinclination, indeed complete inability, of the system to change in line with the will of the people, despite the fact that the liberal democratic system's primary attraction is its supposed ability to do precisely that. The system's refusal to change reveals that the emperor is naked, and we become consciously aware that the radical egalitarianism of electoral democracy is an illusion that has served to disguise the perpetuation of the oligarch's state and the reallocation of wealth and power from the majority to the super-rich. So, although Occupy's reformism appeared to reference its inability to go any further in advocating a comprehensible political and economic alternative to liberal capitalism, it is worth considering the possibility that its reformism contained within it a hard kernel of unrealised revolutionary potential.

When addressing the suggestion that Occupy was a post-ideological political movement, we should keep in mind that it hoped to advance the interests of the majority of the population and challenge the domination of capital over all of our lives. Sure, Occupy did not construct or attempt to construct a realistic alternative to contemporary liberal capitalism, but it did not slavishly follow liberalism's destructive and fragmented ideologies that proliferated in the era of identity politics, where ideology did not die but shattered, into not a tolerant pluralism but a shifting constellation of hostile, separatist, alienated and post-political subject positions. Occupy forcefully asserted that a universal alternative was possible and must be pursued. It did not recruit the depoliticised ex-working classes to the cause, but it advocated a politics that would have advanced the interests of that group. It just could not be clear about what this politics actually might look like, or what it might be called, and it could not bring itself to jettison its symbolically obsolete and alienating counter-cultural regalia.

The movement disintegrated as quickly as it had arisen, and no political victory was achieved, but it did suggest the ability of the Left to move beyond identity politics and single-issue protests, and it did further evidence the surfeit of anger and dissatisfaction that exists in Western neo-liberal societies. So, we can reasonably conclude that Occupy failed, but perhaps, following Beckett, we should note that it *failed better*, in fact a good deal better, and that some genuine signs of progress can now be discerned. This is *almost* our optimistic conclusion, but perhaps we should fight free of the injunction to accept perpetual failure and actually begin to consider what victory might look like, and how we might effect it. Perhaps we should be a little more demanding and a little more urgent in our desire for change. The goal of the Left should not be to produce another moment of sublime failure; the goal should be to win.

7

SPAIN AND THE INDIGNADOS

Spain remains in the grip of a crippling economic crisis. Young people have been hit particularly hard. In the summer of 2013, youth unemployment reached 56 per cent (Burgen, 2013). Understandably enough, with no sign of a sustained recovery on the horizon, people have begun to talk of a 'lost generation' of Spanish young people who are to be denied any sense of optimism about the future. Many talented young Spaniards are leaving the country in search of reasonably secure work, and many more young people have a clear sense that they will be denied the entitlements of the recent past. For example, Jorge, a thirty-two-year-old graduate from La Coruña, told us that:

> It is bad [the economic situation]. I ask myself, how can I be this age and not have a job or even a career? I am lucky enough to get a part-time temporary job for cash. What life am I leading?

Jorge suggested he felt almost as if he were trapped in limbo and unable to really begin to live his life. Instead, he felt cast in the perpetual shadow of the better life he always believed would be his. This prevailing sense of absence and being stuck drove Jorge, and many of his contemporaries, out on to the streets in 2011 and 2012.

Older generations have not escaped hardship. In early 2014, the official jobless rate was over 26 per cent (Burgen, 2014), and somewhere in the region of 6 million people were unemployed (see Burgen, 2013). Spain is a country with an overall population of around 46 million. This represents a genuine and ongoing social and economic crisis, but it is one that has scarcely registered in the US and British media. As in many other European nations, Spanish public-sector workers have seen significant reductions to their wages and entitlements. A concerted attempt to curb public expenditure is under way, and the people are being squeezed still further by tax rises, most notably VAT.

We will not recount the details of the Spanish crisis in detail, but we should note that the rapid deflation of the country's property bubble prompted Spain's economic descent. When the crisis first hit, the thriving building industry quickly ground to a halt, and unemployment rates – which were already high – grew even further. Spain's huge tourist industry also crashed, as foreigners tightened their belts and cancelled holidays. The downturn in the building and tourist sectors and the collapse of house prices prompted a number of large property companies, who had overextended themselves during the boom times, to go bust. Whole housing developments stood empty as the economic circumstances of potential buyers changed and investors waited for the market to hit rock bottom. Rising unemployment prompted mortgage defaults to surge. The number of families in negative equity rose sharply (see Smith and Penty, 2013). Banks quickly found themselves carrying debts that would not be repaid.

A series of bailouts and bank mergers followed. The Spanish economy was the fifth largest in the EU and couldn't be allowed to fail. Before the crisis, it seemed to be a model for neo-liberal economic management, but its deceptive and partial successes quickly turned into abject failure. Poverty and unemployment grew, and new political movements formed that hoped to dispense with the political and financial elites who seemed to carry most of the blame for getting the country into this mess.

The indignant ones

The most notable of these were the Indignados – 'the indignant ones' – who aligned themselves with no ideology and instead directed their indignation at the political system and the corruption of political elites. Beyond those concerns, the Indignados lacked a clear focus, and no clear, politically articulate voice emerged from the movement. They remained determinedly non-violent and, importantly, they appeared to be just as dissatisfied with the political Left as they were with the political Right. Some of the public proclamations made by the group appeared to express the hope that the polity could be held to account and forced to change tack. Others hoped that their movement could foment a politics that placed the interests of people above the interests of money and profit. It is certainly true that other things appeared to unite the protestors. They were clearly against the state's austerity policies and they wanted something to be done about the country's staggering unemployment figures. However, no clear image of a post-capitalist social order emerged. A cacophony of voices could be heard on the squares in which the Indignados gathered, and the goals of the movement remained vague. In some cases, dazzling contradictions emerged that reflected the diverse interest groups that had come together to form such a huge, multi-site protest movement. The protestors were angry at the social effects of neo-liberalism and financialisation and they wanted change, but how change would occur and what the protestors hoped to change the current system into could neither be agreed nor articulated.

Certainly, indignation and anger did not spur the production of a blueprint for a better world. Instead, anger and indignation were directed at the political system in the most general sense. Many believed the entire political system to be corrupt and assumed that mainstream politicians were in it for the money. Juan, from La Coruña, expresses a broadly felt sentiment and one that we heard often from those to whom we spoke:

> Let me tell you about these people [politicians]. These people have fifty new Mercedes cars to take them from place to place. They have a driver for each. But rarely do they use these services. They waste money on stupid things. They dream up ideas and spend money on unimportant nothings. Like when they spent millions of Euros on sand to put on one of our beaches. Within months the sea had washed most of it away. No one can touch them either. They do it in our faces. In Spain, you see, they do these things and get away with it, not like in the UK where they resign because of the shame or embarrassment. It's like they are proud of it. This is why our city sits in pieces.

Joaquin is in his mid forties and lives in Madrid. He has worked all of his life and wonders what kind of legacy his generation is leaving for the one that follows. He has this to say about Spanish politics:

> We will never escape this crisis because we shoot ourselves in the foot. Our politics are too corrupt. We can make all the changes we want to the structure of the council but we will still be in debt. Do you know that around 70 per cent of Spanish politicians who have been prosecuted for corruption were subsequently re-elected in the most recent local elections? And corruption costs our government billions of Euros each year.

Albert, who is in his late twenties, was involved with the Indignados from the very beginning. He displayed a good grasp of Spain's difficult political and economic system and was quite frustrated at the Indignados's lack of direction and their inability to take the next step. Below, he expresses a commonly felt anger at political corruption and failure:

> Both political parties commit vast amounts of fraud. It is all between the banks and the politicians. Imagine the news. One day we see corruption on the news. The next we see more corruption and how much millions of Euros are involved. No one seems to be responsible. What you see as well is that these parties are supposed to offer campaigns with different policies. What do people do? Not much. There are no options, no alternatives. Money talks and we are talking about a capitalistic democracy.
>
> People thought they are living in good times. The banks were loaning easily, 'here take this money, pay it back with low interest, you can't afford

it really but we are making it available to you', said the banks. People thought 'I can ask for credit, buy a nice car, nice house' but this was when the economy was going well, before the crash. People didn't anticipate debt. People were buying and spending and the banks were exploiting them. Then came the crash, the markets collapsed and we are where we are now. People realised that they can't pay for cars, mortgages, and they supposed the government would help them, but they couldn't. Instead the government started schemes to encourage spending to stimulate the market but then the banks seized up.

The Indignados are not a determined group of people. It's a form of reaction to what has happened. It is, basically, I suppose, technically, not a political group, because it is not left or right, but it is a platform for people to say 'the politics of our country are not working'. They are organised in that they protest in attempt to make the country better. We are asking the government to respect democracy that is supposed to be part of our constitution. The Indignados is for anyone really who has a message for the government that things are not working. It is to represent indignation at what is happening.

They started then to camp out at Sol [a large public square in Madrid]. I was there. There were many movements. Left people, right people, radicals, everyone. 15M was based on a response, people were protesting, such as through organisations such as Democracia Real Ya, trying to establish the constitution again because people could not see any democracy. All they saw was political corruption. No one could attack the political party in power because people started to realise they were the same . . . 15M is more a protest, more of a way of getting things said but not necessarily done. It says what it wants in that moment rather than having a vision for how a political system should be. When the politics disappears, as it has, people lose interest. They are in limbo, they are left with their thoughts, with rubbish television or Madrid versus Barcelona. Here the political system doesn't work.

Elizabeth is in her late twenties and lives in Malaga. She is unemployed. Here she tries to explain the reasons why so many of her peers supported the Indignados movement:

Look, in Spain almost everyone is in discontent. Many people are out of work. People are going to university for no reason. Before the crisis, unemployment was bad but now it is far, far worse. I am unemployed and can't get work. I know people who have left for the UK where there are jobs. People I know are getting cash in hand jobs or in shops but don't keep them long. Others just do temporary work before they are practically begging off their families.

The problem is the banks and the political system. They got us in this mess and they are asking us to pay for it. What they have done here is opened businesses in places like China because it is cheaper, which makes for a surplus population of people who have no work and are not qualified to do anything else than what they know. But they have cut so much, and what is next? Education and Health. They have sacked doctors, professionals, services. In education, teachers, specialists, educational workers. All have lost their jobs.

The Rajoy government came in with all these promises of rebalancing the economy and saving Spain but they have made it much worse. Before they were saying they wouldn't increase taxes, before they were elected, but what do they go and do – increase the taxes. Then they blame the previous party for Spain's situation and the opposition are blaming them for their new measures.

The indignant ones demanded that their indignation be recognised, but their preferred social, political and economic destination remained unclear. They hoped that others would enact change on their behalf, and the change they wanted was strictly negative, in the sense that they simply wanted to rid Spain of those things they were against. And further, the movement failed to produce a general accord on those things that were to be opposed. Spokespeople could only offer abstract platitudes that could not be brought down to earth to structure serious proposals for reform or revolution. Suggesting that the interests of people be placed in front of the interests of capital sounds noble and quite strident, but who would oppose such a sentiment? Certainly not the politicians in government, anxiously watching events unfold from the parliament buildings close by. Everyone from Jesus Christ to Margaret Thatcher would have agreed with the Indignados on this point. The entire political spectrum, from Marine Le Pen, Geert Wilders and Nikos Michaloliakos on one side to Owen Jones, Alexis Tsipras and Jean-Luc Mélenchon on the other, advocates the dominance of people over capital. However, without an accompanying analysis of what this might mean in ideological and practical terms, the phrase is entirely meaningless.

Again, it is the total absence of an alternative that ensures these protestors are limited to simply shouting into the skies, as a vague gesture to signify that they want something better. The non-existence of positive political symbolism hangs over events like toxic smog. Everyone shouts, but no one can see where they actually are. Most of those who had been active in the movement talk of the initial positivity falling away. In time, they understood that something was missing; some vital ingredient that could have driven the group forwards was not present. They were unsure what this vital ingredient was – although some identified the absence of leadership as a crucial factor – but the anger and initial enthusiasm of the crowd could not compensate for it. Of course, it is not difficult to imagine these events working out very differently. All of this anger could have fuelled a genuine political intervention geared towards creating a new world of positive freedoms, security and equality, completely free from those things that cause such social and personal distress today. This anger could have done this, *if* they had had access to an alternative ideology that spoke, not just of the harms of capitalism and the vacuity of liberal democracy, but also of the positive substance of an alternative social world. Instead, the unfocused, desperate desire for something else simply could not be moulded and disciplined by the structures of a named ideology. In times of really existing politics, when it was indeed possible to positively imagine an alternative to capitalism, a movement such as the Indignados, animated as it was by a genuine sense of anger and a strong desire for change, would have produced genuine dialectical movement. However, in the post-political present, the Indignados could not fill the gap left by the absence of ideology. All they could do was register their dissatisfaction and hope the political class would change course.

Inevitably, the movement faded from view, and the protestors headed home. Some of our respondents resolved to keep trying. Others gave up and are cynical about the prospects for change. They could see no positive outcome, only their own wasted effort. Sergio and Ines, for example, both in their early thirties and from Madrid, were convinced that protesting was pointless. The politicians would simply continue doing what they had been doing, and there was nothing the Indignados could do that would stop them. If the protestors became more strident in their opposition, they would be beaten up by the police. Why waste time sitting around in a square when nothing changed? Ines in particular wanted to draw our attention to the tragic comedy of it all: the expectation that the entire edifice of parliamentary capitalism could be remoralised by a few noble souls camping out in a public square. Why on earth would entrenched power transform itself at the sight of such events? The politicians had clearly not been shamed into adopting a more pro-social bearing, and capital continued its mad dance, completely divorced from the suffering it visited on diverse populations across the country. For Sergio and Ines, and many others, the initial excitement that existed at the start of the protests had long gone. For them, if this was 'the revolution', it sucked.

From indignity to proto-politics . . . and back again

The 15M movement and Democracia Real Ya grew alongside the Indignados. It would be churlish to claim that their collective efforts have been for nought. Recently, a new political party has emerged that appears to draw much of its strength from the protest movements that arose between 2010 and 2013. Podemos – which means 'we can' – formed in 2014 under the leadership of Pablo Iglesias, a political science professor at Complutense University of Madrid. The party hopes to create a new politics in which all citizens can participate. Podemos received 1.2 million votes – almost 8 per cent of all votes cast – in the 2014 European elections, despite being only a few months old (see Burridge, 2014; Kassam, 2014). The party came third overall, and the domination of the two main parties – the People's Party and the Socialists – declined significantly.

The Indignados' initial expectation that the power elite would buckle at the sight of popular opposition appears to have given way to the sober recognition that it will take a great deal of hard work and personal sacrifice to change Spanish politics. The revolutionary transformation desired by so many can only come into being if it is supported by organisation, mobilisation and careful planning. The rapid rise of Podemos appears, therefore, to be a huge leap in the right direction.

Podemos, on the surface of things, appears to be a party of the Left, despite the fact that it grew out of a protest movement keen to transcend the old binary of left–right politics. Its leftism draws together a social democratic drive to regulate markets and narrow income inequalities with a hazy liberal desire to boost freedom and the toleration shown to minorities. Its members display a concern for the environment and hope to reinvigorate democracy by opening up key institutions to democratic control. They plan to tackle tax avoidance and combat the worst effects of profit-seeking, and they are committed to reducing poverty and 'recovering solidarity'. Ultimately, they hope to 'win, for the first time, equality and freedom' (see Podemos, 2014). The strong liberal humanist element to the Podemos manifesto seems like an almost inevitable addition to what would otherwise be a radical socialist programme for economic and social transformation. The focus it places upon democracy suggests that it clearly has a great deal of faith in the people to make the right choices. Podemos assumes that the people already know the truth and have an organic drive to create a more just society. They just need to be given a voice. The political goal, therefore, is to encourage more people to get involved and to ensure that the views of the people are freely expressed and valued and contribute to the nation's political future. Socialism mixes with liberalism, and the politics of cultural specificity is interwoven with the politics of universalism. We will withhold our standard critique of the paradoxes of this arrangement and instead reiterate that Podemos, if it can retain its radicalism in the face of what will be sustained political and economic opposition, has the potential to at least begin the process of rejuvenating the commons and challenging the dominance of capital over all our lives. Podemos is not yet as advanced as SYRIZA, as we shall see in the next chapter, but the two parties appear to be heading in a broadly similar direction.

A number of those who participated in the various protest movements were aware of the lack of ideological coherence and political momentum.

Alba is in her early thirties and lives in Madrid. Despite being highly educated, she can only find work as a waitress. She earns around €800 per month. Roberto is also in his early thirties and lives in Madrid. He is unemployed, but occasionally manages to get some cash-in-hand work. He continues to rely greatly on his parents, and this clearly causes him considerable discomfort.

Alba:

> Democracia Real Ya were organising protests and I heard about it. They advertised it online and people were talking about it to get the people involved and we united in response. We started to camp out in Sol Square in Madrid and they moved us. But this happened in most cities in Spain, they started to protest and camp out in all these cities. Never had people seen protests like this. It started so small but it had moved the whole nation.

Well, for me, the 15M movement and Indignados spoke to me, gave me the confidence to speak up, to say things were bad, and that the crisis of the capitalist system was not just in our country but across the world. I liked the way we were critical of the system and that we shouldn't be accepting of it; that's why I was involved. So it gave me that confidence, for people like me who are not really that politically active to be interested and say something and send a message to the government.

Without believing in something, how can you participate? But most people were like this in 15M in that they believed in saying things were wrong. No one had left or right views – we were saying 'No'.

Roberto:

We were camped out for a month and a half in one place, not Sol, another place. Other cities, they camped out for longer. There were many people there in the first days. Hundreds but only perhaps forty camped out. In the camp, people were debating and discussing all the issues and trying to think of what system we would put in place. We were trying to establish a consensus. You would like to think that you are doing something towards something, so this is what we were doing; trying to see if our views on things could work out. We felt like we had a hand in something, that we could start the change. But we were only a small group of people in the end.

There are still lots of people involved but they have different opinions. Although everyone was standing up and saying they had had enough, we couldn't agree on things. People here were taken aback with this new position of feeling like they were able to do something. The problem I guess was that we were different people. It wasn't like people from one class who were angry or one particular sector, like teachers. It was larger than that so it came with different points of view. The debates were good but we weren't going to change anything from being in a square. And also we started to fear a little the government. We weren't going to change anything really. It was a great experience though. I suppose people remembered the reality of their responsibilities and had to get on with it, providing for the family, and so on.

Roberto and Alba agree that the movement lacked a clear identity. As time passed, and people began to drift away, the movement began to run out of steam. They believe that the main reason for this was the movement's inability to clarify its mission and continue moving forwards. Roberto talked about the absence of a clear, unambiguous ideology. Although, at first, the diversity of views appeared positive, democratic and refreshing, in time it just became talk, with no clear end or goal in sight. No agreement could be reached, and no authority existed capable of making a final decision on the goals and principles of the movement.

Alba:

> It's true and it comes back to what I was saying about the different people. Someone comes to protest who is an anti-capitalist and says 'down with capitalism'. Then someone else comes and says something else. And now there are not many protests. Probably because of what happened in Plaza de Cataluna, where people sat around and protested and the police came along and beat them up. They were trying to do something but they couldn't. I mean how do you interfere with parliament by protesting in a square? How do you change a voting system and political process to represent you by being in a square?

Roberto in particular is disgusted by the vacuity of mainstream politics. He sees that being given a choice between two groups that are essentially the same has become a means of enforcing the dominant socio-economic model. Of course, voting is the only legitimate means of expressing one's displeasure. For him, the Indignados were attempting to move beyond this restrictive system. Roberto believes that, ultimately, beneath the cacophony of voices and radically different points of view, the movement wanted to encourage the rejuvenation of electoral democracy. However, simply asking the system to change proved not to be enough. Theirs was a non-violent protest that hoped to spur change, but, as the protest dragged on, and it became increasingly clear that the government would not act to address the concerns of the protestors, the movement gradually lost its initial momentum. The initial spark of excitement and the sense of possibility were quickly extinguished, and the dejected protestors trudged home.

Roberto:

> This is part of the problem. They call it democracy, the government, but it isn't. This is why we have organisations that were part of 15M, like Democracia Real Ya, which were calling for democracy. We have a dictator in power. The problem is, as people we are small and we don't know enough about politics. It doesn't help particular classes, like us, and it is confusing. We are not talking about a fair social system. We are talking about a system where we vote but people don't represent us. The truth is the different parties are actually the same. PSOE and PP are the same; they are the same shits ... For me, the 15M, the problem is that it is not a party. There are subjects, there are individuals and we are people who want something but we are not organised like a political party is.
>
> The problem is political and no one politician is connected to social life – that is, what goes on in our lives. You vote because you are choosing someone to represent you, but it goes against you, because capitalism doesn't recognise the real problem, and nor does 15M, because capitalism is so embedded that it is difficult to see a clear way out – including me. I have no idea. When we elect we look at a party to represent us and what we may

have in common with them, but even though 15M was something similar, it could never represent all the differences.

Some of those we spoke to insisted that the absence of a hierarchy within the movement produced a robust interchange of ideas and approaches. Roberto and Alba disagree. They feel that the movement lacked a leader capable of drawing the disparate elements of the movement together, clarifying its goals and taking it forward to the next stage. Everyone was allowed to air their views, but, ultimately, no consensus could be reached. There was a lot of talk, but no resolutions, no policies and no plan of action. Below, they describe how many lost interest or resigned themselves to defeat.

Alba:

> The movement has died down in the last eighteen months. They have stopped attempts to reform or to change the class system for the better. It is activism rather than commitment. It is too variable and there is no agreement. Currently, many people have stopped organising things and lost some confidence.

Roberto:

> We exist in a social system which expects us to be well-educated about making our points of view. Because of that we feel we don't need to use violence. It is ironic really because we [at the bottom] don't use any violence but the people at the top, controlling things, use all sorts of violence to stay there – look at the images of the police beating people like us. It is the problem of civil society and how the subject of politics has disappeared from public action.
>
> [15M is] a collective of people, but there are not many people who are committed to this now but continue in their organisations to fight particular issues, like unemployment. But as a unit they don't really organise themselves as much.

Laura is in her mid twenties and lives in Malaga. Over the last few years, she has been in and out of work, usually low-paid jobs in the service sector. She has been involved in a number of protests organised by 15M and continues to display a degree of commitment to the movement. Here, she describes what motivated her to join the Indignados:

Laura:

> I became involved because I identified with the values of the Indignados, it made me feel indignant – the situation, the crisis, and that it had to stop. The indignation of the fact that we are paying for other people's mess. We have no blame and no power. My friends told me and I found out by Facebook about the movement and there was advertised a protest against this suffering. I wanted to participate because I was in agreement.

The politics in this country do not represent us. Not only me. In Spain in general, most people that I speak to, they continue to vote but say to themselves 'what else can we do?' Many people are now voting for PP who voted PSOE because of the economic conditions, but PP has made it worse! Everyone in Spain is paying for the State and the banks.

You see more people in hospitals but there are no beds and not enough doctors. Everyone has to pay for their healthcare now. But many people don't have the financial resources. More people are homeless now; you see them in the street. People don't use electricity or gas because they can't afford it. On some of the seasides, apart from the English, many restaurants are empty.

People in Spain these days are concerned about plasma TVs, looking nice, good car, and they don't want to lose it. People vote in democracies to keep what they have, so they think 'I vote so someone who will ensure I have a job and can buy things, have a holiday' and people are content with that. This is what they care for.

Now they realise the debt they have accumulated. Even me. I have a job now but I had to move back in with my parents because I couldn't afford to live by myself. It is continuous uncertainty.

The police and firemen are protesting because public service wages have been reduced by 7 per cent, even some of the council workers because they are making cuts in local government as well. All they say is that we need to tighten our belts but they don't realise that they caused this. I don't know how this capitalist system is going to work or when it will end. We are so much in debt that we will be on our knees to Europe. They always deny it as well. They say we don't need help then they ask for a bailout. It doesn't make sense.

Laura continues to protest, despite a growing awareness that support for the Indignados is falling away. Her drive to do something, anything, rather than meekly accept the dominant order is quite striking.

Laura:

We are in the street protesting but it doesn't affect the government. It makes no difference we are in the street. Maybe we come back the next month but it's the same. I go to the 15M or larger ones but there are separate ones protesting against cuts in education. I go to the ones which are organised against the government.

Question: And how do you feel after protesting?

Laura:

It makes me feel impotent. I don't see anything. I see no change. But I can't stay at home. I have to do something but I feel redundant. So many different people with the same feeling, we are all there – old, young – and after all this, where is the change? They continue sacking people and unemployment grows. They continue to destroy things.

Question: Do other people feel like you?

Laura:

> Yes, they all feel the same. Deceived. They don't know who to believe or which party to vote for. They only know what is available to them and they are fearful of the alternatives to democracy. We are scared of anarchy or a dictator, we don't want that.

Question: And what do you think of the results of the movement?

Laura:

> Poor. It was good but insufficient. More and more there are gaps between the classes so it is not surprising that the differences when protesting will come out. But it is not anarchy. It's that people don't know where to turn. One minute people are voting left but when it didn't work they vote for the opposite, the right. Neither works. There is no clarity. People are confused. Politicians are confused. In my view 15M is not about destroying democracy, it is about making it real, because we have no democracy at the moment. It is so corrupt at the moment. We need to clean up the system and basically start again.

Question: So how do you do that?

Laura:

> I don't know. I have no idea. I would like to say throw them all in prison but what result is that? Make them accountable when they commit crime, fraud, indecent acts, make it law to protect us and not protect them. But the system is corrupt in every way, politicians, judges, everyone.
>
> I'm not sure where the movement is going. It's all very well to go to the street and make a noise but we end up going home. Sometimes I feel we are stuck, that there will be no change. What do we do? In fact, what do the politicians do, because I'm not sure they know either. It is a horrible form of capitalism. Well, I believe in capitalism in some ways, in that I like to be able to go shopping, but there needs to be some balance so that inequality does not spread like a cancer like it is now.
>
> It's like people are stuck in lives where they follow football matches and go shopping. I blame the TV, for example. People watch it to escape the daily crap they have to experience, it takes them away from the realities of their lives. So many channels are dedicated to, just rubbish.

Laura's desire for a less damaging version of liberal capitalism was shared by many other interviewees. They spoke out against the horrors of capitalism, but they did not want to fully rid themselves of it. Few of those we spoke to were genuinely committed to radical social change. The only alternative they could think of was communism, and a shift in that direction was unthinkable. Communism for them remained irredeemably tarnished. Communism meant oppression, dictatorship, war and starvation. They like consumerism and new media and saw these things as gifts provided by capitalism. Ultimately, they wanted to accentuate the positive and eliminate the negative. They wanted reform not revolution, and they were perfectly clear about this.

Jóse, who is in his mid forties and from Madrid, did not join the protests, but he was an interested and concerned spectator. He is dismissive of the movement.

Jóse:

> The Indignados just stopped being indignant. They went back to their *casas* and chalets, or off to the beach. They got bored. It was never a serious movement. What did they do apart from come here and sit around and smoke? There was no organisation and they didn't get anywhere. People were coming here, 'ah lets protest!', and they had all this Dolce and Gabbana and all the stuff, 'look how supercool we are, we are going to protest'. What are you doing here I ask them, and they say they are Indignados, but they don't have a clue. No one was in agreement with anyone.

We talked to a pigeon-food seller, Pepe, who works in one of the main squares where the Indignados gathered. He watched on as the movement grew and then disintegrated. He has this to say:

> The main problem I have is that there were just some really silly messages, like people protesting for rights for cats and dogs, people trying to bring forward laws on anal sex, stupid things. People came who were cultured, poor, all sorts, and I liked the way they got together to say 'there is a problem here' but the messages were just so, so stupid it kind of took the legitimacy out of it.
>
> The first week [there was lots of positivity] but when people saw nothing was happening and they weren't getting anything, this is when the silly things developed. Then came people offering free food, then people started drinking in the square and this attracted homeless people and they were, I suppose, part of the campaign, but too many different people started to come and it got messy, people lost their vision. Well, if they ever had one. This is when the stupid messages started to appear, and I ask what the fuck are you if you can't understand the basic principles of a revolution? You need to be united. They needed to be more political.
>
> 'Spain's revolution' they were saying. You know the media appeared and they interviewed me on a programme, on TV, and they asked me how

beautiful I thought it was, but I said it was shit because it was not being led, it was not attacking the politics enough. The Indignados were not representing anyone, they had no leader, no visible person who could sort out the mess, get rid of the silly messages and take the serious ones forward. Some people were concerned with eradicated mortgages while others wanted free schooling and healthcare. When you have a political leader, you can sort out these agendas and you have a way into the system but just sitting around and protesting does nothing. Look, I am with them in that I have a business, I suffer, I have to put food on the table for my family and send my children to school, but people were taking the piss. One week protesting and, yes, I am with you, but after ten, fifteen days, what are you doing? Where is this going? This is one reason why it just died, people got bored, went on holiday. It was good to start with and they were doing me a favour in that first week because I was with them. [Eventually] people were taking the piss, just like the government.

I don't want to sound too negative because it was good they were saying how the government is corrupt and were criticising the imbeciles who were running the country. But, you know what they did, they did a gallery of the photos from the protest and put it in a shop and all the stuff around it was how amazing it was, but it did nothing. Nothing has changed. I just got tired of it, it was pissing me off. My balls are already full [this expression means 'I've got my hands full']. It was good that all different classes, ages, like children and old people, came, but no one had any way of uniting them past actually being in the same place. It's like the politicians were thinking 'we'll just leave them to it' because it was obviously nothing serious to them. It's sad really.

The triumph of capitalist realism in Spain

Again, we find that anger exists in abundance, and again we find that – in the absence of adequate leadership, clear political symbolism and a vision of a better world – this anger results only in impotence, exhaustion and the continuation of the present by default. Clearly, the people we spoke to wanted change. In some cases, they were willing to camp out on the street for weeks on end to further this goal. However, the change they wanted remained frustratingly out of reach. They had been poorly served by politicians and intellectuals and, on the whole, they were distrustful of those identified as potential leaders. The absence of an alternative totally transformed the potential of the movement. The goals of the Indignados inevitably became goals that were positioned within the constellation of contemporary parliamentary capitalism. Rather than striving for the Good, they debated how they might make the present a little less bad. In many respects, they were an anti-capitalist movement that did not want to overcome capitalism. Their discourse was shaped by the political catastrophism carefully diffused throughout the West by liberal ideologues in the post-war period, and they remained convinced that capitalism was the best available socio-economic system. Sure, it had its problems, and it was vital that politicians seek to work these problems out, but, even after an enormous economic crash that impoverished millions, capitalism still appeared better than communism or fascism. No space beyond parliamentary capitalism could be opened up from which the protestors might be able to see capitalism's totality and what capitalism's continued supremacy might mean for the Spanish people.

Even liberal capitalism's most determined critics remained committed to electoral democracy. They wanted more choice at election time. They wanted a nicer capitalism. They wanted a fairer society. They wanted less corruption in both local and central government. They wanted things to be better. Ultimately, they wanted a version of the present minus its perceived excesses. Yes, capitalism, but a less beastly version of capitalism. Yes, democracy, but a rejuvenated democracy that better reflects the views of the people. Yes, consumerism, but cheaper prices. Yes, the wage form, but higher wages. Ultimately, the Indignados and the other protestors were reformers rather than revolutionaries. At a deeper level, they wanted what the revolutionary wants, but they could not begin to conceive of a positive future in which both capitalism and democracy were absent.

We are certainly not criticising the protestors for failing to orchestrate a radical break, or for wanting a less harmful capitalism and a rejuvenated democracy. Our point is simply that parliamentary capitalism simply cannot deliver what the protestors hoped for. Austerity is already established as the new normal. There will not be a new industrial revolution in Western Europe that brings back high-paying jobs. We are unlikely to discover new and easy-to-exploit oil fields. The sustained economic growth of the past is at an end. Even mainstream economists such as Thomas Piketty (2014) have acknowledged that runaway financialisation will continue to concentrate capital in the hands of the super-rich. If capitalism could deliver improved consumer lifestyles to a greater proportion of the world's population, if it could reintegrate marginalised populations, if its democratic system could be rejuvenated and if its governments could begin a sustained attempt to address poverty and the ecological crisis, then we would be happy to remain within capitalism and dedicate ourselves to encouraging capitalism's continued ethical overhaul. However, this cannot happen. The Left's reformism simply isn't bearing fruit. It is time for some tough decisions to be made.

The problems faced by our respondents were, of course, very real, but the reforms the Indignados proposed were overly abstract and imprecise. Some of the proposals made by radical left liberals, especially those that related to sexual freedom, appeared to alienate working-class Spaniards, whose primary motivation was to curb unemployment and poverty. In truth, beyond vague abstractions, they simply didn't know what they wanted. All they knew was that they wanted things to be better. Phrases such as 'more freedom', 'more democracy', 'less corruption' and so on simply disappear into the ether, unless they are attached to a concrete and principled political programme that attempts to clarify goals and put plans into action.

The absence of much-needed politics suggests that the most important outcome of the Indignados movement is clearly the formation and rapid rise of Podemos. The great promise of Podemos is to drag some of the abstract chatter of the Indignados down to earth with grounded policies and concrete goals. This is not simply a process of gathering together the various concerns of the protestors and setting them down clearly in one document. In fact, the act of constructing a manifesto in this way serves to instruct the Indignados in what to believe. It is an act of clarification and instruction: 'Enough talk', the manifesto says, 'this is what we believe'. Henceforth, when a protestor is asked what they want and what they believe, rather than simply recounting their own private concerns and motivations, and rather than offering forth only vague abstractions, they will be able to say, quite simply, that they believe in Podemos.

It is still early days for the party, and its continued rise is by no means guaranteed. However, what is crucial is the determination to organise, to clarify goals and then to seek to educate and grow. The limitations of remaining within the liberal democratic system are real, and, should Podemos find itself in government with a clear mandate from the people, it will have to fight very hard simply to remain true to its principles. As we have already said, 'we can' can quickly become 'we can't'. Principles can quickly crumble under the weight of expediency, and, if an economic miracle is not forthcoming, popular support can rapidly evaporate to leave only despondency and cynicism. Time will of course tell, but until then we will remain cautiously optimistic, buoyed by the willingness of those at the forefront of the movement to at least make an attempt to instigate a new social democratic revolution.

8

THE TROUBLE WITH THE GREEKS

Between a rock and a hard place

On 4 April 2012, Dimitris Christoulas, a seventy-seven-year-old retired pharmacist, left his small apartment in Athens and began to make his way to Syntagma Square. Christoulas, a genial, educated and dignified man, had been struggling to cope financially. He had been active in the anti-austerity movement, and a banner proclaiming 'Can't pay, won't pay' hung from his balcony. Christoulas had always been interested in politics, but, late in his life, the economic crisis that began in 2008 had turned him into an activist. His pension had been cut to the extent that he could barely afford to feed himself. He felt his dignity slipping away. When he arrived in Syntagma Square, he stood under a pine tree close to the parliament building, in the very place that he had pitched his tent during protests in the square in 2011. After gathering his thoughts, he proclaimed, 'This is not suicide; they are killing me', and promptly shot himself in the head.

Christoulas's suicide drew the attention of the world's media and sparked further protests in the square. In his suicide note, Christoulas had said that he refused to be reduced to foraging in dustbins for his sustenance and preferred to end his life immediately. He felt that old age prevented him from aggressively targeting those he believed to be responsible for his plight. Christoulas's death quickly became a symbol of the price the Greek people were paying for the aggressive austerity measures imposed on them by their elected representatives and the bureaucrats of the Troika, the tripartite committee of the European Commission, the European Central Bank and the International Monetary Fund.

Christoulas's death was powerfully symbolic and served to draw attention to the suffering of the Greek people, but it was by no means an isolated incident. In 2011, recorded suicide in Greece shot up by 40 per cent from the previous year (Smith, 2011). Further, Antonakakis and Collins (2014) believe that they have identified a clear correlation between fiscal austerity and the rising suicide rate in

Greece. Middle-aged men have been particularly affected. Antonakakis and Collins claim that the deaths of 551 men between 2009 and 2010 can be linked directly to austerity. That is more than one suicide per day – all men driven to utter despair by their inability to support themselves and their families. Few of these deaths were as dramatic as Christoulas's, and none of them drew the same level of attention, but each of these men would have had a story to tell of unemployment, bankruptcy and growing financial pressure breaking apart relationships and families. All would have been able to talk about the destruction of a positive social identity and the humiliation that result from the inability to feed one's family. Christoulas drew the headlines, but the forces that drove him to act were broadly felt among the Greek people.

Of course, the tragedy does not end there. Stuckler and Basu (2013) have identified a 200 per cent increase in HIV infection in Greece since 2011, and alcoholism and serious addictive drug use have also shot up. A whole range of preventable diseases have quickly spread as medical funding has been stripped back. Recorded cases of malaria are at a record high. It is, of course, very difficult to identify precisely the number of people who have died because they have been unable to access medicine, but we should expect the figure to be quite significant. Stuckler and Basu (ibid.) are quick to point out that it is not simply the contraction of markets that prompts such deep social harms. Of course, during the Keynesian era, periodic recession often prompted governments to boost spending and employment in order to get the economy moving again. This kind of interventionist response to crisis, Stuckler and Basu claim, can have an immediate beneficial effect upon suicide rates and public health. It is austerity specifically that causes widespread despair and produces a broad range of negative social outcomes.

Hunger and malnutrition have also risen rapidly. Frontline charities report that up to 90 per cent of families in the poorest neighbourhoods rely on food banks and soup kitchens (Smith, 2013). The Greek Orthodox Church is said to feed upwards of 55,000 people daily (ibid.). The president of UNICEF in Greece, Lambros Kanellopoulos, has noted that approximately 600,000 children in Greece live below the poverty line, and 322,000 children are unable to meet their basic daily nutritional needs (see Papantoniou, 2013). Forms of acquisitive crime have increased significantly. Burglaries, for example, appear to have risen by more than 50 per cent (Hadjimatheou, 2012), and many previously legitimate business owners have been drawn into illegality in order to make ends meet (see Antonopoulos and Hall, 2014). All of this is happening in a developed European nation, a nation with the thirteenth largest economy in the EU, a nation that had, in the years leading up to the crisis, shown significant and sustained growth in its GDP. Greece had been a model for neo-liberal economic development, but, by 2008, as the global economy went into a tailspin, all that was at an end. George Papandreou admitted that the financial situation faced by the Greek state was much worse than they had hitherto admitted, and the country's patina of neo-liberal respectability rapidly disintegrated. Two questions occur to us. First, how did Greece fall so far, so fast? And second, what do events in Greece tell us about what the future holds?

Before we begin, let us be clear about one thing: a choice has been made between the well-being of the Greek people and the relative economic stability of the Eurozone. Rising levels of suicide, hunger and poverty, and widespread desperation, have been judged a price worth paying to restore balance, assuage markets and reconstruct the country's reputation for economic management. However, in order to fully understand the nature of this choice, we must first acknowledge that the Greek economy has not been stabilised as a result of austerity measures. Even now, in 2014, five years into austerity, the economy remains in deep crisis. It has contracted by more than a quarter since the crisis began (see Bouras, 2014). Perhaps more to the point, the IMF officials who sanctioned the bailout that kept Greece afloat as the crisis unfolded appear to have known full well that the imposition of draconian fiscal austerity measures would work against economic recovery and prevent the Greeks from repaying the debt in a timely manner (Elliot *et al.*, 2013). They knew that the austerity requirements were against almost everyone's interests, but still they went ahead.

How can we understand an economic and political situation that effectively requires all parties to partake in this kind of self-flagellation, in which the only apparent choice available is a choice with no obvious beneficiary? Who or what is the higher authority that compels so many to act against their interests? The IMF itself admits that, as a result of the austerity requirements that accompanied the bailouts, 'market confidence was not restored, the banking system lost 30% of its deposits and the economy encountered a much deeper than expected recession with exceptionally high unemployment' (ibid.).

Of course, the great concern of the Troika was to avoid a contagion that could split apart the EU. Those whose job it was to guide global financial markets clearly believed that such an event was indeed possible, and, if it came to pass, it would be catastrophic for the global economy. Markets would collapse, living standards would fall dramatically, and faith in parliamentary democracy would fall away. To preserve the system, everything that could be done had to be done. The gravity of the situation meant that, for the bureaucrats at the epicentre of the Troika, everything was on the table. They needed to respond swiftly and imaginatively to the crisis. Ideology and a commitment to the purity of economic principles were luxuries they could not afford.

Of course, future-facing pragmatism of this kind always involves ideology, even if ideological commitment is consciously disavowed. Pragmatism, in any frame, is constructed upon an ideological foundation. It grows from the basic truths that help us to construct our understanding of social reality. At the very moment when the crisis demanded that all potential options were fully considered, some options remained totally inconceivable. Only those options that fitted within the dominant ideological field appeared to possess any potential to placate markets, boost investment and weather the storm about to engulf the Eurozone.

The hegemony of the market remained. The market continued to assert its dominance, despite the attempts by various states to buy up debt and push money back into the economy. The ultimate goal was to re-establish normality, and of course the normality they hoped to re-establish was one dominated by neo-liberalism and the primacy of investment and profit over the interests of labour and society.

Markets needed to be reassured so that confidence might return. As soon as the initial panic ended and it became clear that the EU would hold together no matter what the cost, capital investment would pick up, and the economic situation would stabilise. Banks would start lending again, employment would slowly increase, and the crisis would be at an end. The issue then becomes one of attempting to second-guess markets. What can politicians and bureaucrats do that will be interpreted positively by markets? What will inspire investors to push capital back into circulation? How can the investment class be encouraged to believe that it will see a return on its investments? Here, the EU's financial experts use the allure of secure investment and renewed profits to encourage implacable abstract markets to get moving again.

It is not simply that markets can respond in ways that would have been difficult to predict, and it is not simply that markets remained governed by 'animal spirits' (Keynes, 1965) and display an obvious tendency to irrational bursts of activity. Rather, abstract financial markets represent the core aspect of global capitalism today and they can be placed firmly in the Lacanian category of the obscene Real. They defy immediate comprehension. They exist beyond our rationality. They display a merciless indifference to us. We offer up sacrifices and beg to be granted their favour. Some even revel in the conceit that they have been chosen to instruct us how best to assuage the markets' capricious nature. But, to the markets, we are nothing. Even those at the very top of global financial organisations fail to see the complex forces that can shift the entire edifice of global capitalism without warning. With total indifference to our existence, the markets have the capacity to completely reshape our lives. They seem entirely divorced from our everyday social experience and yet they have the power to completely redefine it, to turn our lives upside down or to rip away those things that are of value to us.

It is true that these markets often appear, from time to time, to advantage specific localities and populations over others, but the key issue here is, of course, the titanic power these markets possess and our apparent unwillingness to exert any reasonable control over them. For over thirty years we have been instructed to marvel at the markets' capacity to create growth, but, throughout this time, the neo-liberal project has been unable to recreate the sustained growth of the Keynesian years. We have been told that, if markets are given free rein, they will boost the lifestyles of all. Sure, there may be a few bumps along the way, but the pleasures of advanced consumerism and technological innovation are worth it. Even after the crash, our politicians have displayed very little desire to produce new control systems capable of acting against the markets' tendency towards aggressive risk-taking. Instead, they prefer to induce the markets to get back to the reckless profit-seeking activities that appear to produce high profits and high tax receipts. The activities of our politicians are something like a brave man attempting to coax a great wild bear along a path with a bag of sweets. As the bear takes the sweets, the brave man briefly appears to be in control. But the bear retains the ability to wander off at any moment and create utter mayhem for any human settlement he stumbles upon. If we cannot bring ourselves to shoot the bear, surely it behoves our politicians to place it in some kind of regulatory cage that protects the human world from its next unpredictable outbreak of wanton destruction?

So, we must note that contemporary financial markets are an abstraction, but they are an abstraction with very real effects. A flurry of market activity, the devaluation of a currency or the flight of capital from state bond markets can completely change the texture of everyday life for huge numbers of people. In the vast majority of cases, those people have no understanding of the forces that have caused such disturbance. The dominance of culturalism in intellectual and educational life and the trivialisation of the mass media actively maintain this condition of ignorance. All people know is that everything that once appeared reasonably stable has come crashing down to the ground.

Politicians, academics and activists attempt to explain events to the people. Many identify individuals, social groups or institutions as the objects of blame. However, none of this activity troubles the markets. The markets remain entirely cut off from the social and ecological costs of their activities and protected from any reaction. The generalised 'market' is inhuman. It has no consciousness, no self-conception and no moral sense. It is simply the amalgamation of asocial investment activity, the sum total of the profit-seeking behaviours of the investment class. Even Marx and Engels (1992) marvelled at the capacity of this inhuman marketplace to drive forward living standards at a remarkable rate, while retaining the power to destroy aspects of social life that are integral to civilisation. For many decades, we have been so attached to the first effect – the market's ability to boost living standards – that we have ignored or excused the latter. Even now in 2014, still in the grip of a global downturn that has impacted upon the lives of millions, this amorphous, abstract and destructive thing continues to call the tune to which we all must dance.

In this realm of supposedly objective and doggedly pragmatic economic analysis that appeared to inform the Trioka's response to the Greek crisis, the politics of national interest clearly exerted considerable influence. Germany, the primary surplus economy in the EU, remained committed to the EU and its shared currency. However, the German population appeared unwilling to accept any responsibility for the debts of the struggling PIIGS group (Portugal, Italy, Ireland, Greece and Spain). Southern Europeans were often depicted as lazy and disorganised, the polar opposite of the industrious German people, who had borne their own hardships to turn their nation into the region's economic powerhouse. The Greeks' debt problems were presented as the inevitable result of incautious government spending, endemic tax avoidance and lax bureaucratic organisation. Ultimately, these were Greek problems to which the Greeks themselves needed to find answers. What was the use of giving the Greeks money if they were not forced to correct the very practices that got them into this mess in the first place? Enthralled by the illusion that the economies of nations and continents were roughly equivalent to those of the family home, and that the best policy was to enforce fiscal responsibility and to curtail spending in order to pay down debt, the German people appeared willing to lend a hand, but they certainly didn't want to hand the Greeks a blank cheque.

Europe remained a loose coalition of independent sovereign states who shared a currency. Debts accumulated by member states were theirs alone. The failure of these states to move further towards full integration, the act of stopping halfway in order to placate opposition at home, set the stage for the crisis of the Eurozone. Sharing a currency, but allowing all members to make their own decisions with regard to spending and the accumulation of debt, inevitably produced significant risks for the entire Union. Here, hard-nosed economic pragmatism crashes against the political will of democratic electorates across the continent. Further integration would, on the whole, provide a greater degree of economic security, but all nations appear resolute in their commitment to retaining as many sovereign powers as possible. Understandably enough, no nation-state is particularly keen to hand over further powers to the bureaucrats of Brussels.

We should also note that significant levels of economic competition continue to exist between EU member states. The shared currency has certainly not put a stop to this competition, but it has relieved nation-states of the power to adjust exchange rates. A state struggling with higher inflation cannot devalue in order to boost export markets, and so one of the modern era's primary fiscal responses to a deep and sustained economic downturn was, in the years following the crash, no longer available to struggling nations on Europe's periphery.

The Troika's emphasis on austerity also plays a role here. The dominant logic is that states should cut costs to make themselves as efficient and competitive as possible. However, if one nation possesses a competitive advantage, this inevitably means that neighbouring states are at a relative disadvantage. If one of the stronger EU economies successfully cuts costs, boosts productivity and grows export markets, its competitors tend to lose out. However, all nations are tied together in monetary union, and the stronger economies, especially Germany, clearly have a vested interest in boosting growth in the weaker ones. Germany has also taken on the logic of austerity, partly in order to convince other member states that it can swallow the medicine it prescribes to others and partly out of what appears to be a fetishistic attachment to neo-liberal theory and a desire to 'balance the books'. Germany's austerity programme is especially regrettable, because the continent needs its most powerful economy to spend in order to boost production and consumption and thus kick-start an economic recovery across the Eurozone.

The tangle of competing and shared interests is further complicated by the rapid growth of nationalism across the Eurozone and an insistent call to have sovereign powers returned to national governments. All of this, when considered alongside some of the issues we outline below, seems to reinforce the view that the Eurozone is set for a long period of static or very low growth, in which national governments, especially at the periphery, will need to keep interest rates at a historic low and scale back spending still further just to remain afloat.

Surplus recycling

Varoufakis (2011; see also Varoufakis *et al.*, 2013) argues that, as the Eurozone's key surplus economy, Germany should have loosened the purse strings and advanced a much greater amount of money to the continent's deficit economies as a means of recycling its capital surplus. Pursuing this course would have had the added benefit of tying Europe's national economies more closely together. Germany has a highly productive and competitive economy, but its economic strength will not continue if those who currently buy its products can no longer afford them and cannot access sufficient credit to maintain consumer lifestyles.

This is how the global flows of trade and finance work. After years of running a huge surplus that allowed it to supply struggling European nations with the money they needed to rebuild after the war, the USA switched strategies to become the globe's principal debtor, a hugely powerful Hoover capable of sucking up capital surpluses from around the globe. During the 1970s, 1980s and 1990s, the USA's manufacturing base shrank enormously. It moved from being the world's workshop to its shopping mall. It is often said that US industry won the Second World War, but, by the time Reagan took office, its might had already significantly waned. In the decades that followed, it would wane further still. Pay levels atrophied, and inequality raced forward, but a general sense of affluence was maintained by a constant inflow of cheap foreign goods from Germany, Japan and, later, China. Similarly, a constant supply of cheap credit allowed millions of Americans to buy their own homes. Wages were low, but consumer products were cheap, and banks and corporations were lining up to offer credit.

Money from the globe's key surplus economies flows into Wall Street to the tune of around $5 billion per day (Varoufakis, 2011). This creates a powerful surplus absorption process that provides US citizens with the ability to keep buying goods manufactured abroad while, at the same time, keeping surplus economies productive and offering them a means of investing their surplus. Basically, and in a roundabout way, US citizens buy using credit advanced to them by China, Germany and other economies that run large trade surpluses, and China, Germany and others immediately have customers for the goods they produce and a useful investment market for the capital that accrues from the sale of those goods. This contemporary form of global neo-liberalism is dependent upon the maintenance of this global financial arrangement, but this arrangement is also dependent upon belief in the system's strength and its ability to continually reproduce itself.

The strength of the dollar is of course crucial, but much of the strength of the dollar is purely perceptual. The dollar is strong because people believe it to be strong, and also because there does not appear to be an obvious challenger for its global hegemonic role. In turbulent economic times, if the dollar doesn't provide a measure of surety, then what does? If the dollar is not strong, or if America is not judged a safe bet, and money does not continue to flow into its financial markets, the whole system breaks down, leaving America with unpayable debts and the production plants of China and Germany at a standstill, without a market for their goods. Workers would be made redundant, capital flows would grind to a halt, and money would wither away in offshore bank accounts, as investors become guarded and unsure about where to invest their money. Tax revenues would dry up, and everyone would want the money they were owed to be repaid, but no one would have the money to do it. The entire global economic system would seize up, and in truth something approaching this happened in 2008–9, although the ultimate cause was not the perceived weakness of the dollar.

An immediate conclusion should be quite obvious, and it addresses the role of politics within contemporary neo-liberalism. As such, it fits neatly together with the central thesis we have tried to advance throughout this book. A crash of this magnitude results from the inherent flaws of our global economic system, and it is exacerbated by the inability of academic economics to fully come to terms with the motives that actually drive people to act in the world. We can talk about lax regulation, cultures of endemic greed and absurd risk-taking, and the growing gap between the financial services industry and the real productive economy in which people find their work. Much of this has a great deal of relevance in helping us to understand why the crash happened and why it took the form that it did. However, the point we need to bear in mind as we excavate some of the details in the coming pages is this: the market, once it entered crisis, had no mechanism to correct itself. Those who have identified the market's fundamental drive to continue, and its willingness to destroy everything in its path so that it might do so, are absolutely correct. But the market needs to domesticate politics to do all of this. Democratically elected politicians and their hirelings in the International Monetary Fund, the World Bank, the World Trade Organisation and the European Central Bank responded swiftly to save the system. In a process that looked like a postmodern version of a socialism reserved only for the rich, politicians across the globe socialised debt, flooded money markets with cheap cash, rapidly reduced interest rates and rushed to the assistance of corporations, banks and sovereign nations who appeared on the brink of collapse.

We should keep in mind the political commitment and energy it has taken to keep the global capitalist economy moving in a way that is broadly similar to its pre-crash model. We should keep this in mind especially when neo-liberals talk about the inefficiencies of the state and the need to roll back its frontiers to advance the freedoms of its citizens. When they tell us about the market's tendency to a natural equilibrium, we should consider what would have happened in 2008 if the supposedly sclerotic state, with its overbearing bureaucracies and its restrictive regulations, had not responded so rapidly to the crisis. When Darwinian neo-liberal purists tell us that they would have favoured an approach that allowed lame ducks to go to the wall, they leave out any consideration of the human costs. If the state had not assisted banks and corporations, our entire economic system might have collapsed, and we would have witnessed a social catastrophe on a much larger scale.

Politics these days seems inextricably connected to liberal capitalism, connected in its very being to the system's continuity. Capitalism remains a barely comprehensible totality, but, in order to maintain its supremacy, it needs to extract the substance from genuine politics, hollowing it out to leave only a shell of management and administration in its place. Instead of genuinely political arguments about what is Good and how society might move towards this end, now only domesticated arguments exist about how best to manage capitalism, how best to divide up the spoils, or how to curb its excesses, and so on. The point, surely, is to reconfigure politics, to rip it away from these moorings, so that it can once again become a field upon which we make collective decisions for which we can take full responsibility. Only then will politics provide us with a reasonable vantage point to assess capitalism and possible alternatives to it.

The time for decisions is already upon us. We need to decide what, if anything, will be done to mitigate the effects of climate change. We need to decide to what extent we will allow the field of biogenetics to advance. We need to decide what, if anything, will be done to reintegrate marginalised populations. We face historic decisions and we need the field of politics to be fully operative if we are fully to face up to them. The market's domination of politics actively prevents us from making any headway. This, ultimately, is what neo-liberalism is about: it is not just about the free market and the minimal state; it is about transforming politics to the extent that politics becomes the free market's handmaiden.

Play the part and you shall become

To return to our discussion of global trade and surplus recycling, we should also recognise that US military power remains crucial. The USA remains the world's most dominant military superpower, and its politicians and bureaucrats seem dedicated to maintaining its military strength, even in times of austerity. This military strength is crucial for many reasons, but one of these is that it inspires confidence and encourages other nations to believe that the USA is a safe economic bet, a debtor always able to pay back what it owes.

The scale of the USA's borrowing becomes such that no one is able to call time on it. It would be self-defeating for the Chinese to ask the Americans to settle up, and, of course, US military strength reminds its creditors that it will not be pushed around or threatened. Instead, we arrive at a situation akin to the peace of mutually assured destruction. Surplus economies need to keep pumping money into US markets, and the nation needs to keep hoovering up as much debt as possible.

Varoufakis *et al.* (2013) argue that Germany's major mistake was not to establish a similar surplus recycling system in the Eurozone. Doing so would have cushioned Europe from the worst of the crisis and provided an immediate means of getting the continent's economy back on its feet. Instead, a sovereign debt crisis ensued in Greece. Debts piled up on top of debts. Private debt was transformed into public debt, which in turn ensured that a growing proportion of GDP was taken up by servicing existing debt, which in turn cut down on the money available to pay for the welfare state, which in turn produced widespread desperation and social crisis. This situation was then exacerbated by the unwillingness of capital markets to advance further money to struggling southern European states, or at least not at serviceable rates of interest. Greek debt was reduced to junk bond status, and investors assume that, ultimately, Greece will default on the debt, or that investors will have to take a severe haircut in order to access at least some of the money advanced to the Greek state.

Germany, Europe's key surplus economy, then rides to the rescue of its European partner. Its economic strength means that it doesn't really need to curtail its own spending or welfare programmes in order to assist the Greeks: it can simply borrow at very low rates of interest, and this money can then be advanced to the Greeks in order to protect their shared currency and maintain the integrity of the Union. Again, fear of economic contagion is key, and supposedly practical economic measures are inevitably shaped by the politics of nation. Greece is advanced money on the assumption that it will pay it back, but this debt continues to weigh upon the Greek economy. Varoufakis's basic suggestion is that a European version of the Marshall Plan is needed. Fixing the problems of the crisis-stricken southern states is clearly in the best interests of all, but shackling these states with titanic debts is really not the help that they need. Instead, we should completely cast aside the assumption that the crisis faced by the southern states is in any way similar to the crisis we might face as individuals if we were to get into financial difficulties. Following the logic of Varoufakis's argument, and against common sense, it is not really in the interests of Germany or the German people to ask for the money back. The debts should be written off, and every effort should be made to turn Greece and other indebted countries back into relatively self-sufficient trading partners capable of absorbing Germany's surplus. Pursuing this course would ensure that the Greeks have money to spend and that the production plants of Germany can continue to churn out the goods purchased by its European neighbours. We may assume that this is an overtly 'leftist' response, but, if so, it is a leftist response that seeks to save capitalism from itself. Only a radically new approach to the organisation of global trade can ensure the market's continuity.

All of this, the entire debate about crisis in the Eurozone and the future of the EU, reflects the continued dominance of a ruling ideology that goes about its business by convincing all that we are indeed deep within a post-ideological era. Time and time again, we hear that this is not about politics: it's about ensuring a return to normality; it's about the practical economic measures we need to take in order to ensure that the EU doesn't disintegrate; it's about tackling sovereign debt now, so that future generations don't have to pick up the tab. The great desire of all concerned is to re-establish something that passes for stability. However, the model of stability that all parties seek to re-establish is the 'unstable stability' of global neo-liberalism, with its staggering inequalities and its propensity for boom and bust. There is clearly a common drive to ensure liberal capitalism's continuity. There is now opposition at the margins, but that opposition can be found on the right as much as it can on the left. Of course, the rise of new nationalist movements across the continent threatens both the EU and the towering achievements of the European tradition. The paradoxes of the contemporary Right in Europe tell us something about what lies in store for us.

Cancelling the debt

As the IMF itself admits, Greece's initial bailout simply had to go ahead, even though it knew Greece's debt was unsustainable and that austerity measures would damage the Greek economy still further. The response of the Troika and the major European leaders was confused and riven with mistakes born of fidelity to the logic of neo-liberal market strategy. A burst of Keynesian interventionism, in which states bought up private debt and pumped huge amounts of money into the economy with quantitative easing programmes, was followed by a pan-continental commitment to reducing state deficits. Many struggling European states reduced interest rates as much as possible and then squeezed their national economies by increasing taxes and cutting spending. Higher taxes were felt mostly by the middle and working classes, and spending cuts were felt mostly by the poor. Jobs became increasingly scarce, and those that were available tended to be insecure, part time and poorly paid.

Electorates were told that, above all, the state's debts needed to be repaid. Precisely why this was the case was rarely discussed. Instead, misperceptions about the nature of sovereign debt abounded. It was assumed that paying back the debt was simply a matter of honour. The money had been borrowed and spent, and now it was time to pay it back. Belts would need to be tightened. Welfare spending needed to be cut, publicly owned assets needed to be sold off, utilities would have to be privatised, and public-sector pay, employment and pensions needed to radically decrease. All of this was presented as a regrettable inevitability. Ultimately, the Greek people would be forced to suffer in order to reassure markets that a new era of fiscal responsibility was under way. Interest rates on government debt needed to be brought back under control, and markets needed to be convinced that money advanced to Greece and other struggling EU nations would see a return.

The success of neo-liberal ideologues in convincing the majority that the sovereign debt crisis results from left-of-centre governments who spent beyond their means during the growth years is truly staggering to behold. The inherent instabilities of new abstract markets are rarely considered. Taxes needed to rise; public spending needed to decrease. Efficiencies needed to be sought across the board. Markets needed to be reassured, so that pre-crisis capital flows could recommence, and the entire continent could move back slowly to something that looked like 'business as usual'.

SYRIZA and change

Throughout much of this book, we may have given the reader the impression that we are cynics, dismissive of the capacity of much of today's radical politics to effect genuine socio-economic change. This is, of course, a simplification of our position. It is certainly true that we are entirely dismissive of the contemporary Left's focus on identity politics, and we have little sympathy for the myriad reformist groups on the left who seek only to get a better deal for their own particular micro-community. We have argued repeatedly that many contemporary political movements that appear to oppose capitalism are in fact integral to its continuation. A great deal of contemporary radical politics is dominated by pseudo-activity: activity that covers up a deeper inactivity. Waving placards and moaning about the government are all well and good, but, if no benefit accrues, if policy doesn't shift, and the system rumbles onwards blithely unconcerned with our dissatisfaction, then we must, in the standard dialectical manner, consider the possibility that this domesticated oppositional activity actively benefits the system we believe ourselves to oppose. Žižek has argued that, if we are indeed serious about holding capital to account and effecting genuine change, we should display the courage to withdraw from this pseudo-activity. Carlen (2014) appears to consider this a capitulation to social oppression and mocks the suggestion that critical academics withdraw from the immediacy of social and political critique to rethink the situation and identify the diverse groups involved in their own inimitable ways in the system's reproduction. However, even thinkers as radical as Marx and Engels (1977: 573) noted the presence of people in their orbit who 'ostensibly engage in indefatigable activity' but ultimately 'do nothing themselves [and] try to prevent anything happening at all except – chatter'. Action and talk, without prior coherent thought and direction, are always politically worthless and often counter-productive.

The neo-liberal state depends upon the perpetual criticism of the domesticated Left. It secretly solicits the work of campaign groups who argue for policy change. Žižek's point is that, if one truly wants to subvert the neo-liberal state, it is better to stand mute and refuse to be active than to engage in an endless cycle of pseudo-activity that ultimately legitimises parliamentary capitalism, enabling it to keep on presenting itself as subject to the democratic will of the people. Withdrawal has been a reasonably successful strategy in the past, most notably in the labour movements of the industrial era, and it can be so again. Žižek ultimately wants to draw our attention to the distinction between activity and the act. In politics especially, we can busy ourselves with frenetic activity that appears to others – and, consciously, to ourselves – as important productive labour with a particular goal in mind. However, we must be aware of those occasions when we fill in time with activity precisely because we hope to avoid an encounter with the central issue that must be resolved, and acted upon, if genuine change is to occur. It is the job of intellectuals to shift our mode of engagement and identify what truly needs to be done to effect change. Žižek (2006: 223) suggests that such a strategy of passive aggressivity is 'a proper radical political gesture'. He compares this favourably to the 'aggressive passivity' of the contemporary Left, in which 'we are active all the time in order to make sure that nothing will happen, that nothing will really change' (ibid.).

To stand mute in front of neo-liberal power cuts off the public conversation that sustains the pretence of contemporary liberal democracy. A mass refusal to vote would challenge the legitimacy of government. The neo-liberal state would then, one imagines, desperately solicit a response from the ominously mute subject and then scramble around to interpret the meaning of its passivity. What do the people want? Why won't they participate? Is it too outlandish to imagine the state responding with violence and repression, attempting to round up the terrorists who are attempting to destroy democracy? Wouldn't the power disguised by democracy then emerge and fully reveal itself to the people?

We have (see Winlow and Hall, 2013) also suggested that it is incumbent upon critical academics to withdraw from the pseudo-activity of campaigning, rethink our situation and begin to construct models for a post-market society. How will the economy work? How will the field of politics be organised? What can be retained, and what must be jettisoned? These are questions of huge importance, and academics should take a lead in attempting to answer them, or at least provide the ideas and logical analysis that might service a productive debate about what comes next. Our point, of course, is to encourage our colleagues, and some political groups, to withdraw from pseudo-activity so that real activity – the activity of genuine transformation and progress – might begin. The creation of an appealing alternative is essential if we are to free ourselves from the ties that bind us to the present.

An alternative gives us a choice. It removes us from the enclosed space of contemporary political discourse and allows us to reconsider the pros and cons of liberal capitalism. It creates a dynamic tension that can spur the refinement of social models and politicise a much greater proportion of the population. Demanding that more is done to assist those struggling to remain afloat in times of austerity is important work, but it is not work that necessarily demands the involvement of legions of academics. Similarly, encouraging government to address injustice is important, but there is no reason why so much of the social sciences needs to be devoted to this task, especially when we consider that the collective efforts of campaigning academics don't appear to be doing a great deal to influence the major decisions of parliamentary capitalism. Harms continue to pile up on top of each other, and it must surely be time to reconsider the primacy of piecemeal social reform. Significant change is needed if we are to avoid catastrophe.

So, it's true that we see little in contemporary radical politics to be truly optimistic about. There are certainly some signs of life, but the majority remains deeply embedded in the ruling ideology and cannot imagine a world beyond capitalism and democracy. Many are angry and increasingly dissatisfied with our political and economic systems, and that's a start, but, for the most part, across Europe and North America the Left has failed to fully capitalise on this anger and dissatisfaction.

However, in Greece things appear more positive. A series of protests, strikes and riots followed the 2010 bailout and the resulting austerity measures. Like the English riots of 2011, these riots exhibited a palpable sense of anger, but this anger seems to have been accompanied by genuine desire to move politics forward. We are certainly not suggesting that the rioters were fully conscious political actors, driven by a desire to dethrone capital, but in these riots there existed something beyond blind anger and frustration. They cannot be simply dismissed as a collective scream for recognition. The Greek rioters had identified their enemy, and an embryonic alternative ideology and social model were beginning to creep into Greek politics. The indignant citizens' movement drew some international attention after the 2010 bailout, but the real positivity for the political Left in Greece is the rise of SYRIZA. In this final substantive chapter, we want to skip the fine details of the protests and protestors and move straight to the positive political momentum that today can be discerned in Greece.

The establishment of SYRIZA was not a product of protests. It was a product of realist thought, communication and organisation in extremely difficult times. It began as a coalition of leftist political parties. The social effects of austerity were becoming quite obvious by 2010. SYRIZA's popularity grew quite rapidly from this point. For the most part, its growing popularity involved the movement of voters from the centrist parties, who promised only to be trustworthy custodians of the system, towards those on the fringes, who proposed more radical measures. Disgusted at the main parties' capitulation to the Troika and suffering the pain of austerity, the people opened themselves up to the idea of change. Of course, as we have already seen, this popular disgust at the political mainstream has fuelled radical parties on the right as well as those on the left, and this is certainly true in Greece. However, things look positive for SYRIZA. In the second democratic election of 2012, they registered as a single political party and secured more than 25 per cent of the votes, becoming the official opposition party in the Greek parliament. In 2014, they won the European parliamentary elections. There is now a genuine chance that an organised political party of the radical Left can take power.

To us, watching from our homes here in Britain, one of the most appealing aspects of SYRIZA's rise has been its obvious willingness to *actually take control*. Make no mistake: if it does find its way into office in the near future, it faces a huge job in rebalancing the relationship between the economy and civil society. SYRIZA's leader, Alexis Tsipras, talks passionately about his desire to hold capital to account. He appears to be a pragmatist in the true sense: he recognises that radical action is needed to restore stability and reasonably civilised community life to Greece. Forging a new path is difficult, and to take on this task is usually judged idealistic and unwise, but the true pragmatist recognises that continuing on the old path leads only to further harm and suffering. SYRIZA recognises that it is better to face the pain of fighting to create a positive future than to face the pain of a ceaseless neo-liberal present.

When media commentators tell us that the election of SYRIZA might prompt capital flight from the country, and that further economic catastrophe awaits, we should not dismiss them entirely. The mainstream media have waged a campaign to undermine SYRIZA, and sections appeared dedicated to the task of convincing the electorate that SYRIZA is too radical and unworldly, and that standards of living will fall still further if it wins office. However, it is certainly true that the global market and key financial institutions would react negatively to the election of SYRIZA and any concerted attempt to tax wealth and regulate markets. If SYRIZA were to cancel the debt, or even a significant portion of it, and if it were to take Greece out of the euro, the consequences would be huge, and not just for Greece. Certainly, we should not underestimate the repercussions for the Greek people if SYRIZA takes power and begins a radical overhaul of the Greek economic system. The initial burst of happiness at securing a historic victory must quickly give way to the hard work of reconstituting the country's economy on a more equal footing, while minimising the harms that are likely to be visited upon the Greek people. Greek civil society might suffer greatly, but these harms must be placed next to the harms that are already under way and those the Greek people will face in the future, if neo-liberal pragmatists remain in office. It is not too difficult to imagine the leading lights of the global economy rubbing their hands together in glee at the prospect of the further immiseration of the Greek people: if wages plummet, if employers have immediate access to Eurozone export markets, if the state continues to allow large-scale tax avoidance, if the tendency to turn Greece into a global green zone continues, then things look good for liberal capitalism in Greece – at least until the next crisis, which some far-sighted economists can already see developing on the horizon (Keen, 2011; Varoufakis, 2011).

The unwillingness of key national economies to create new global surplus recycling mechanisms means that, post-2008, our global economy is drifting aimlessly. A sustained recovery seems unlikely, and, perhaps more to the point, no political will, SYRIZA apart, exists to reconstitute the social democratic entitlements of the past. In this respect, it is worth considering the possibility that SYRIZA, with a clear political mandate and a determined will, might actually set about tackling some of the country's grotesque imbalances and, in so doing, prepare the ground upon which a new post-crash prosperity might grow. In short, rather than offering a revolutionary challenge to capitalism, SYRIZA effectively promises to *save capitalism* by enforcing a new disciplinary and regulatory system geared towards a more just dispersal of wealth and an unwavering commitment to the primacy of civil society over capital. We must now realise that, if the European polity remains wedded to the model of neo-liberal financialisation, then further tragedy awaits.

For the moment, it is not clear if SYRIZA is dedicated to continued membership of the EU, and there will no doubt be calls from hardliners to drop out, re-establish the drachma and restore the sovereignty of the Greek state. Pursuing this course would radically change the place of Greece within the global economy, and things could get a good deal worse for the Greek people. There is certainly no guarantee that SYRIZA will continue to have the support of the Greek people through the years of turbulence that lie ahead. Things will be hard. The radical alternative proposed by SYRIZA is drawing supporters now, but this can change. Will SYRIZA be able to manufacture genuine signs of progress before another election rolls around?

For years, there have been many on the left who have claimed that the best strategy is to avoid taking power; instead, the Left should take up a position of permanent critique (see, for example, Holloway, 2002). The timidity of the Left throughout much of the neo-liberal period, and perhaps back a good deal further than that, has contributed to the development of new harms and injustices and the desperate position faced by the poor everywhere. SYRIZA has forged a new path and it has done so in full recognition of the forces that will line up against it. It is attempting to take power, despite knowing that there is a good chance it will fail.

If it finds its way into office in the near future, it will face a huge deficit, crippling debt obligations and an economy on its knees. It will have to set about the task of cleaning up the mess left after twenty-five years of aggressive neo-liberal restructuring and it will have few friends in Europe willing to assist it. And, despite all of this, it remains absolutely dedicated to taking power and attempting to take Greek society in a new direction. The public proclamations of SYRIZA and Tsipras are admirably straightforward and overtly ideological. In Tsipras, the Greek Left appears to have an intelligent leader capable of inspiring commitment and dedicated to the creation of a positive future for Greece from which the gross injustices of the present are absent. Many difficult decisions lie ahead for the party and the country, but to remain within the present framework will ensure that no positive change can come.

9

CONCLUSION

The dialectics of change

There is now considerable agreement that more needs to be done to regulate abstract financial markets (see Elliot, 2014). Politicians of every stripe line up to tell us how they plan to protect civil society from the market's interminable boom and bust cycle, which itself, in an age of declining resources, is destined to bump along the bottom rather than reach the high points of capitalism's post-war industrial heyday. Even those on the neo-liberal right who remain inextricably tied to the logic of deregulation tell us that we need new forms of regulation that control potentially harmful practices. As long as regulation does not impede the diligent and socially responsible wealth creators who constitute the majority of the financial services community. The majority, after all, should not be held responsible for the criminal behaviours of a disreputable few.

Many people across the Eurozone now know that liberal capitalism is dangerously unpredictable and grossly unfair. The 2008 crash remains with us, and its scale and destructiveness will not easily be forgotten. However, this knowledge of capitalism's dark side has not prompted a drive to replace it with something else. Like the man besotted with an inappropriate and unruly lover, we are so intoxicated by the thrill of the good times that we are willing to put up with the bad. We ignore the infidelities and forgive the hurtful remarks because we remember the good times as truly exceptional. Our errant and capricious lover might yet rehabilitate herself, and the good times will return.

We know that capitalism has the power to radically disrupt our lives and cause us great pain, but we also believe that capitalism equips us with wondrous gifts that act as compensation. After we have sat waiting for hours, with dinner spoiling in the oven, our lover turns up with an apology and the gifts of mass consumption, technological innovation and something that looks like boundless cultural novelty and diversity. Of course, these gifts are not really capitalism's to give, but we are so besotted that we say 'thank you' and give our lover another chance. We hope things will improve, but secretly we know they will not, because, ultimately, our lover cannot return our love.

Resigned to our fate, we learn to live with the ups and downs and try to convince ourselves that we are adventurers and gamblers at heart and, therefore, thrilled by the unpredictability of it all. We believe that this is how it is, how it has always been and how it always will be. We lie to ourselves and dismiss stability as stultifying and uninteresting. We stop hoping for something better. Indeed, we begin to doubt that such a thing really exists. We cynically dismiss those who tell us that another way is possible and convince ourselves that we are fulfilled by the good times we get from capitalism. However, in our more contemplative moments, there is a growing recognition that the good times really aren't that good anymore, and the compensatory gifts really don't compensate for the sense of absence and lack that gnaws away at those who allow themselves to feel and think, knowing but not wanting to know that something else, something better, really can be brought into existence.

In the contemporary intervallic period, we know that capitalism and liberal democracy are far from perfect. We know of the deep harms they produce. We know about the inequality and injustice, the continued degradation of the natural environment, and capitalism's steadfast refusal to use its titanic strength to address the manifold problems that blight the developing world. However, we remain attached to capitalism, as it appears to be better than the alternatives. By comparison, everything else seems monotonous and dull, and, as we have been at pains to stress, every political system that is not built upon fair electoral practices appears tyrannical, oppressive and 'inhuman'.

So, we know that capitalism cannot be placed firmly in the category of the Good. It is simply the 'least worst' (Badiou, 2009; Žižek, 2009, 2010). It is too aggressively individualistic. It is too competitive, and, in capitalism's interminable competition, few appear to spare much of a thought for the losers. Growing numbers of people are cut adrift from mainstream economic life. Billions continue to live in desperate poverty (Davis, 2007). We know that it is impossible for liberal capitalism to overcome its own internal contradictions or humanise its cold logic, and we know that its markets cannot truly be set to the task of solving the problems of contemporary economic globalisation. However, we are also convinced that all alternatives were worse and will continue to be worse. In keeping with the faithless cynicism of our times, we in fact assume everything to be flawed: every idea, every strident ideologue, every political party, every movement and every radical attempt to improve what exists. Our lethargy and our distrust of ideology and change ensure that capitalism remains. Certainly not perfect, we conclude, but on balance probably the best of a bad bunch.

The historical dialectic has stalled. The contradictions inherent in the existing thesis have been disavowed or covered over, the antithesis has become fragmented and fudged, or for many simply abandoned, and, therefore, no genuine synthesis is possible, and the initial thesis – the existing system, with all its logical imperatives, contradictions and inevitable deleterious outcomes – simply continues onwards. It is in this shapeless and becalmed political interregnum that the often quite desperate and aimless logic of contemporary riot and protest is played out. The protestors want change, but in most cases they cannot conjure up an image of something else that is free from the flaws that appear to beset every political idea. They have not been equipped with a positive image of the new. So many protests these days are structured in relation to the protestors' desire for some authority to enact change on their behalf. Many protests continued to be structured in relation to the needs and wants of specific micro-communities, and little consideration is given to others. Even the new protest groups of the radical Left that appear to want to actually move beyond capitalism often end up asking corrupt elites to rehabilitate themselves before taking the lead on reducing those things the protestors most dislike about the present. The same is true of many contemporary riots. In many cases, no progressive politics exists within the frame of the riot, and there is no seductive image of an ideological alternative for people to rally around. Instead, the riot is driven forward by an incoherent rabble of pissed-off individuals incapable of joining together to form a genuine political community. In the context of the post-political present, the riot is more a depressive acting out of deep, objectless frustration and anger than a concerted proto-political intervention demanding change. In most cases, the only vague hope we have been able to identify among contemporary rioters is the desire to be re-included into the very socio-economic system that excluded them in the first place. Many of our peers continue to romantically misconstrue riots as spontaneous political action driven by some mythical rebellious predisposition. They also tend to argue that we must abandon dialectical sophistry and discard philosophical abstraction. We must recognise and combat our own disabling cynicism, put down our books and head out on to the streets to register our moral dissatisfaction with the existing order of things. If a genuine victory for the Left is to come, we are told, it will be won on the streets, and not in the lecture theatre or even in the old party form. The moral weight of the crowd will bear down upon our political leaders until they succumb to the pressure, embrace the marginalised and reconfigure the relationship between the state and the market.

These ambitions are entirely reasonable, and it is certainly true that, if genuine change is to come, it will push past philosophical abstraction without a care. But shouldn't critical intellectuals be ready with a few ideas for new political and socio-economic frameworks in which these ambitions can actually be realised? Is it really a waste of time to think about how a post-capitalist economy might be structured? Is spontaneous action, without prior positive thought and clearly outlined purpose, really the way to go about things? Should we simply demand justice and wait for it to be handed to us by a reinvigorated and suddenly benevolent political class, or should we perhaps think through in some detail what kind of justice we want and how it might realistically be brought about? What we need is a positive programme for change. We need to aspire to something different, something less scarred by the injustices of the present, and we need to work hard to define this new world and make it comprehensible and attractive to everyday people. Expressing our dissatisfaction with the present order of things will not lead to the change we need. Piecemeal reform will not save us.

Many complex issues that could shape a qualitatively different future need to be investigated. Is it possible to maintain our current lifestyles in the face of an ongoing energy crisis and impending resource wars? Can we put history into reverse gear and re-establish the modern social democratic state, at a time in which the real economy appears to be reaching its objective material limits? Is it possible that the nation-state could be carefully democratised and retreat from the unforgiving cut and thrust of the global marketplace, to focus upon new, sustainable systems of national production and distribution, and do so in peaceful relations with other states? Could we re-establish comprehensive welfare states, while at the same time creating new global and regional surplus recycling mechanisms? With the advent of sophisticated IT, is it possible to be even more ambitious and consider some sort of hybrid central–devolved democratic control of the financial economy? Is a steady-state economy possible? Could a citizens' wage be introduced in Western nations in a way that avoids economic crisis? How could such a thing be funded, and how might the state prevent further debilitating capital flight? How can we deal with new advances in technology and orient them to social needs? How can we create enough meaningful jobs in the West to ensure full economic and social participation? The issues that demand attention appear endless, and answers to these questions are far from clear. Whereas so many of those around us insist that now is the time for action, for us it is a time for critical reflection, fully engaged social research and deep thinking.

What counts as a radical intervention these days?

The Left is failing to centralise these crucial questions in its debates, research programmes and academic literature. Its popular spokespeople continue to argue with consummate vagueness and celestial piety that more needs to be done to help the poor and the marginalised and to reduce the injustices of the current order. However, this simple negative discourse fails to fully account for the global economic context, and it fails to create a meaningful alternative for everyday people to aspire to. In pursuing these arguments in the absence of a genuinely transformative political agenda, our popular spokespeople join their competitors on the liberal right in enforcing a horizon of the possible. The liberal Left argues vaguely that capitalism needs to be controlled to a greater degree, and the liberal Right argues that it needs to be freed from state intervention. The limitations of this domesticated political jousting must now be clear for all to see. It is now incumbent upon the political Left to rejuvenate its discourse and transform itself into something that inspires young people to believe that something better can actually be brought into existence. What the Left really needs is a *realist utopianism*, a utopianism that connects a genuine faith that a better world can be created to a doggedly realistic understanding and appreciation of just how difficult this task is and the scale of the work needed to make it possible. The first step for the Left is to abandon its debilitating and divisive attachment to identity politics and construct new accounts of universalism. We need to stop dreaming about our own personal freedoms and rediscover our historic commitment to the common good.

Social democracy remains the political philosophy of choice for the pragmatic postmodern socialist. The refusal to look beyond capitalism and the aggressive denunciation of all those who propose a genuine return to history ensure that our economy and society remain inextricably bonded to the profit motive. It transforms the dialectics of change into a debate between the parliamentary Left and the parliamentary Right about the degree to which the state intervenes to regulate the destructive and asocial drive for personal gain. We are told that we must accept that the market remains capable of productive and organisational wonders. We must accept that the people remain committed to democracy and consumer culture and have no desire whatsoever to move on to an alternative socio-economic system. If capitalism cannot be dispensed with, the job of the Left then becomes a ceaseless process of carefully calibrating regulation and control, in the hope that capitalism's inevitable harms can be curtailed without reducing its ability to drive innovation, while at the same time ensuring that government does all it can to defend human rights and reintegrate marginalised groups.

We are happy to admit that a programme of social democratic control of capital would offer a revolutionary break from the present, roughly equivalent to the first social democratic revolution that followed the Second World War. Here, we mean revolutionary in the weak sense, in the sense that, in comparison with the towering inequalities and injustices of the pre-war period, the rise of social democracy represented a genuinely progressive intervention. However, the market remained. Capitalism was merely regulated; it was not defeated and replaced with something else.

We see this agenda at the core of SYRIZA in Greece and Podemos in Spain. These political parties possess considerable potential, and they represent a genuine challenge to the current neo-liberal order. However, as with any revolutionary intervention, we need to acknowledge the considerable power of the forces of reaction. We took pains to point out earlier that, of all the European movements emerging in the midst of contemporary crisis, it was SYRIZA that offered the most radical, clearly outlined and economically literate political programme. However, if it wins office in the near future, it will face significant pressure to abandon key elements of reform and water down many of its policies. There will be threats and bribes, those at the forefront of the movement will be subjected to continuous media criticism, and, in the background, the immensely powerful forces of neo-liberalism will gather their strength as they wait for the earliest opportunity to retake power. Because SYRIZA will be isolated in its attempt to contravene at least some of the rules of the global market, that opportunity will come sooner rather than later, and SYRIZA must be prepared for it.

SYRIZA will also be forced to confront intractable systemic problems in economy and culture. We should not simply assume that a return to social democracy would mean a return to the sustained growth of the post-war social democratic period. The specific factors that spurred post-war economic growth are absent in our own time. It will be very difficult for today's radical social democrats to engineer identifiable gains before they find themselves back before an electorate keen to see improvements in its standards of living. Five years of economic stagnation, even when they are accompanied by policies that seek to equalise social relations and combat inequality, might well boost support for neo-liberal parliamentary parties who promise immediate gains. Perhaps it is best to seek to reform what exists, rather than completely abandon it in favour of something else. Perhaps the best the Left can hope for these days is to regulate the market to a much greater degree. We would not vigorously dispute this point. We are certainly not against a sustained regulatory drive to extinguish capitalism's blazing excesses. However, this is not the only route open to us.

Social democracy would be a significant improvement upon what currently exists, but we should not settle upon social democracy as a transformative horizon. There is a world beyond this horizon, if we are willing to explore it. One of the key lessons of critical theory is that the seemingly impossible can happen. It seems impossible to imagine a world beyond capitalism, but a world beyond capitalism can come into existence. What is, in the here and now, totally inconceivable can come to fruition. Only in the future, once the event has come to pass, are we granted the privilege of being able to identify the forces that made possible the transformative event.

We have tried, throughout this book, to marry a pessimism of the intellect to an optimism of the will. We need to cling on to utopianism, and we need to fight hard against those who would place limits on our imagination and our desire for something better. We should, of course, acknowledge the dismal state of contemporary leftist politics and the ideological incorporation of the majority, but we also need to believe that a better world is possible. Walter Benjamin's (1999) analysis of historical change in his 'Theses on the Philosophy of History' suggests that the failures of today can be redeemed in the future. Our failure to act in the present – our reticence and fearfulness, our abortive and failed attempts to enact change – does not collapse into complete non-existence. The series of setbacks the Left experienced during Benjamin's time did not fully close off the possibility that, at some point in the future, things could be very different. For Benjamin, a future radical event can transform and rehabilitate our failures and their place in history.

Since the start of the neo-liberal era, the Left has gone from defeat to defeat to defeat. The Left today, in Britain especially, is in total disarray. However, the crucial point is that the nature of its failure has changed. As it reformed, fragmented and softened itself in the post-war era, it did not incrementally fail better, but in fact *failed worse*. In the process of liberalisation and decline, as we have argued throughout the book, the Left abandoned many of its core principles and lost touch with the sectors of the population it purports to represent. Key constituencies on the left have capitulated to the logic of the deregulated market, and most on the left today accept liberal democracy and its faux-egalitarianism. Multicultural tolerance, the discourse of rights and the primacy of defensive individualism have replaced the traditional principle of universal egalitarianism. The Left and the Right have, in recent years, both succumbed to an insubstantial liberalism totally incapable of delivering its promise of panoramic freedom.

In the vacuum created by the evaporation of the Left, the triumph of neo-liberal capitalism appears all around us. This triumph has been such that, across the continent, most mainstream leftist parliamentary groups accept the inevitability of the free market. The diaphanous liberalised Left offers no clear alternative. However, despite all this, the future is not written. Following Benjamin, the pattern of leftist failure and defeat can be broken. Each passing day offers the opportunity to radically change things. The impossible can happen. For it to do so at some point in the future, the Left must learn once again to take advantage of the inevitable crises that the capitalist market will cause. It must learn to fail better and thus transform its trajectory from decline to incline. Then, rather than blindly rioting and protesting in a negativistic manner against our various dissatisfactions, we would rediscover in our intellectual life something concrete to aspire to and campaign for.

BIBLIOGRAPHY

Aas, K. F. (2007) *Globalization and Crime*, London: Sage.

Agamben, G. (2005) *State of Exception*, Chicago, IL: University of Chicago Press.

Akram, S. (2014) 'Recognizing the 2011 United Kingdom Riots as Political Protest: A Theoretical Framework Based on Agency, Habitus and the Preconscious', *British Journal of Criminology*, 54, 3: 375–92.

Althusser, L. (2005) *For Marx*, London: Verso.

Althusser, L. (2008) *On Ideology*, London: Verso.

Althusser, L. and Balibar, E. (2009) *Reading Capital*, London: Verso.

Anderson, P. (1992) *A Zone of Engagement*, London: Verso.

Antonakakis, N. and Collins, A. (2014) 'The Impact of Fiscal Austerity on Suicide: On the Empirics of a Modern Greek Tragedy', *Social Science and Medicine*, 112: 39–50.

Antonopoulos, G. and Hall, S. (2014) 'The Death of the Legitimate Merchant? Small to Medium-Size Enterprises and Shady Decisions in Greece During the Financial Crisis', in P. van Duyne, J. Harvey, G. Antonopoulos, K. von Lampe, A. Maljević and A. Markovska (eds) *Corruption, Greed and Crime Money*, Oisterwijk, Netherlands: Wolf Legal.

Arblaster, A. (1971) 'Vision and Revision: A Note on the Text of Isaiah Berlin's *Four Essays on Liberty*', *Political Studies*, 19, 1: 81–6.

Arendt, H. (1973) *The Origins of Totalitarianism*, New York: Harcourt.

Arendt, H. (2009) *On Revolution*, London: Penguin Classics.

Badiou, A. (2002) *Ethics*, London: Verso.

Badiou, A. (2007) *The Century*, Cambridge, UK: Polity Press.

Badiou, A. (2009) *The Meaning of Sarkovy*, London: Verso.

Badiou, A. (2010a) *The Communist Hypothesis*, London: Verso.

Badiou, A. (2010b) 'The Idea of Communism', in S. Žižek and C. Douzinas (eds) *The Idea of Communism*, London: Verso.

Badiou, A. (2011) *Being and Event*, London: Continuum.

Badiou, A. (2012) *The Rebirth of History*, London: Verso.

Bale, T. (2011) *The Conservative Party*, Oxford, UK: Polity.

Balibar, E. (1991) 'Is There a "Neo-Racism"?', in E. Balibar and I. Wallerstein, *Race, Nation, Class*, London: Verso.

Barofsky, N. (2013) *Bailout*, New York: Free Press.

Baudrillard, J. (2007) *In the Shadow of the Silent Majorities*, Los Angeles, CA: Semiotext(e).

Bauman, Z. (2011) 'The London Riots: On Consumerism Coming Home to Roost', *Social Europe Journal*, 9: 08.

Bell, D. (2014) 'What Is Liberalism?', *Political Theory*, DOI: 10.1177/0090591714535103.

Benjamin, W. (1999) *Illuminations*, London: Pimlico.

Berlin, I. (2002) 'Two Concepts of Liberty', in I. Berlin, *Liberty*, Oxford, UK: Oxford University Press.

Berlin, I. (2013) *The Crooked Timber of Humanity*, London: Pimlico.

Bird, K. (2000) *The Color of Truth*, New York: Touchstone.

Bloch, E. (1995) *The Principle of Hope*, Vol 1, Boston, MA: MIT Press.

Boltanski, L. and Chiapello, E. (2007) *The New Spirit of Capitalism*, London: Verso.

Borabaugh, W. (1992) *Berkeley at War*, Oxford, UK: Oxford University Press.

Bouras, S. (2014, 14 February) 'Greek Economy Contracts Less Than Expected', *Wall Street Journal*.

Bourdieu, P. (1990) *The Logic of Practice*, Cambridge, UK: Polity.

Bridges, L. (2012) 'Four Days in August: The UK Riots', *Race and Class*, 54, 1: 1–12.

Briggs, D. (ed.) (2012) *The English Riots of 2011*, London: Waterside Press.

Burgen, S. (2013, 13 August) 'Spain's Youth Unemployment Reaches Record 56.1%', *The Guardian*.

Burgen, S. (2014, 23 January) 'Spain's Unemployment Rise Tempers Green Shoots of Recovery', *The Guardian*.

Burgum, S. (forthcoming) 'On Occupy and the Problem With Post-Political Cultural Resistance', PhD Thesis, University of Warwick.

Burridge, T. (2014) 'Spain's "We Can" Party Proves It Can', BBC website, available at: www.bbc.co.uk/news/blogs-eu-27579898

Butler, P. (2014, 28 January) 'Food Banks: An Inconvenient Truth for the Government', *The Guardian*.

Carlen, P. (2014) 'Review: *Rethinking Social Exclusion*, by Simon Winlow and Steve Hall', *British Journal of Criminology*, 54, 3: 490–3.

Cohen, A. (1955) *Delinquent Boys*, New York: Free Press.

Cohen, S. (2001) *States of Denial*, Oxford, UK: Polity.

Cook, P. D. (2010) *Allied War Criminals of WWII*, New York: Xlibris.

Cooper, C. (2012) 'Understanding the English 'Riots' of 2011: 'Mindless Criminality' or Youth 'Mekin Histri' in Austerity Britain?', *Youth and Policy*, 109, 6: 6–26.

Copsey, N. (2010) *The English Defence League*, London: Faith Matters.

Crowley, L. and Cominetti, N. (2014) *The Geography of Youth Unemployment*, London: The Work Foundation.

Davis, M. (2007) *Planet of Slums*, London: Verso.

Dejours, C. (2003) *L'évaluation du travail à l'épreuve du réel*, Paris: Editions Quae.

Denham, A. and Garnett, M. (2001) *Keith Joseph*, London: Routledge.

Dworkin, D. (1997) *Cultural Marxism in Post-War Britain*, Durham, NC: Duke University Press.

Ehrenreich, B. (2010) *Nickel and Dimed*, New York: Granta.

Eichhorst, W. and Neder, F. (2014) 'Youth Unemployment in Mediterranean Countries', IZA Policy Paper No. 80.

Elliot, L. (2014, 27 May) 'Carney and Lagarde Acknowledge City's Primeval Will to Survive', *The Guardian*.

Elliot, L., Inman, P. and Smith, H. (2013, 5 June) 'IMF Admits: We Failed to Realise the Damage Austerity Would Do to Greece', *The Guardian*.

Fink, B. (1995) *The Lacanian Subject*, Princeton, NJ: Princeton University Press.

Fioramonti, L. (2013) *Gross Domestic Problem*, London: Zed Books.

Fisher, M. (2009) *Capitalist Realism*, London: Zero.

Freud, S. (2001) *Complete Psychological Works of Sigmund Freud*, Vol 14, London: Vintage.

Friedman, T. (2000) *The Lexus and the Olive Tree*, New York: HarperCollins.

Frost, D. and North, P. (2013) *Militant Liverpool*, Liverpool, UK: Liverpool University Press.

Garland, J. and Treadwell, J. (2010) 'No Surrender to the Taliban! Football Hooliganism, Islamophobia and the Rise of the English Defence League', *Papers from the British Criminology Conference*, 10: 19–35.

Girard, R. (1989) *The Scapegoat*, Baltimore, MD: Johns Hopkins University Press.

Glenny, M. (1996) *The Fall of Yugoslavia*, London: Penguin.

Goss, S. (2014) *Open Tribe*, London: Lawrence & Wishart.

Gould, P. (2011) *The Unfinished Revolution*, London: Abacus.

Gough, R. (2006) *A Good Comrade*, New York: Tauris.

Graeber, D. (2011) 'Enacting the Impossible: Making Decisions by Consensus', in S. Van Gelder and the staff of *Yes! Magazine* (eds) *This Changes Everything: Occupy and the 99% Movement*, San Francisco, CA: Berrett-Koehler.

Gray, J. (2013) *Isaiah Berlin*, Princeton, NJ: Princeton University Press.

Green, J. and De La Motte, B. (2009) *Stasi Hell or Workers' Paradise?* London: Artery.

Greenspan, A. (2013) *The Map and the Territory*, London: Allen Lane.

Hadjimatheou, C. (2012) 'Greeks Confront Crime Wave Amid Austerity', BBC website, available at: www.bbc.co.uk/news/world-radio-and-tv-19269891

Hall, S. (2012a) *Theorizing Crime and Deviance: A New Perspective*, London: Sage.

Hall, S. (2012b) 'Don't Look Up, Don't Look Down: Liberal Criminology's Fear of the Supreme and the Subterranean', *Crime, Media, Culture*, 8, 2: 197–212.

Hall, S. (2012c) 'The Solicitation of the Trap: On Transcendence and Transcendental Materialism in Advanced Consumer-Capitalism', *Human Studies*, 35, 3: 365–81.

Hall, S. (2012d) 'Consumer Culture and the Meaning of the Urban Riots in England', in S. Hall and S. Winlow (eds) *New Directions in Criminological Theory*, Abingdon, UK: Routledge.

Hall, S. and Jefferson, T. (eds) (1976) *Resistance Through Rituals*, London: Hutchinson.

Hall, S. and Winlow, S. (2013) 'The English Riots of 2011: Misreading the Signs on the Road to the Society of Enemies', in F. Pakes and D. Pritchard (eds) *Riot: Unrest and Protest on the Global Stage*, Basingstoke, UK: Palgrave Macmillan.

Hall, S. and Winlow, S. (2015) *Revitalizing Criminological Theory: Towards a New Ultra-Realist Perspective*, Abingdon, UK: Routledge.

Hall, S., Winlow, S. and Ancrum, C. (2008) *Criminal Identities and Consumer Culture: Crime, Exclusion and the New Culture of Narcissism*, Cullompton, UK: Willan.

Harvey, D. (1991) *The Condition of Postmodernity*, Oxford, UK: Wiley-Blackwell.

Harvey, D. (2007) *A Brief History of Neo-liberalism*, Oxford, UK: Oxford University Press.

Harvey, D. (2010) *The Enigma of Capital*, Oxford, UK: Oxford University Press.

Harvey, D. (2014) *Seventeen Contradictions and the End of Capitalism*, London: Profile House.

Harvie, D. and Milburn, K. (2013) 'The Moral Economy of the English Crowd in the Twenty-first Century', *South Atlantic Quarterly*, 112, 3: 559–67.

Hayward, K. and Yar, M. (2006) 'The Chav Phenomenon: Consumption, Media and the Construction of a New Underclass', *Crime, Media, Culture*, 2, 1: 9–28.

Hebdige, D. (1979) *Subculture*, London: Methuen.

Hegel, G. W. F. (2010) *The Science of Logic*, Cambridge, UK: Cambridge University Press.

Heinberg, R. (2011) *The End of Growth*, London: Clairview Books.

Hennessey, P. (2007) *Having it So Good*, London: Allen Lane.

Hiscock, G. (2012) *Earth Wars*, London: John Wiley.

Hitchens, C. (1998) 'Moderation or Death', *London Review of Books*, 20: 23.

Hobsbawm, E. (1964) *Labouring Men*, London: Weidenfeld.

Hobsbawm, E. (1995) *Age of Extremes*, London: Abacus.

Hobsbawm, E. (2012) *Nations and Nationalism Since 1780*, Cambridge, UK: Cambridge University Press.

Hoggart, R. (1969) *The Uses of Literacy*, London: Pelican.

Holloway, J. (2002) *Change the World Without Taking Power*, London: Pluto.

Horsley, M. (2014) *The Dark Side of Prosperity*, Farnham, UK: Ashgate.

Ignatieff, M. (2000) *Isaiah Berlin*, London: Vintage.

Jacoby, R. (2013) *Picture Imperfect*, New York: Columbia University Press.

James, O. (2007) *Affluenza*, London: Vermilion.

James, O. (2010) *Britain on the Couch*, London: Vermilion.

Jameson, F. (1992) *Postmodernism: Or, the Cultural Logic of Late Capitalism*, London: Verso.

Jenkins, S. (2007) *Thatcher and Sons*, London: Penguin.

Judt, T. (2010) *Post-war*, London: Vintage.

Kassam, A. (2014, 27 May) 'Podemos Hopes to Cement Rise of Citizen Politics in Spain After Election Success', *The Guardian*.

Kautsky, K. (2014) *Bolshevism at a Deadlock*, Abingdon, UK: Routledge.

Keen, S. (2011) *Debunking Economics*, London: Zed Books.

Keynes, J. M. (1965) *The General Theory of Employment, Interest and Money*, London: Harcourt.

King, M. (2013) 'Birmingham Revisited: Causal Differences Between the Riots of 2011 and 2005?', *Policing and Society*, 23, 1: 26–45.

Klare, M. (2002) *Resource Wars*, New York: Owl Books.

Klare, M. (2012) *The Race for What's Left*, New York: Picador.

Lacan, J. (2000) *The Seminar of Jacques Lacan: On Feminine Sexuality, the Limits of Love and Knowledge*, Book 20 (ed. J. A. Miller), New York: Norton.

Lacan, J. (2007) *Ecrits*, New York: Norton.

Laville, S. (2011, 6 September) 'Riots Cost Taxpayer at Least £133 Million, MPs Told', *The Guardian*.

Laville, S. (2013, 12 May) 'Oxford Gang Found Guilty of Grooming and Sexually Exploiting Girls', *The Guardian*.

Lenin, V. I. (1993) *What Is to Be Done?* New York: International.

Lenin, V. I. (2010) *Imperialism: The Highest Stage of Capitalism*, London: Penguin Classics.

Levitas, R. (1998) *The Inclusive Society?* Basingstoke, UK: Macmillan.

Lloyd, A. (2012) 'Working to Live, Not Living to Work: Work, Leisure and Youth Identity Among Call Centre Workers in North East England', *Current Sociology*, 60, 5: 619–35.

Lloyd, A. (2013) *Labour Markets and Identity on the Post-Industrial Assembly Line*, Farnham, UK: Ashgate.

Losurdo, D. (2011) *Liberalism: A Counter-History*, London: Verso.

Manuel, F. and Manuel, F. (1979) *Utopian Thought in the Western World*, Boston, MA: Harvard University Press.

Marcuse, H. (2002) *One Dimensional Man*, Abingdon, UK: Routledge.

Marx, K. and Engels, F. (1977) 'Circular Letter', in D. McLellan (ed.) *Karl Marx: Selected Writings*, Oxford, UK: Oxford University Press.

Marx, K. and Engels, F. (1992) *The Communist Manifesto*, Oxford, UK: Oxford Paperbacks.

Matthews, R. (2014) *Realist Criminology*, London: Palgrave Macmillan.

Miles, S. (2014) 'Young People, "Flawed Protestors" and the Commodification of Resistance', *Critical Arts*, 28, 1: 76–87.

Miller, J. A. (1977) 'Suture (Elements of the Logic of the Signifier)', *Screen*, 18, 4: 24–34.

Millington, G. (2013) ' "Anti-riots" *und Postpolitik in der neo-liberalen Stadt: London im August 2011*', *Berliner Journal für Soziologie*, 23: 51–73.

Milne, S. (2004) *The Enemy Within*, London: Verso.

Mirowski, P. and Plehwe, D. (2009) *The Road From Mont Pelerin*, Cambridge, MA: Harvard University Press.

Moxon, D. (2011) 'Consumer Culture and the 2011 "Riots" ', *Sociological Research Online*, 16, 4: 19.

Muir, H. (2011, 6 September) 'In Search of the Spark that Turned Tension in Tottenham Into Flames', *The Guardian*.

Neville, S. and Treanor, J. (2012, 6 December) 'Starbucks to Pay £20m in Tax Over Next Two Years After Customer Revolt', *The Guardian*.

Newburn, T. (2011, 5 September) 'There Is a Pressing Need for Credible Research Into the Riots', *The Guardian*.

Newburn, T. and Prasad, R. (2012, 1 July) 'Policing the Riots: Fear, Frustration – and a Deep Sense of Pride', *The Guardian*.

Orwell, G. (2013) *Nineteen Eighty-Four*, London: Penguin Classics.

Papantoniou, M. (2013, 23 May) 'UNICEF: 600,000 Children Below Poverty Line in Greece', *The Greek Reporter*.

Pearce, F. (2013) *The Landgrabbers*, London: Eden Project Books.

Picketty, T. (2014) *Capital in the Twenty-first Century*, Cambridge, MA: Harvard University Press.

Platts-Fowler, D. (2013) ' "Beyond the Loot": Social Disorder and Urban Unrest', *Papers from the British Criminology Conference*, 13: 17–32.

Podemos (2014) '*Podemos: Documento Final Del Programa Colaborativo*', available at: http://podemos.info/wordpress/wp-content/uploads/2014/05/Programa-Podemos.pdf

Popper, K. (2002a) *Unended Quest*, Abingdon, UK: Routledge.

Popper, K. (2002b) *The Poverty of Historicism*, Abingdon, UK: Routledge Classics.

Popper, K. (2005) *The Logic of Scientific Discovery*, Abingdon, UK: Routledge.

Popper, K. (2011) *The Open Society and Its Enemies*, Abingdon, UK: Routledge Classics.

Popper, K. (2012) *After the Open Society*, Abingdon, UK: Routledge Classics.

Prasad, R. (2011, 5 December) 'Rioter Profile: "I Saw an Opportunity to Take Stuff" ', *The Guardian*.

Reiner, R. (2007) *Law and Order*, Oxford, UK: Polity.

Ross, K. (2004) *May '68 and Its Afterlives*, Chicago, IL: University of Chicago Press.

Sassoon, D. (1997) *One Hundred Years of Socialism*, London: Fontana.

Saunders, F. S. (2000) *Who Paid the Piper?* London: Granta.

Saunders, F. S. (2013) *The Cultural Cold War*, London: The New Press.

Seldon, A. (2005) *Blair*, London: Free Press.

Service, R. (2010) *Stalin*, London: Pan.

Seymour, R. (2012) *The Liberal Defence of Murder*, London: Verso.

Shaxson, N. (2012) *Treasure Islands*, London: Vintage.

Sloterdijk, P. (2012) *Rage and Time*, New York: Columbia University Press.

Smart, B. (2010) *Consumer Society*, London: Sage.

Smith, H. (2011, 18 December) 'Greek Woes Drive Up Suicide Rate', *The Guardian*.

Smith, H. (2013, 6 August) 'Greece's Food Crisis: Families Face Going Hungry During Summer Shutdown', *The Guardian*.

Smith, O. (2014) *Contemporary Adulthood in the Night-time Economy*, Basingstoke, UK: Palgrave Macmillan.

Smith, S. and Penty, C. (2013) 'Spanish Defaults Surge as Banks Forced to Come Clean: Mortgages', Bloomberg.com, available at: www.bloomberg.com/news/articles/2013-12-17/spanish-defaults-surge-as-banks-forced-to-come-clean-mortgages

Southwood, I. (2011) *Non-stop Inertia*, London: Zero.

Stuckler, D. and Basu, S. (2013) *The Body Economic: Why Austerity Kills*, London: Allen Lane.

Sutterlüty, F. (2014) 'The Hidden Morale of the 2005 French and 2011 English Riots', *Thesis Eleven*, 121, 1: 38–56.

Taylor, P. A. (2013) *Žižek and the Media*, Cambridge, UK: Polity Press.

Tempest, M. (2002, 10 June) 'Mandelson: We're All Thatcherites Now', *The Guardian*.

Tester, K. (2012) 'August in England', *Thesis Eleven*, 109, 1: 4–10.

Thompson, E. P. (1975) *Whigs and Hunters*, New York: Pantheon.

Thompson, E. P. (1978) *The Poverty of Theory and Other Essays*, London: Merlin.

Thompson, E. P. (2013) *The Making of the English Working Class*, London: Penguin.

Topping, A. and Bawdon, F. (2011, 5 December) 'It Was Like Christmas: A Consumerist Feast Among the Summer Riots', *The Guardian*.

Toynbee, P. (2003) *Hard Work*, London: Bloomsbury.

Treadwell, J. and Garland, J. (2011) 'Masculinity, Marginalization and Violence: A Case Study of the English Defence League', *British Journal of Criminology*, 51, 4: 621–34.

Treadwell, J., Briggs, D., Winlow, S. and Hall, S. (2013) 'Shopocalypse Now: Consumer Culture and the English Riots of 2011', *British Journal of Criminology*, 53, 1: 1–17.

Turner, C. (2010) *Investigating Sociological Theory*, London: Sage.

Varoufakis, Y. (2011) *The Global Minotaur*, London: Zed Books.

Varoufakis, Y., Hollands, S. and Galbraith, J. K. (2013) 'A Modest Proposal'. Available at: http://yanisvaroufakis.eu/euro-crisis/modest-proposal/

Vinen, R. (2010) *Thatcher's Britain*, London: Pocket Books.

Wain, N. and Joyce, P. (2012) 'Disaffected Communities, Riots and Policing: Manchester 1981 and 2011', *Safer Communities*, 11, 3: 125–34.

Watt, N. (2013, 12 November) 'David Cameron Makes Leaner State a Permanent Goal', *The Guardian*.

Webb, R. (2013, 30 October) 'Dear Russell, Choosing to Vote is the Most British Kind of Revolution There Is', *The New Statesman*.

Whitehead, P. and Crawshaw, P. (2013) 'Shaking the Foundations: On the Moral Economy of Criminal Justice', *British Journal of Criminology*, 53, 4: 588–604.

Whitehead, P. and Crawshaw, P. (2014) 'A Tale of Two Economies: The Political and the Moral in Neo-liberalism', *International Journal of Sociology and Social Policy*, 34, 1/2: 19–34.

Wilkes, D., Warren, L. and Davidson, L. (2011, 18 October) 'Portrait of a Very Middle Class Protest: A Poet, a Mother and Even an Extra From Downton . . . Just Who Is at the Tent City Demo?', *The Daily Mail*.

Williams, R. (2005) *Culture and Materialism*, London: Verso.

Winlow, S. and Hall, S. (2006) *Violent Night: Urban Leisure and Contemporary Culture*, Oxford, UK: Berg.

Winlow, S. and Hall, S. (2009) 'Living for the Weekend: Youth Identities in Northeast England', *Ethnography*, 10, 1: 91–113.

Winlow, S. and Hall, S. (2012a) 'What Is an "Ethics Committee"? Academic Governance in an Epoch of Belief and Incredulity', *British Journal of Criminology*, 52, 2: 400–16.

Winlow, S. and Hall, S. (2012b) 'A Predictably Obedient Riot: Post-politics, Consumer Culture and the English Riots of 2011', *Cultural Politics*, 8, 3: 465–88.

Winlow, S. and Hall, S. (2012c) 'Gone Shopping: Inarticulate Politics in the English Riots of 2011', in D. Briggs (ed.) *The English Riots of 2011: A Summer of Discontent*, London: Waterside Press.

Winlow, S. and Hall, S. (2013) *Rethinking Social Exclusion: The End of the Social?* London: Sage.

Žižek, S. (1992) *Looking Awry*, Boston: MIT Press.

Žižek, S. (1995) *Tarrying with the Negative*, Durham, NC: Duke University Press.

Žižek, S. (1997) 'Multiculturalism, Or the Cultural Logic of Multinational Capitalism?', *New Left Review*, I, 25 September–October.

Žižek, S. (2000a) 'Melancholy and the Act', *Critical Inquiry*, 26, 4: 657–81.

Žižek, S. (2000b) *The Ticklish Subject*, London: Verso.

Žižek, S. (2002) *Welcome to the Desert of the Real*, London: Verso.

Žižek, S. (2006) *The Universal Exception*, London: Continuum.

Žižek, S. (2008) *Violence*, London: Profile Books.

Žižek, S. (2009) *In Defence of Lost Causes*, London: Verso.

Žižek, S. (2010) *Living in the End Times*, London: Verso.

Žižek, S. (2011) 'Shoplifters of the World Unite', *London Review of Books*, 19, 08.

INDEX

Aas, K. F. 126
absolutism 41
academia 99
acquisitiveness 29
activism 2, 9, 83, 178
administration 80, 193
advertising 66
Agamben, G. 6
agency 39–40, 43, 46, 48–49, 51–52, 83, 95, 107
aggression 81, 119
Akram, S. 147
alcoholism 186
Althusser, L. 21, 25, 45–48, 54
altruism 51, 137
Americana 39, 41
anarchism 160, 163
anarchy 180
Anderson, P. 92
Antonakakis, N. 185–186
Antonopoulos, G. 186
apolitical 26, 56, 98, 137, 142, 146
apologism 142
Arblaster, A. 92
Arendt, H. 32, 39, 83–85
aristocracy 63
aristocrats 106
artists 39
asceticism 63
asylum 128
atomisation 132, 136, 158
atrocities 21, 61
Auschwitz 35
authenticity 122

authoritarian/ism 6, 38, 41, 49, 77, 86, 89–91, 96, 123, 140, 146
authority 41, 43, 58, 95, 107, 121, 154, 164, 176, 187, 203
autonomy 44, 125, 142

Badiou, A. 4, 23, 33, 38, 160, 163–164, 202
Baldwin, S. 63
Bale, T. 64
Balibar, E. 48, 126
banking 8, 12, 20, 136, 187
bankruptcy 186
barbarism 7, 30–31, 33, 35–38, 40, 154
Barofsky, N. 151
Baudrillard, J. 158
Bauman, Z. 139, 143
Bawdon, F. 55, 135, 138
Beckett, S. 168
Bell, D. 39, 96
Bellamy, E. 32
benevolentism 126
Benjamin, W. 63, 94, 206–207
Bentham, J. 94
Berlin, I. 8, 10, 32, 39, 83–84, 91–96
Berlusconi, S. 20
Bevan, A. 50
biogenetics 193
Bird, K. 93
Blair, A. 50, 65–71
Bloch, E. 32
blogs 153
BNP see British National Party
Bolshevism 212

Boltanski, L. 3, 21
Borabaugh, W. 51
Bouras, S. 187
Bourdieu, P. 147
bourgeoisie 7
Briggs, D. 136
British National Party (BNP) 113, 128
Britons 128
broadcasters 71
Brown, G. 50, 71
Bullingdon Club 20
Bundy brothers 93
bureaucracies 77, 192
bureaucrats 124, 185, 187–188, 190, 193
Burgen, S. 169
burglaries 186
Burgum, S. 163
Burridge, T. 174
business 12, 14, 44, 50, 56, 66, 68–69, 71,
   77–78, 92, 100, 113, 125, 145, 158,
   173, 182, 186, 194–195
Butler, P. 10
Butler, R. 64
Butskellism 63

Cameron, D. 20, 71, 141–142
Carlen, P. 196
carnival 127, 153
Cataluna, Plaza de 177
catastrophism 102, 182
cathexis 17
Catholic Church 132
censors 99
censorship 37
Central Intelligence Agency (CIA) 38–39
centralisation 15
CEOs see Chief Executive Officers
Chamberlain, N. 63
charismatic leader 121, 124
Chiapello, E. 3, 21
Chief Executive Officers (CEOs) 66–67
Christ 107, 112, 173
Christianity 15, 63, 111, 119, 161
Christoulas, D. 185–186
CIA see Central Intelligence Agency
citizenship 26, 42–43, 97
civilisation 20, 25, 30, 36–37, 95, 141,
   189
Cohen, A. 45
Cohen, S. 21
cold war, the 3, 22, 39–40, 56, 62, 90,
   93, 132, 145, 167
collectivisation 36
collectivism 27, 91
Cominetti, N. 2

commodification 52, 131, 136, 212
commodity 39, 52, 56, 139
commoners 63
communism 22, 37–41, 43, 49, 90–91,
   146, 160–163, 166, 181–182
concentration camps 86
Congress for Cultural Freedom 39
consciousness 2, 36, 46, 50, 64, 75, 99,
   139, 148, 154, 189
consensus 9, 11, 34, 37, 42, 56, 63–65, 73,
   82–83, 87, 160, 176, 178, 211
conservatism 63–65, 71, 161
Construction Skills Certification Scheme
   (CSCS) 113
consumerisation 5
consumerism 20, 22, 24, 31, 33, 39,
   55–56, 67, 107, 118, 136, 139, 141,
   143–144, 181, 183, 188
consumption 43, 46, 52, 54–56, 68, 71,
   100, 122, 190, 201, 211
Cook, P. D. 61
Cooper, C. 141–142
Copsey, N. 105
corporatism 122
corruption 20, 41, 73, 136, 156, 164,
   170–172, 183, 209
cosmopolitanism 126
counterdemonstrations 112
Crawshaw, P. 71
creativity 44, 49, 54, 121, 167
criminality 45, 73
critical rationalism 85
critical theory 83, 206
Crowley, L. 2
CSCS see Construction Skills Certification
   Scheme
cultural Marxists 127
Cultural Revolution 37
cultural turn 148
culturalism 142, 189

Daily Mail, the 143
Davis, M. 202
De La Motte, B. 37
deconstruction 7
defeatism 101
deficit 6, 166, 191, 195, 200
deflation 170
Dejours, C. 157
Democracia Real Ya 172, 174–175, 177
democratisation 55, 71, 204
demonisation 121
denazification 61
Denham, A. 64
dependency 10, 65

depoliticisation 14, 19, 45, 47, 50–51,
    55–56, 80, 142, 145–147, 152,
    154–155, 157–158, 163–164, 168, 197
depression 18, 63, 79, 140, 151
deregulation 201
Descartes, R. 88
despotism 95
dialectic 44, 201–202, 205
disorder 30, 56, 135, 165, 213
Disraeli, B. 63
diversity 3, 22, 31, 33, 43, 51, 62, 66, 92,
    126–127, 176, 202
dogma 1, 38, 48, 70, 106
Dolce and Gabbana 181
downsizing 48
downturn 170, 189–190
drunkenness 115
Duggan, M. 135, 138
Dworkin, D. 53–54

Eastern Bloc 36–37
Eastern economies 56, 62, 145
economism 52
economists 53, 74, 183, 199
egalitarianism 5, 15, 19, 31, 37–38, 40–41,
    126, 140, 160, 168, 207
Ehrenreich, B. 68
Eichhorst, W. 2
elitists 33
Elliot, L. 22, 187, 201
empiricism 45, 47, 54, 138
Engels, F. 189, 196
Englishmen 122
Enlightenment, the 11, 53, 88, 97
entrepreneurs/entrepreneurship 44, 59,
    64–65, 71, 128
ethnic minorities/identities/conflict 22,
    42–43, 54, 62, 82, 106, 115–117, 127,
    133, 152
ethnocentrism 62
ethnographic research 138
European Central Bank 185
European Commission 185
Eurozone 187, 190–191, 193–194, 199,
    201
expansionism 97
exploitation 6–7, 21, 41, 44, 53, 79,
    118–119, 128, 144, 157
extermination 162
extremists 106

Fabian reformers/liberals 87, 140
Facebook 178
factionalism 71
factories 48, 66, 107–108, 113

faithlessness 165
falsifiability 85
falsification 89
Farage, N. 20, 76
fascism 49, 62–63, 86, 91, 111–112, 114,
    123, 133, 182
fatalism 47, 49
fetishistic disavowal 75, 99
fidelity (ideological) 23, 32, 75, 78, 117,
    121, 130, 158–159, 195
financialisation 9, 70, 170, 183, 199
Fink, B. 121
Fioramonti, L. 70
firefighters 67
Fisher, M. 20
football 105, 114, 128, 180
Ford Foundation 93
Fourier, C. 32
fragmentation 7, 80
Frankfurt School 52–53
Freud, S. 130–132
Friedman, M. 72, 88
Friedman, T. 12
Frost, D. 68
fundamentalism 23, 106, 127

Gaitskell, H. 64
Garland, J. 105
Garnett, M. 64
gay marriage 112
GDP *see* Gross Domestic Product
gender 43, 51, 152
genocide 96
Gilroy, P. 54
Girard, R. 125
girls: exploitation of 118–119
Glenny, M. 62
globalisation 11, 70, 131, 202
Goss, S. 115
Gough, R. 37
goulash communism 37
Gould, P. 65
Graeber, D. 153
graffiti 8
Gramsci, A. 21, 46
Gray, J. 93
Greed 1, 20, 24, 68, 124, 192, 209
Greenspan, A. 31
Griffin, N. 121
Grillo, B. 74
Gross Domestic Product (GDP) 69–71,
    186, 193

habitus 147, 156, 209
Hadjimatheou, C. 186

Hall, Stuart 45
Harvey, D. 8, 26, 70, 151
Harvie, D. 55–57, 136
Hayek, F. 72
Hayward, K. 56
healthcare 179, 182
Hebdige, D. 45, 54
hedonism 97, 139
Hegel, G. W. F. 53, 85–86, 106
hegemony 7, 23, 46, 117, 124, 143, 187
Heinberg, R. 6, 32, 59, 79
Hennessey, P. 64
heritage 76, 125
heterosexuality 16, 122
hierarchy 41, 51, 55, 64, 124, 153–154,
  178
Hiscock, G. 6
historicism 45, 47, 54, 85–86, 89
Hitchens, C. 93
Hitler, A. 32, 91
HIV 186
Hobbes, T. 92, 94
Hobsbawm, E. 36, 62, 106
Hoggart, R. 54
Holloway, J. 44–45, 199
Holocaust, the 35, 62, 86
homosexual marriage 16
Honecker, E. 37
Horsley, M. 151
humanism 43, 46, 48

iconoclasm 3–4, 7, 12, 20, 25, 64, 121,
  144
idealism 11, 13, 53, 159
identification 65, 74, 80, 131–132, 156,
  159, 162
Ignatieff, M. 91, 93
immigrants 62, 76–78, 81–82, 108–109,
  111–114, 116, 118–120, 122–128, 152
immigration 15–16, 62, 76–77, 109, 114,
  123, 125, 128–129
immiseration 16, 38, 56, 162, 199
imperialism 51
incrementalism 49
indigenous population 114, 118, 120, 123
individualism 2, 19, 22, 27, 39, 57, 68–69,
  75, 97, 100, 144, 158, 165, 207
industrialisation 56, 67
industrialism 66, 68, 83
insecurity 14, 33, 62, 67, 70, 77–78, 83,
  97, 137, 156
instrumentalism 125
intelligentsia 37, 39, 53–54, 87
interpassivity 20
interpellation 54

interventionism 65, 78, 96, 101, 186, 195
invasions 70
investment 8, 12, 14, 26, 34, 67, 70, 80,
  89, 151, 187–189, 191
investors 70, 170, 188, 192, 194
Iron Curtain 36
Islam 118–120, 125, 129
Islamism 109, 112, 119
Islamophobia 211

Jacoby, R. 3, 92
James, O. 18
Jameson, F. 8
Jefferson, T. 45
Jenkins, S. 64
Jew, the (as stereotype) 62
Johnson, B. 20
Jones, O. 173
Joyce, P. 136
Judt, T. 36, 62

Kadar, J. 37
Kanellopoulos, L. 186
Kant, I. 92, 95
Kassam, A. 174
Kautsky, K. 106
Keynes, J. M. 188
Keynesianism 11, 34, 64, 186, 188, 195
Khrushchev, N. 36–37, 48
King, M. 141
King, M. Luther 3
Klare, M. 32, 79
Klu Klux Klan 132

Lacan, J. 105, 119, 121, 124
Lacanian theories/concepts 115, 118, 158,
  188
Laville, S. 118, 135
Le Pen, Marine 173
leadership 63–64, 71, 153, 160, 173–174,
  182
legislation 11, 35, 40
Lehman Brothers: collapse of 151
Lenin, V. I. 50, 106
Levitas, R. 69
liberalisation 70, 106, 206
libertarianism 3, 10, 21, 40–44, 87, 96, 102
livelihood 81–82, 152, 161
Lloyd, A. 68
Locke, J. 94
London School of Economics and Political
  Science (LSE) 138
looters/looting 55, 58, 135–136, 138, 141,
  143, 148
'losers' 57, 117, 202

lost generation 169
lost object 130–132
Losurdo, D. 91
LSE *see* London School of Economics and Political Science

machismo 49, 66
Mandelson, P. 69
Manhattan occupation 160
manufacturing: demise of 107, 191
Mao Zedong 32, 37, 162
Marcuse, H. 163
marketisation 69
Marshall Plan, the 194
Marx, K. 21, 46, 48, 51, 53, 85–86, 93, 98, 189, 196
Marxism/Marxist 37, 39, 45–46, 48, 51–55, 57–58, 83, 85–86, 127
materialism 48
Matthews, R. 55
McRobbie, A. 54
media coverage 15, 39, 57
melancholy/melancholia 106, 129–132
Mélenchon, J-L. 173
meltdown 1, 12
meritocracy 39, 71
metaracism 126
metropolitan liberal left 16–17, 50, 69, 76, 87, 107, 125–126, 135
Michaloliakos, N. 173
migrants 119, 123, 126
migration 62, 123
Milburn, K. 55–57, 136
Miles, S. 143
Miliband, D. 50
Miller, J-A. 105, 119
Millington, G. 136, 140, 145–146, 148
Milne, S. 38
Mirowski, P. 88
mobility 25, 31, 44, 66, 68
monetarist economic policies 65
Mont Pelerin Society 88–89
Moxon, D. 143
Muir, H. 135
multiculturalism 62, 65, 114–115, 120, 122, 126–127, 129, 215
Muslims 15, 109–110, 114, 116–119, 123, 125–126, 128–130

narcissism 48, 211
National Health Service (NHS) 71
nationalism 62–63, 77, 81, 106, 117, 120, 125, 127–128, 190, 194, 212
naturalisation 24
naturalism 19

Nazism 32, 36, 47, 61–63, 83–84, 86–87, 91, 128
Neder, F. 2
negation 106, 125, 158, 161
neighbour 107, 116, 194
neighbourhood 107–108, 120, 125, 129, 133, 137, 142, 147, 186
neoclassicism 34
neoliberalism 8, 78, 122, 166
Neville, S. 63, 100
Newburn, T. 138
NHS *see* National Health Service
nihilism 136

Obama, B. 155
objectless anger 17, 142, 148, 203
offenders 119
offshore bank accounts 192
oligarchs 9, 25, 98, 145, 168
ontology 32, 53
open borders 62
open society 84–87, 90–91
optimism 13, 25, 34–35, 49, 52, 68, 168–169, 184, 197, 206
organic politics 7, 38, 45, 51, 53, 98, 108, 137, 147, 175
Orwell, G. 31, 39, 90
Osborne, G. 20
otherness 127

paedophiles 114, 119
Pakes, F. 211
Papandreou, G. 186
Papantoniou, M. 186
parliamentarianism 3, 15, 18, 22–24, 29–31, 33, 35–37, 44, 47, 58, 72, 74, 79, 91, 98–99, 141, 144, 153, 155–156, 159, 167, 173–174, 177, 182–183, 185, 187, 196–198, 205–207
participatory economics 8
Partido Socialista Obrero Español (PSOE) (Spanish Socialist Workers' Party) 177, 179
paternalism 10, 63, 95
patriarchy 25
Pearce, F. 6, 32
Penty, C. 170
pessimism 97, 206
phenomenology 53
philosophy 41, 43, 48, 52–54, 85–86, 88, 91–93, 95, 205–206
Picketty, T. 74, 140, 151, 183
PIIGS group *see* Portugal, Italy, Ireland, Greece and Spain (PIIGS) group
Plato 53, 85–86

Platts-Fowler, D. 141–142
Plehwe, D. 88
pluralism 91–96, 141, 146, 168
podemos 174–175, 183–184, 205
Pol Pot 32, 162
police/policing 67, 85–86, 108–109,
   111–114, 116, 135, 138, 141, 143–144,
   148, 174, 177–179
political correctness 76
Pollock, J. 39
polls 65, 71–72
Popper, K. 32, 83–91
populism 91, 97
Portugal, Italy, Ireland, Greece and Spain
   (PIIGS) group 189
positivity 38, 132, 141, 144, 173, 181, 198
postmodernism 21–22, 24, 65, 75, 146
postmodernity 165, 211
pragmatism 5, 10–13, 33, 35, 49–50, 56,
   62, 71, 88–89, 93, 99–100, 124, 160,
   166–167, 187, 190, 198–199
Prasad, R. 138
precariousness 100, 145
preconsciousness 147–148
predestination 40, 146
privatisation 12–13, 65, 68, 97, 195
productivity 11, 34, 70, 88, 190
profit 4, 11, 17, 21, 26, 35, 43–44, 56,
   58–59, 66, 68, 70–71, 78, 100, 102,
   170, 175, 188–189, 205
profiteering 66, 72, 124
progressivism 88
proletariat 43, 52–54, 59, 101, 128, 130
prosperity 13, 34–35, 38, 62, 90, 199, 212
protectionism 78
pseudoactivity 196
PSOE *see Partido Socialista Obrero Español*
psychoanalysis 53, 106, 115, 118, 130, 132

race 59, 67, 96, 209–210, 212
racism 43, 54, 76–77, 105, 109–110, 113,
   119, 122, 126–128
radicalisation 114, 119
radicalism 30, 35, 49, 83–85, 87–88, 125,
   158, 175
rage 78, 88, 137, 141, 213
Rajoy government 173
rationalism 53, 84–85, 95
Reagan, R. 10, 191
realism 19, 56, 79, 99, 167, 182, 198, 204
recession 68, 186–187
recovery: economic 90, 169, 187, 190, 199
reflexivity 122, 147–148, 165–166
reformism 30, 38, 167–168, 183
Reiner, R. 36

relativism 23, 106
religion 15, 22–23, 43, 62, 94, 116,
   118–119, 152
rentiers 66
repossessions 151
repression 19, 37–38, 43, 86, 96, 197
reproduction of capitalism 24, 43, 131,
   142, 144, 155, 196
resistance 8, 14, 43, 45–46, 48–49, 52,
   146, 158, 163
respect 16, 31, 70, 73, 107–108, 121–122,
   126–127, 146, 152, 172, 182, 199
respectability 139, 186
respondents 115, 118–120, 122–123, 125,
   129–130, 133, 174, 183
revisionism 3
revolution 14, 35–37, 40, 44, 56, 64,
   86–87, 91, 100, 133, 160, 173–174,
   181, 183–184, 205, 209, 211, 214
revolutionary 5, 51, 83, 101, 133, 140,
   145, 151, 168, 174, 183, 199, 205
Riksbank Prize in Economic Sciences 88

sacrifice 2, 18, 30–31, 75, 86, 92, 94–95,
   137, 155, 159, 174, 188
Sassoon, D. 25
Saunders, F. S. 39, 83, 91, 110
Scapegoat/scapegoating 123, 125
securitisation 6
security 10, 12, 17, 96–97, 107, 115, 151,
   154, 173, 190
Seldon, A. 66
separatism 146, 168
sexism 43, 54, 122
sexuality 42–43, 119–120, 152, 181
Seymour, R. 91
Sharia Law 106, 110, 114, 128
Shaxson, N. 67
Sloterdijk, P. 157
Smith, H. 19, 94, 110, 170, 185–186
socialization 8, 106, 141, 192
socialism 34, 38, 40–41, 43, 56, 61, 65, 69,
   71, 85–86, 146, 160–163, 174–175,
   192, 205
sociology 26, 135, 148
sociopath 26
solidarity 10, 19, 39, 41, 47–48, 50–51, 67,
   97–98, 106, 130, 137, 140, 157, 175
solipsism 9
Southwood, I. 68
sovereign 10, 40, 123, 141, 190, 192–195
sovereignty 42, 161, 199
Soviet Union 30, 36–37, 39, 41, 62, 87
speculation: financial 58
stagnation 70, 206

Stalinism 30, 32, 36–37, 41, 47–48, 83–84, 161–162
Stigler, G. 88
stigmatisation 141
Stuckler, D. 186
subjectivity 3, 7, 17–18, 27, 48, 52–53, 56, 80, 147, 157
surplus 26, 43, 97, 101, 117, 173, 189, 191, 193–194, 199, 204
survival 10, 16, 59, 85, 97, 127
sustainable economy 6, 8, 20, 83, 98–99, 204
Sutterlu_ty, F. 57
Swastika 128
sweatshops 56, 116
symbolism 20, 22, 36, 52, 56–57, 62, 66, 74, 116, 139–141, 148, 159, 173, 182
Syntagma Square 185
SYRIZA 101, 175, 195, 198–200, 205

taxation 1, 10–14, 20, 26, 42, 44, 63, 65–69, 77–78, 80, 99–102, 111, 113, 118, 141, 158, 167, 169, 173, 175, 188–189, 192, 195, 198–199
taxpayer 12, 22, 135, 153
Taylor, P. 165
technocrats 7
technology 204
Tempest, M. 69
terrorism 29–30, 114, 119, 124, 129, 197
Tester, K. 139, 143
Thatcher, M. 10, 64–66, 68–71, 76, 173
Thatcherism 51, 69–70, 77, 142
there is no alternative (TINA) 76
Thompson, E. P. 45–48, 51, 53–56
TINA *see* there is no alternative
Tito, J. B. 62
tolerance 16, 22, 25, 39, 62, 65, 96, 105–106, 116–117, 126–128, 133, 168, 207
Topping, A. 55, 135, 138
Tory/Tories/Toryism 49, 63–64, 66, 69, 110
totalitarianism 1, 12, 29–32, 36, 40–41, 44, 61, 83, 85–86, 90–91, 96–97, 102, 106, 154, 156, 162
Tottenham riots 135
Toynbee, P. 68
tradition 16, 32, 41, 46, 49, 53–54, 63–64, 117–118, 131–132, 135, 194
transcendental being/ideal 23, 39
Treanor, J. 100
Treaty of Lisbon 62
Treblinka 35
tribe 115–116

Troika, the 185, 187, 189–190, 195, 198
Tsipras, A. 173, 198, 200
Turner, C. 12
tyranny 29, 32, 35–38, 41–43, 62, 90

UAF *see* United Against Fascism
UK Independence Party (UKIP) 76–78, 81–82, 110, 120, 122–123
Ulbricht, W. 37
underemployment 6, 9, 24, 71, 151
UNICEF see United Nations International Children's Emergency Fund
unionism 14
Union of Soviet Socialist Republics (USSR) 36
United Against Fascism (UAF) 111, 127
United Nations International Children's Emergency Fund (UNICEF) 186
universalism 67, 92, 106, 117, 132, 141, 152, 159, 175, 205
upheavals 35, 123
USSR *see* Union of Soviet Socialist Republics
Utopia 29–30, 32, 39–41, 43, 82, 89–90, 92, 95, 115, 132
utopianism 5, 13, 29, 32, 34, 41–42, 45, 61–103, 115, 204, 206

Varoufakis, Y. 6, 70, 191, 193–194, 199
victimisation 80
Vietnam, war in 93
Vinen, R. 65
von Mises, L. 88

Wain, N. 136
Watt, N. 12
wealth 10–12, 15, 20, 44, 57, 59, 65, 69–70, 74, 93, 97–98, 101–102, 156, 161, 167–168, 198–199, 201
Webb, R. 31
Weimar Republic 91
welfare 2, 10–14, 20, 24, 34, 63, 66, 69, 72, 78, 98, 100–101, 108, 118–119, 123, 125, 128, 139, 141, 145, 148, 152, 166–167, 193–195, 204
welfare dependency 14, 118, 120
Westminster: Palace of 67, 76, 125
Whitehall 69
Wilders, G. 173
Wilkes, D. 151
Williams, R. 54
Willis, P. 54
Wilson, H. 50
Wolfson College 93
workforce 50, 56, 58, 65–66, 71, 83

working class 78, 82
workplace 71, 100, 145, 157

Yar, M. 56
youth 2, 114, 119, 132, 142, 169

Žižek, S. 3, 6, 21, 23, 25, 75, 80, 105, 115, 118, 123, 126–127, 131–132, 141, 143, 157, 165, 168, 196, 202
zombie politics 17, 147
Zuccotti Park 151